NFL BRAWLER

A Player-Turned-Agent's Forty Years in the Bloody Trenches
of the National Football League

RALPH CINDRICH

Guilford, Connecticut

An imprint of Rowman & Littlefield

Distributed by NATIONAL BOOK NETWORK

British Library Cataloguing in Publication Information Available

Library of Congress Cataloging-in-Publication Data Available

ISBN 978-1-4930-0523-9 (hardcover)
ISBN 978-1-4930-1944-1 (e-book)

♾™ The paper used in this publication meets the minimum requirements of American National Standard for Information Sciences—Permanence of Paper for Printed Library Materials, ANSI/ NISO Z39.48-1992.

To the three angels in my life for their love: my mother Stella, my Zia Rosa (Great-Aunt Rose Scriva), and the love of my life, my wife, Mary. And for showing me the way and just being there when needed most, my Little League coaches, Mario and Ab.

It is not the critic who counts; not the man who points out how the strong man stumbles, or where the doer of deeds could have done them better. The credit belongs to the man who is actually in the arena, whose face is marred by dust and sweat and blood; who strives valiantly; who errs, who comes short again and again, because there is no effort without error and shortcoming; but who does actually strive to do the deeds; who knows great enthusiasms, the great devotions; who spends himself in a worthy cause; who at the best knows in the end the triumph of high achievement, and who at the worst, if he fails, at least fails while daring greatly, so that his place shall never be with those cold and timid souls who neither know victory nor defeat.

—THEODORE ROOSEVELT

Contents

NOTES AND ACKNOWLEDGMENTS

The language used in this book was not the language I used around my family. It was not how I was brought up. I would have received a back-hand from my dad for speaking that way. It is not OK with me to use now. But the game of football, both on the field and off of it, requires confidence, conviction, and occasionally a few choice words. Or, maybe I was just too stupid to figure out the other alternatives.

I am most grateful I've had the opportunity to thank many throughout this book who have been so kind to me over the years.

Special thanks to Nate Wilkinson who acted as a final contributor for me. I first came in contact with Nate through his book, *Draft Daze*. He provided organization, balance, and a theme to this book. He worked to make this a story.

To Matthew Vaughn, longtime attorney in the office, who first took the mess of all my stories and helped organize and edit them. Many thanks for keeping me organized throughout.

To Ed Bouchette of the *Pittsburgh Post-Gazette* who reviewed and edited this book with a Pittsburgh and expert viewpoint. With his help, I was ready to sign off on the finished product.

To Curtis Eichelberger, who edited a draft at the end. To Kevin Cook for urging me to take a broad look at the NFL and Gene Collier for getting me started.

Thanks to all of my great clients for their loyalty and for referring their teammates and others. To character guys like Corey Raymer, or Bob Landsee, who kicked my car when I picked him up at the airport, but delivered his bud, Paul Gruber. Bob kicked my car because it was crap while other agents picked him up in town cars. To Barry Warner, Rich Salgado, and so many others in the media and the NFL . . . many thanks.

Thank you to all my coaches mentioned here or not; to Al Abrams (RIP); Avella High School; Mousey Danna—a great leader (RIP); the University of Pittsburgh; the South Texas College of Law; Dean Walker (RIP); Roger McGill (RIP); Willie Meyers; Mouse McCullough; the

New England Patriots; the Houston Oilers; the late Mark McCormack of IMG; Peter Johnson of IMG; Eddie DeBartolo; my youth football coaches Abby Rush & Mario Gabrielli (RIP)—I miss you, pal; Ray Bazzoli (RIP); Dick Novak; Ray Campanelli (RIP); knucklehead wrestling coach Dave Adams; Bum Phillips (RIP); Bud Adams (RIP); writer, Len Pasquarelli . . . to all of you, I'm most indebted and appreciative.

Finally, and most importantly, to my late mother and father, Stella and A. J.; my wife, Mary; son, Michael, and family; daughter, Christina; brothers, Ron and Bob; sisters Rita and Rebecca; and extended family too numerous to mention . . . thank you for your love and support.

Introduction

"THE PITCH"

IT'S ALMOST TIME.

Someday soon, I'll make a couple of calls and schedule a meeting with some Hollywood big shot. I'll sit across an expensive desk, in the shadow of a massive ego and some shelves lined with shiny awards, and for once make a pitch for myself.

I'll stare the guy straight in the eye—just as I always did with those NFL owners—and sell him on the best story he could ever tell.

My own.

"What kind of plot lines do you like?" I'll ask.

Conflict?

I almost punched a Super Bowl–champion coach, only to have the fight broken up by Cowboys owner Jerry Jones. I got into a drinking contest with Colts owner Bob Irsay, a guy so universally hated that his own mother called him the devil. I spurned Penn State legend Joe Paterno after he traveled through bitter weather to recruit me, spawning a feud that would linger for a few years afterward.

That's not enough? You want something rags-to-riches?

Go back to where I was born. I grew up in Avella, Pennsylvania, a rough-and-tumble coal-mining town that went bust long before I arrived, a place once considered to be one of the poorest in the country. But my upbringing gave me enough grit to advance far beyond it. I was an All-American in college, a professional football player for four years, and before long a big-time agent in a billion dollar business, securing million dollar deals almost every time I signed my name.

Or maybe you want something softer, like a love story?

My eyes found Mary Rose across the room at a frat party in college, and I fell in love right then. We've been together ever since, married for four decades, with two kids and an everlasting love, one of those make-believe romances that only happens in fairy tales.

How about something with a harder edge. Sex. Drugs. Rock-and-roll?

My Houston Oilers team covered most of those themselves. We had a first-round defensive end who seemed to be pumped full of everything and other players who found an avalanche of cocaine every time they went out on the town. And then there's the agent business too, an industry that was overtaken by the Mob for about half a decade, a profession often infested by unethical people who recruit players with cash, cars, and women in varying degrees of clothes.

Maybe that's not it. Maybe you need something more wholesome?

The vast majority of my clients were the professional football players you never hear enough about, guys who were involved with their families and active in their communities, a bunch of people who put their teammates and others far ahead of themselves. Guys like Mark May, Al Toon, Paul Gruber, and a whole bunch more. I represented Kent Hull, who stood up for a teammate in his darkest moment, after a Super Bowl–winning kick went wide right. And on top of that, I was pretty damn ethical too—an outlier in my slimy business—someone who still believed in rules, morals, and the promise of a spoken word.

You want some memorable characters too?

My youth football coach was a standout athlete who lost a leg in World War II, but never entertained excuses for himself or any of the numerous players he coached. I worked with Herschel Walker, one of the biggest names in football, a downtrodden youth who became a college legend, and eventually became involved in the biggest trade in NFL history. And I knew the Chief, Art Rooney, a benevolent guy who loved cigars and horse races, but never missed a single day of Catholic mass. He founded the Pittsburgh Steelers as a young man and built the team into a powerhouse that made him the most beloved person in town.

And if that's not enough, every buzzword that you've ever heard attached to football appears in my story too.

Painkillers. Concussions. Violence.

I've seen it. Endured it. And advised my clients on how to handle it themselves.

My story has it all.

People are going to love it. And it could make you a lot of money. But if you're not interested, I'll walk out of this office right now and find someone else who is.

You want to hear more?

Put your feet up. Get comfortable. Pour yourself a drink.

I'll tell you the whole damn thing.

———

"We'll see what an impact Ralph Cindrich has on this draft right away. . . ."

It's 1985.

The NFL Draft is live on ESPN and a 24-year-old kid named Mel Kiper Jr. is firing off phrases like machine gun rounds, shooting names and information to a nationwide audience that's becoming more invested every year. Soon, Kiper and all the other analysts are speeding into a conversation about the draft's biggest storylines.

And I'm near the top of the list.

I'm only a few years into my career as an agent and not far removed from a contract war with the Washington Redskins over my client Mark May.

It was time to enter the arena again. With a lot of work and a little luck, I landed two of the draft's biggest names—Bill Fralic and Al Toon, two high-profile players who deserved to be top 10 picks.

Fralic was the son of a steel mill worker and a monster offensive tackle from the University of Pittsburgh who received 81 Heisman Trophy votes in his senior season. Toon was a wideout from the University of Wisconsin who rewrote the school's receiving records in football and was also a two-time All-American in the triple jump.

The draft would decide their fates in a matter of minutes.

And I was trying to hijack the whole thing.

Fralic wanted to play somewhere warm, which sure as hell wasn't in Minnesota, which owned the No. 2 pick. And both Toon and I believed Indianapolis could derail his career. The Colts were only a year away from their midnight escape from Baltimore and had gone 4-12 in 1984. So I was doing my best to scare off both teams, having sent cautionary letters to each franchise. But I still hoped to get my clients drafted early in the first round by someone else, with all the prestige and contract dollars that the players deserved.

"We'll see if those teams shy away from Fralic and Toon," Kiper continued, his trademark black hair slicked back and stationary. *"We will see if Cindrich has a direct impact on the draft...."*

Every career, perhaps every life, has a few tipping points.

Mine had arrived. With a great draft and a couple of quality contracts, I'd be on my way as an agent, a proven commodity in a burgeoning business. But if the draft or my ensuing negotiations went bust, my career might too.

With the cameras rolling and televisions tuned in at home, my success or failure was about to be broadcast live.

What would happen next?

No one knew. And I had plenty of reason to worry.

I told Fralic to go golfing that day and skip out on the entire thing. Mike Lynn, the general manager of the Vikings, had made his money with movie theaters. He was notoriously cheap and seemed to enjoy screwing players over, often squeezing them for every last dollar he could get.

I thought for sure he'd take Fralic.

Time passed. The tension grew. With the first pick, the Buffalo Bills took Bruce Smith, an explosive defensive end from Virginia Tech. Then, the Vikings exhausted the entire draft clock at No. 2.

Time was up. What happened next would determine the course of my career.

Commissioner Pete Rozelle stood in front of the podium, ready to deliver the verdict.

"With the second pick in the 1985 Draft ..."

One way or another, my next battle was about to begin. And I wasn't about to back down. My entire life up to that point had been filled with conflict—tackles and takedowns, arguments and adversaries.

I'd been fighting the odds and everything else since the day I was born....

Avella

The Homestead

My hometown's roughneck spirit started forming before our country was born.

The first settlers in Avella were colonists on the edge of the frontier, people pushing the limits of established boundaries and encroaching on Indian lands. According to local historian Mark Mamros, the western edge of Pennsylvania hadn't been drawn in the 1760s, so settlers bold enough to build homes there did so without any formal protection.

No soldiers. No militias. Nothing.

The families settling western Pennsylvania back then were on their own. They clustered together and built forts—about 30 to 40 of them in the area overall—to protect themselves from Indian attacks.

Wars ensued, boundaries were drawn, and eventually some of those clustered forts became Avella, Pennsylvania, the town where I grew up. The railroad arrived in the early 1900s and an abundance of opportunity rode in on its rails. Large beds of coal and wide swaths of profits were waiting underground. Companies began building one mine after another, confident that railroad cars could carry out their hauls. At the beginning, there was a lot more coal than miners, leaving an excess of work and wages.

Immigrants from Europe—my grandparents included—arrived on a seemingly endless stream of boats and chased that opportunity all the way into western Pennsylvania, crawling after the American dream in those underground mines. The population of Avella started swelling, taking on more immigrants, more homes, and more life early in the 20th century.

The entire town was transformed. Something happens to a place when a large part of the populace starts each day by descending underground, and moves forward in incremental inches, collecting more calluses and more dirt every minute. Throw in the obvious dangers of such strenuous work—cave-ins, clogged lungs, and errant explosions, to name just a few—and it's not long before the toughness becomes way too big to remain trapped underground.

It escapes into the outside air and slams against the sweat on a farmer's brow or the boots of a steel worker that were almost melted by the mill. Toughness gathered everywhere in Avella and multiplied among its peoples.

Hands were heavy. Hearts were hard. Backbones were thick. The meek might inherit the earth, but they sure as hell weren't easy to find in Avella.

In 1922, about 400 miners from the area stormed a nonunion mine in nearby Brooke County, West Virginia, hoping to close down the entire operation. A battle ensued and before it ended, the sheriff of Brooke County was dead, eight miners were imprisoned, and many more were killed, buried in crude unmarked graves in the woods between both mines.

Another oft-told true story involved the Ku Klux Klan and a couple of burning crosses. Klan members in Avella hated the immigrants and were often angry that the newcomers took the jobs and occasionally their women too. A Klan member burnt a cross on the hill above our town in protest. The next day, a Klansman was dead. A little later, a second cross was set ablaze—and a second Klansman was dead. The message got through. The Klan and their burning crosses were never seen in Avella again. That story survived for years though, a legend for kids both in town and beyond about what it meant to be from Avella.

That renegade spirit, resolve, and toughness got embedded in the kids of my hometown and soon turned the blue and gold Avella Eagles into an athletic powerhouse. It actually started in soccer, when little old Avella won two straight youth soccer national championships in 1939 and 1940. A little bit later, high school coach Ray Fiorini and all the Pee Wee coaches underneath him brought life to the football teams in town. (I always called him Coach even though he was never really my coach.)

Fiorini served in World War II, then settled in Avella, inheriting a football program that was often a punching bag for bigger teams.

But Fiorini saw past the mere numbers to the assets lying underneath. Those kids of coal miners and laborers and farmers had hard edges that others didn't. And a hunger too. They thought nothing of sweating through three practices in a single day, with the only breaks arriving when the kids stripped off their clothes and splashed down in a nearby creek. Since the amenities afforded to other kids were often missing, it seemed an abundance of camaraderie helped close the gaps.

"It's a funny thing, it was kind of a classless society," my brother Bob said. "Everyone was poor. There was no wealthy section. We were all working people. You didn't notice the fact that you were poor because everyone else was too. We were all in the same boat and all had a desire to get out of it."

Fiorini turned all that togetherness, toughness, and determination into a football dynasty, a local source of pride that had four undefeated seasons, four league titles, and two Western Pennsylvania championships in a 10-year stretch.

A proud town puffed its chest out even more. And every kid who wore blue and gold played with a chip on his shoulder pads, propped up by a proud tradition and bleachers full of screaming fans.

My parents, A. J. and Stella Cindrich, arrived in Avella right in the middle of the athletic glory, their old-fashioned values and hard-nosed sons sustaining the status quo in town and the success on the playing fields too.

My dad was the son of a Croatian butcher whose parents crossed the Atlantic and settled in Slovan, Pennsylvania, just down the road from Avella. Many Croatian immigrants enjoyed the hills of western Pennsylvania because the rolling landscapes reminded them of home. But the life they encountered there was hard on almost everything outside the eyes.

A. J. Cindrich was built like a beer barrel with big, meaty hands weathered by a whole bunch of blue-collar work. He grew up in the shadow of a steel mill, and worked a few shifts there in his younger years. But then World War II broke out and he became a paratrooper, returning home even harsher than when he left. He started an excavation business and then a utility pipeline company, making his living with a lot of hard labor.

He nearly lost a few fingers once, when a machine he was working on smashed them, leaving them bloody, mangled, and hanging by a thread. He missed a few months of work, but his fingers unfortunately held on, making all the backhands I got later in life a few digits worse.

My mother Stella Sfara was born on a boat coming to the United States from Calabria, Italy. She was the youngest of three sisters and a very bright girl, smart enough to skip a grade in school. Stella's parents ran a bar in the heart of Avella, a place that had a huge dance hall and a number of hotel rooms too. For a time it was one of the most popular hangouts in Washington County, with plenty of room for young people to knock back a few beers and dance to some jukebox songs with anyone who might catch their more forgiving eyes.

A. J. was a somewhat legendary drinker who would occasionally visit Sfara's to socialize with friends and quench his persistent thirst. One day, he met my mother there and the two probably shared a few looks, then a dance, a drink, a moment, and then everything else that sends you quickly off into love. Stella's kind heart softened the edges of A. J.'s exterior just long enough for romance to take root. The two were married a little bit later.

They eventually settled into a white, one-story house on a bend in the road just outside town, only a few miles away from the bar where they first met.

The children of immigrants would live there for years, filling the next several decades with a lot of labor, love, and Avella's version of the American dream.

Before long, they'd give birth to five kids.

And one of them would test every single limit they had.

Young Ralph

The Restless Spirit

A. J. AND STELLA WERE IN TROUBLE.

I was born on October 29, 1949, exactly 20 years after the stock market crashed in New York and Lincoln National Bank in Avella went broke.

Soon after I entered the world, I started testing the limits of it.

"He was the cutest kid you ever saw," my brother Bob, who was five years older, remembers. "But he was mischievous. Always into something."

"Damn ornery," my brother Ron says.

One of my earliest memories is of climbing a fence around our house when I was about four years old. We lived in a ranch-style home on an old country road, and I started wandering down it soon after I learned to walk. My parents built a fence about five feet high to pen me in. It didn't work.

I can still remember putting my feet on the fence to climb over it. But I lost my balance in the process, flipped over the top, and landed hard on some gravel, just inches away from the fence itself with a gaping head wound.

It was perhaps my first concussion. Football would give me many more.

My mother was mortified. She couldn't figure out how I escaped, but knew that I'd try again sometime soon. The gate stayed open until they took the fence down.

I was one of five kids in our family's four-room house: Ron, Robert, Rita, myself, and Rebecca. As a kid, I got the nicknames Nunick, from an old comic, and Big Bruiser, from an Easter bunny I drew in elementary school. With all of us living in such close quarters, there was a lot of fun to be had and perhaps a few fights too. But I'm sure my brothers and sisters enjoyed having me around because I seemed to keep a lot of my dad's legendary heat off of everyone else.

Avella was the perfect place for a restless spirit like me. There were rolling hills and woods in almost every direction that I might run. I fell in love with the open spaces around me, and my interest in wildlife began back then too. One time I caught a black snake and carved it up like it was a Thanksgiving turkey, showing it off to a prissy little girl I hoped to impress. Her mother wasn't amused. My dad wasn't either.

But my adventures continued. Times were different back then, when kids were untethered by tablets and television screens. If we didn't have school, we'd spill out of the house early in the morning and only return for lunch, dinner, and bedtime. One time I made a homemade bow and arrow and shot it at a car coming down the road.

Bullseye!

The poor guy almost wrecked. I sprinted into our backyard and over the hill, past my brother Ron who had no idea what the hell had just happened. Ron said it was the fastest 40-yard dash of my life. In a few seconds, I was out of sight and into my hideout, a hillside cave that was really an old coal mine entrance without my imagination. I often fled there when I found trouble. And needless to say, I had a blanket and food inside and made sure it was always stocked.

I was waiting out the trouble when the car I hit pulled in our driveway. A stranger got out. Ron swears he was 6'6".

"Did you see a young boy running around here?" the guy asked.

Ron thought the guy had a drawl, like he was from somewhere out west where vigilante justice works just fine.

"I said, 'No sir I didn't see anyone,'" Ron remembers. "I said, 'Why, what happened?'"

"Someone shot an arrow at my car as I was coming around the curve."

The guy eventually left before he could locate my hideout or find me sweating inside it. Perhaps I was predisposed to trouble, but my dad made sure I got punished for every mistake. Discipline waited for me at the end of every line I crossed.

In 1955, I was about six years old, and I went inside a gas station that sold candy too. Impulse overtook me and I shoplifted some penny candy.

My sister promised not to tell, but ratted me out as soon as we got home. My dad asked me if it was true; I said no.

Wrong answer.

A. J. Cindrich was a man of ethics and integrity, and his word was better than a contract. Seeing his son as a thief and a liar made him lose every last bit of his mind.

He took a belt and beat me senseless. When he was finished, he grabbed the scruff of my neck and the seat of my pants and tossed me out into the front yard. He gave me a razor blade and told me to cut the grass.

Every. Single. Blade. Of. Grass.

Two hours passed. Darkness rolled in.

"ENOUGH!" my mother yelled.

Stella Cindrich was a woman of ethics and integrity too, but she was also a lioness when it came to protecting her young. If she ever felt her family was threatened, she'd grab a butcher knife with every intent to use it. On this particular day, she thought the punishment was starting to exceed the crime. After seeing the extent of my beating and blade cutting, she was pretty sure the lesson had sunk in.

It did. If I've ever taken anything again in my life that is not mine, my mind blocks it out. You would be hard pressed to find anyone who ever said as a man I ever lied, cheated, or stole. Some lessons you never forget.

The beauty of my upbringing was that I had a lot of other adults who influenced me in addition to my parents. My mother made massive spaghetti dinners, a tradition I've continued ever since. The smell of garlic and sauce would slip out of our house and down the driveway, luring 20, 30, or more family members or friends to pop in for a meal.

My mother and father eventually started a pipeline company, putting in gas and other utility lines. They were trying to make a better life for all of us and had to work pretty hard to do it. They woke up early and drove roughly 30 miles to work every day except for Sunday. My mom wasn't around much, so she convinced Aunt Rose to come stay with us and look after me.

Zia Rosa was born in Italy and remembered the town square and the dances there as long as she lived. Over here, she ran a country store in Rochester, Pennsylvania, a rough-and-tumble town a lot like Avella. Zia

Rosa was a kind lady with a very gentle heart. I consider her my angel and still send her occasional prayers and thanks all of these years later. The few soft spots I have somewhere inside me are partly due to her.

But with my penchant for mischief and my father's devotion to punishing it, the good feelings never seemed to last too long in my house. How I lived into adulthood still baffles me some days.

Besides my mother, sports probably deserves the silver medal for saving my ass. My older brothers were great athletes in their own right, and I often tagged along to their practices and games, accelerating my own athletic development in the process. Plus, I eventually grew to a good size, which certainly didn't hurt in sports either.

As I began to excel on the playing field, whether in football, wrestling, or baseball, A. J. couldn't help but swell with pride. And for a few hours, he forgot about kicking my ass. But that doesn't mean he got soft.

In one game when I was about nine years old, my fingers got stomped on by an opponent with sharpened spikes. Blood was pouring out. Both the ligaments and the bone were visible, and the scar persists to this day.

I went to the sideline and my father stopped over to provide his medical opinion.

"Piss on it and get back out there."

I can't remember if my bladder was full enough to consider his treatment, but I was wise enough to know that urine didn't make a great antiseptic. And I didn't have time to waste searching for my dinkle either. In any case, I got back on the field.

And so it went for the remainder of my childhood. My mom instilled the importance of family and provided all the compassion she could. My dad gave me the toughest of loves and enough backhands to keep me in line. Between the two, I got a full complement of old-fashioned values, with unlimited lessons on how to act, work, and make something out of myself.

Those teachings stayed with me long after I left home. And they carried me to my dreams.

Mario Gabrielli

The Hero

IT'S JUNE 10, 1944.

The world is at war, the Nazis are in Europe, and the largest, costliest invasion in modern history is finally complete on the coast of France. Paratroopers who never had a prayer are still hanging in the trees.

My future Pee Wee coach, Mario Gabrielli, had just arrived to hell on earth. What would happen next would forever change Mario's life, and mine, and perhaps a hundred or so others across the ocean in Avella. But no one could have known it then. If it wasn't for his sister Fran Monroe in San Diego who took down his story, the memory of his life would be as silent as the hundreds laid out at Normandy.

Mario (or Gary as we called him when he was our coach) was only 18 then. He was a tough and toned athlete just a few months removed from the campus at Waynesburg College and his pro football dreams.

War interrupted everything.

Gabrielli left college and his previous life and joined the Army in February of 1943. Before long, he was crammed into cattle cars in Africa, carrying bazookas into battle, and scrambling to avoid German artillery in Sicily. On that Italian isle, amid the death and destruction raining from the Mediterranean skies, the fear Mario had been sidestepping since he enlisted finally gained equal footing. Its icy clutches grabbed hold. And it would be months, maybe years, before it ever let go.

"I remember hearing shelling in the distance . . . the cold fear in the pit of my stomach. I didn't allow myself to think . . . to feel anymore. I cared for nothing . . . except the 9th Infantry Division, 60th Regiment Headquarters Company. It rolls off my lips with pride."

The German assault continued. Each explosion shattered Mario's memories of Avella and football and childhood games. But a chance encounter brought a few of them back together. Somewhere in Sicily, Gabrielli found Bill James, a football rival at Trinity High. A few years back, before the war ruined everything, Gabrielli's Class B Avella team beat a much bigger Trinity team 5–0. Mario had scored every point, kicking a 53-yard field goal and tackling an opponent in the end zone for a safety. "That was the greatest moment of my life."

It was perhaps the closest he'd ever get to a shining moment. Teammates carried him off the field on their shoulders. Waynesburg offered him a scholarship that night.

But now in Europe, it was almost impossible to think about anything that had happened across the Atlantic. It all seemed too far away. Mario was fighting for his life, fighting for the remnants of health and humanity that he still had left. He made it out of Sicily only to enter a deeper circle of hell in Normandy, where mankind's worst battle had just been waged.

On June 10, 1944, Mario's company was four days behind the D-Day invasion of the Allied soldiers and following closely in their footsteps. "As soon as we started to move inward, we saw bodies of paratroopers hanging from their chutes in the trees . . . some [were] covered with them on the ground. Gliders were all over the place; smashed bodies clearly seen with no time to move them out. There were many German soldiers left behind."

"I had guard duty and two men had their throats cut, killed the first night. I got my sleep wherever and whenever possible. I wanted to sleep under a tree but [it was] no good, an airburst would get you. I thought about the woods—no. Same [problem]."

Even when all was quiet, it was almost impossible to rest. On June 15, it got even worse. The shelling started at 7:00 a.m. Moments later, Mario's patrol found a platoon of their fellow soldiers fleeing from a gunfight. "The leader, the next soldier, and all 13 men behind him had a bullet in or through them. They tell us we are in no man's land . . . in enemy territory. And there are snipers in the trees, as well as machine-gun emplacements."

Mario dove for cover as bullets began whizzing by. Unfortunately, his fate had already been settled. And there was no foxhole that might save him from it.

"I watched daisies swaying back and forth in the soft breeze. I remember birds chirping. And I started thinking about home, about football, going home."

His patrol started moving again. But then artillery screamed overhead. Three heavy 88-millimeter shells were fired in rapid succession. The first landed over Mario's head. The second shell fell in front of him. "I didn't see or hear the third shell," Mario said years later. The third shell had landed right on top of him. Mario's body went flying through the air and landed with a thud. "I felt no pain. I opened my eyes. I was thinking about a Humphrey Bogart movie I had seen. I thought this is it. I am dying. I said aloud, 'God, don't let me die . . .'"

Mario yelled for the medic. Mike arrived in seconds.

"Mike, will I lose my leg?" Mike worked with Mario in training their champion boxing team. "Mike didn't answer."

"He never looked at me . . . said nothing. My right leg was gone—blown off by the 88-millimeter shell. From then on, it seemed that I kept dreaming of running. I could not stop running. They stuck my bayonet into the ground, a blood plasma bag attached to it. I looked around to see hundreds and hundreds of bayonets stuck into the ground, and all around men crying and groaning."

Mario's first life and his pro football dreams died right there in Normandy. But neither loss was enough to kill him. Even a wheelchair, crutches, and the other implements an amputated leg required weren't enough to shake his resolve. The resiliency of our town ran too deep. His head was high when he crossed the Atlantic and finally returned home.

"The shock and grief was on all the faces of my family and friends. . . . But I was proud. I wore my uniform when they came. I was still Mario Gabrielli of Avella, Pennsylvania, proud to have had a chance to do my part for a better world, for my country, for my family, for my sisters, for my town, for my friends."

Mario's second life would be spent on the sidelines of our local sports teams. And one good leg was more than enough to make him a great coach.

I first met him when I played Pee Wee football. Some thought that he was too hard on us kids. That maybe he was still wounded by the war and taking out his aggression on all his innocent players. Of course we couldn't say it that way; we just thought it. He was just a tough SOB. He had a wooden cane that he used to hobble around, and if you screwed up, you were certain to feel a quick "whack."

The cane would crack your helmet and your head might ring a little. It didn't really hurt, but you sure as hell wouldn't jump offside again. Coach's cane was just giving us discipline and the toughest of loves and we were all better because of it. We knew it even then.

One November day, the Avella sky was spitting freezing rain. It was cold and miserable and the ground was soaked. Our football team huddled by the coal furnace in the basement of the American Legion with spirits high, thinking practice was called off.

Mario sent us out.

We started by stretching, then moved on to grass drills, diving up and down into the sopping mess and doing it over and over and over again. When we finished, Mario picked up a ball, tucked it under his arm, and hobbled over to a spot right next to a massive puddle. He dropped the football right in the middle of it.

"Gentlemen," he said, "We're going live."

The message was clear. Relief wasn't arriving anytime soon. Some of the guys cracked. They started the walk of shame back to the American Legion basement across the tracks, quitting. The rest of us stayed. Giving up was never an option in Avella. We knew the punishment handed out at home would be twenty times worse than anything that might happen out here.

We slogged through the rest of our practice, each raindrop and drill building the kind of character that wouldn't easily wash away.

When it was finally over, we huddled up. And we listened.

"You think I am hard on you?" Mario said. "I've heard the stories. Men, this was about preparing you, toughening you so you don't quit.

If it is cold and rainy, or snowing and icy when you play your game, you will handle it because you have gone through it, and you'll know you can handle it. And the weather will never be as bad when you play as it is today. Because if it is, they will call the game off. Now, get out of here."

A few days later, we played in freezing temperatures on an icy field against a team twice our size. They pranced around in near-perfect pants and jerseys, wearing gloves and winter clothes under their pads. They laughed at our rag-tag team and what passed for our uniforms. But when the game began, we kicked their ass up and down the field. The toughness instilled in us by coach Mario along with head coach Abby Rush's game plan balanced perfectly.

The same lesson that hit home for me that day would be shared with almost every kid who played ball in Avella. My Pee Wee coaches, Abby Rush and Mario, were local legends. After the war, Mario spent his entire life in our hometown, coaching its kids, and working as the postmaster. In time, he met, loved, and married his wife Lillian and had two daughters of his own. And every Memorial Day, he would march at the front of the Avella parade, as tacit messages of pride, sacrifice, and toughness trailed closely behind him.

"My story is just one among thousands of war veterans who return home to resume life," he would say to his sister as she transcribed his story. "It is not that heroic, it is not that dramatic, it is just a life. It is my life and it is a good one."

Mario seemed to know then what the rest of us wouldn't figure out until we were well past our Pee Wee years. His toughness had been embedded in all of us. The old coach had weathered the worst of life's punches and trained us for any that we might encounter on our own.

Perhaps that's why we always kept coming back to his porch. To talk, to thank him, to eat the Italian sausage loaded with enough garlic to make you suck air, and land at least one more meaningful punch before we moved on.

"They still call me Coach," Mario once said, late in the stages of his life. "They still come to see me, to talk about the game. And when we finish talking, they are sure to give me the one-hand punch. It is a reminder to me. It is as if to say: Life hands you many punches, but it is how you take the punch that makes a difference."

My life was only beginning, but Mario gave me a ballast that never went away. His pride, toughness, and tenacity would help carry me out of Avella and onto much bigger things.

"I want your best, Ralphy Boy, that's not your best!"

I hear you Mario, and I miss you pal. Thank you.

And I'd sure as hell know how to take a punch when the time came.

Cindrich vs. Joyner

The Match

IT WAS THE BIGGEST MATCH OF MY LIFE.

With the training and toughness provided by everyone in Avella and some God-given talent and size, I became a dominant force in two sports. Our football team went deep into the playoffs as I created havoc on the interior lines, earning a spot in the exclusive Big 33 all-star game, against a team from Texas coached by NFL legend Bobby Layne. Other awards and accolades soon arrived, along with a steady stream of scholarship offers in my mailbox. A. J. even eased up on me a bit, bursting with pride at everything his rebellious little bastard was accomplishing on the field.

Wrestling season followed football, and I was a maniac on the mat. In my mind, wrestling was in many ways a mental sport, so I fought for a psychological edge as well as a physical one. Matches were often won and lost in the first few seconds. So I usually started mine shaking hands soft and mushy like a wuss, then smacking my opponent's head, locking him up, and driving his ass off the mat—a move that provided dividends far beyond what might get recorded on the scoreboard. Many times, the match was over right then. The opponent would get unsettled or intimidated or both and the spirit would get sucked straight out of him.

As a junior, no one scored a point on me until the regional finals, and I finished as a state runner-up in the unlimited weight class (the precursor to the heavyweight division). I was on a similar steamrolling path as a senior, going unbeaten en route to the Western Pennsylvania championship (for my second straight year) and storming into the state championships. Back then, there were no divisions based on the size of your school. Kids from all over Pennsylvania were thrown together in tournament brackets and settled things mano-a-mano on the mats.

It was 1967. My Pee Wee football coach Ab Rush and about a hundred other people from Avella were in the audience when I stepped out onto the mat for the state final my senior year. The meet was held in State College, on Penn State's campus. I had lost in the same place a year earlier and was hoping like hell to avenge that defeat. I wanted to take home a title for my school and all those hardworking people screaming their support in the stands. No one from my school had ever won a state championship before. It was mine that year. Everything in my life had prepared me for that match.

I had to win it. I thought it was my destiny.

My opponent was Dave Joyner, a talented and well-known rival who would eventually become an athletic director at Penn State. Joyner and I wrestled at a camp the previous summer, and I got the best of him that time. He told me he'd see me again at states. I wasn't even sure that he'd make it that far.

But he did, going deep into the tournament until my name was next to his in the bracket. It was the state final. The biggest match of my entire life. My eyes glared at Joyner across the mat. And somewhere outside my gaze, luck must have snuck over to his side.

Early in the match, we were grappling for position and tumbled off the mat. My right hand landed awkwardly. Something popped. And just like that, two metacarpals were broken.

What? No God, please no. Please don't let this happen . . .

The match was momentarily stopped. A doctor was called over and I heard the bad news.

"You probably shouldn't wrestle. You might still be in shock from the break. But you can't hurt the hand any further . . ."

My coach looked at me.

"Can you continue? I'm just asking and I don't think you should. No one expects you to. I don't know if I would. But it's your call."

I was wrestling.

There was no way I could quit now, even if I was handicapped with one good hand in a sport that required two. Life had landed a punch, but I damn sure knew how to take it.

I fought like hell for the rest of the match and went into overtime with a 1–1 tie. Minutes melted away. With about seven seconds remaining in the extra period, I grabbed his singlet and Joyner received a penalty point for the infraction. It was a controversial call, but perhaps the right one.

And the result was final. I lost 2–1.

Inside that arena, in front of all those people from my hometown, Joyner's arm was raised up. Mine stayed at my sides.

It was the most devastating defeat of my life, a heart-breaking setback that filled me with nightmares and tears and kept me from sleeping for several weeks, maybe months, afterward.

No one expects to lose when you get that close. And certainly not the way I did. Almost 50 years have passed and I've never once watched the film A. J. recorded of that match.

I never will.

For a while afterward, I was angry and depressed and struggling to complete the simple tasks of life.

But no one in Avella let you stay down for long.

Pretty soon I'd have to pick a college.

And before I did, a coaching legend would be coming to my house.

Joe Paterno

The Legend

JOE PATERNO WAS DRIVING TO MY HOUSE.

It was the dead of winter and a massive snowstorm had swept across our little town about 40 miles away from the airport. I was a big-time college recruit with more than 100 letters of interest or offers, in both football and wrestling. Those letters stirred up a lot of pride in my father, and he kept every last one of them, including an eight-page handwritten one from Joseph Vincent Paterno.

Joe Pa's first season as head football coach at Penn State was in 1966, and a year later, he was saving his last scholarship for me. I wanted to concentrate on wrestling and waited until my final high school season was complete before making my choice, forcing Paterno and all the other coaches to chase me deep into the winter of 1967. I wasn't being a dick or a big-timer; I was just laser-focused on wrestling and wanted to be left alone. I was hell-bent on that state championship, but a broken hand wrecked it all just a few miles away from Paterno's home at Penn State.

Now, I was being "wined and dined" as Joe Pa and all the other coaches went to work selling their schools. Paterno's journey out to see me was difficult. Heavy snow was falling and piling up on Avella's rolling country roads, which would never be confused with the Autobahn on the best of days.

Somehow, Joe Pa made it. Even though he was not yet the icon he would become, he was still a head football coach at a major college—and an Italian one at that. My mother, who was born on a boat coming over from Italy, was bursting with pride. She left work early that day and headed to Petrucci's in Burgettstown, the closest supermarket, to collect all the ingredients for what she believed was one of the most important meals she'd ever cook. She spent the rest of the day in the kitchen, boiling pasta, simmering sauces, and perfecting the flavors of her ancestors. My principal, Ray Fiorini, a former coach himself, was pretty excited too, and my father uncorked a special bottle of booze for our honored guest. A. J. enjoyed getting drunk with almost everyone, coal miners and mill workers alike, so drinking with Joe Paterno was just a bonus. We had a huge bottle of Chianti at our house that seemed to be waiting for a special occasion. Something like this one.

A. J. popped the cork.

"I never drink around recruits," Paterno said.

I'm pretty sure that was the case, but my dad could be pretty persuasive, even when he wasn't driving home his point with the back of his hand. Before long, both he and Joe had finished that bottle and were well into a second one—at least A. J. was.

Sometime during the visit, Joe Pa gave us his pitch for Penn State. I wasn't sold on State College after losing the wrestling title up there in such tragic fashion. I knew Dave Joyner was going to Penn State and at the time I just wanted revenge. With a healthy hand, I figured I could beat him out for the heavyweight spot on Penn State's wrestling team, but I wanted to win on a bigger stage than in the back of a wrestling room. And if I went to another school and beat him in the Eastern Championships or at Nationals, revenge would be even sweeter. Plus, I wanted a redshirt year because of my late October birthday and wasn't sure if it would be possible at Penn State. Joe Pa promised me anything I wanted.

"Coach, I'm not sure I can help you. I've always been a year behind with a late October birthday. I want a redshirt year. Or prep school."

We both knew there were technical reasons—compliance reasons—that were supposed to prevent athletes from getting any extra years at his school. But the esteemed coach told me the same thing every other school said—don't worry, you can have your redshirt—there are ways.

"We have redshirts, just not like the other schools you're talking to. There's a legit way around it," Paterno said.

He said he'd make sure I got my extra redshirt year. Even if it was technically against the rules, there were too many other places making it happen. He could find a way at his school too.

"Don't worry about a thing," he said. "You'll be happy at Penn State."

Pitt, West Virginia, and essentially all the other schools that recruited me had offered to skirt the rules on my behalf too, so Paterno wasn't alone. But the lesson wasn't lost that even a beacon of character was a bit flawed.

I was just a college recruit then, but I was becoming convinced that the NCAA, its member schools, and many of its coaches were often corrupt, some of them to significant degrees. Everyone wanted to win, and most people were willing to sidestep some rules along the way. That opinion would only get stronger as I acquired more anecdotal evidence in later years.

Our honored guest eventually left, a little fatter and a little drunker than when he arrived, thanks to the combined efforts of my parents. Soon afterward, I ended up picking the University of Pittsburgh, spurning both Paterno and Penn State, and fueling a rivalry of my own that would continue in the years ahead. But the Nittany Lions did pretty well on their end of things too. That last scholarship went to Jack Ham instead of me, a class guy who became a collegiate All-American, a Pro Football Hall of Famer, and one of the greatest linebackers who would ever wear blue and white. Ham was one of the many Penn State guys I grew to like over the years, players with strong character and sparkling conduct, people who certainly gained some of those values from their old Italian coach.

With Ham on the roster instead of me, I suppose Paterno got the last laugh. And then he tried for another one too.

During my sophomore year—freshmen didn't play back then—I suffered a nasty ankle injury in the first game against UCLA. We got our asses kicked and I decided not to rush back from it, cashing in the second redshirt year that all the schools had promised. It was a legitimate injury that lasted a few weeks and it didn't seem like a problem at first. That feeling ended when I got notice that Pitt's athletic director wanted to see me ASAP. Paterno had reported me to the Eastern College Athletic Conference, saying that my redshirt season didn't fit the strict rules and should not have been granted. It sure as hell seemed like a vendetta. I was plenty pissed.

The case eventually went to a hearing. I won it, but the damage had been done. Paterno and Penn State were on my shit list, and I suppose they all hated my guts too. That same year, they beat us so badly that the refs kept the clock running when people went out of bounds to end it faster. Paterno and I M.F.-ed each other every time we approached each other on the sidelines. I suppose I had a knack for picking fights, even if there was a legend on the opposite side.

My run-ins with Joe Pa were only the beginning.

There would be many more in the years ahead.

Mary Rose

The Thunderbolt

YOU HAVE TO BE LUCKY TO FEEL IT ONCE.

Most people never get the chance. To them, it's nothing but a fable, something that can only happen in fairy tales and fantasy worlds.

The Sicilians call it "the thunderbolt"—a feeling of love and lust so strong that the closest comparison is a lightning bolt that lands atop your head.

That's exactly what hit me the first time my eyes met Mary Rose. I fell in love instantly. And I catch a little bit of it again every time I tell the story. . . .

Mary Rose was born and raised at 905 Fifth Street in Beaver, Pennsylvania, a quaint, old, WASP town on the Ohio River about an hour north of Avella. Her mother was Italian and her father was Jewish, but he converted to Catholicism after he suffered a heart attack and a priest administered the last rites a bit prematurely. Her father miraculously recovered, became a Catholic from that day on, and four-year-old Mary dodged a tragedy that could have destroyed her life.

She grew up in a modest house that was nothing like the mansions built on the river's edge or the large houses sitting high atop the hills. Her mother always talked about those homes and the endless money that seemed to be sitting inside of them. Later in life Mary could have had her pick of them. But back then, her father worked in the mill, so life was simple, humble, and overwhelmingly happy.

Before long, Mary grew into something special. She was pleasant, polite, and refined and enjoyed the kind of upbringing that exists on the edges of a Norman Rockwell painting. Her grandmother owned a fruit stand on a main street in town. Most of her extended family lived within two blocks. She went to Catholic school and believed everything every priest or nun ever told her from the beginning of time until months after meeting me. Trust me on that.

She played the piano, cheered for the high school football team, and did so well in school that she finished first in her graduating class. A bright future waited in front of her, wide open and overflowing with possibility. She hoped to be a doctor someday. And she was pretty enough to be a pageant queen too, winning a competition called the Beaver County Junior Miss.

We still have a framed picture from that pageant, a black and white photograph with Mary wearing a winning smile, a sash draped across a slinky white dress and a tiara atop her head. First prize was a scholarship from state senator Ernest Kline, and it paid for her entire tuition to the University of Pittsburgh.

She was going places, a rare combination of brains and beauty who could make some money in a world finally opening up to women. She was several miles out of my league, deserving the socialite son of some doctor or suit living in one of those grand houses her mom always talked so much about.

But destiny doesn't deal in expectations. And a hard-ass athlete from a coal-mining town was about to cross her path.

Fast forward to a fraternity party during my sophomore year in college. Mary and I might have been the only two people who were sober. I was so frustrated by Pitt's failures in football that I was laser-focused on wrestling. I was teetotalling the entire trimester.

No alcohol. No tobacco. Nothing.

None of that was easy, especially abstaining from snuff, since it was something of a food group down in Avella. All those sacrifices paid off though.

I had just won the Eastern Championships in wrestling and my face got busted up in the process. The National Championships were looming a few weeks later in Utah, and I didn't dare screw up any of my preparations with a bunch of frat house beer. Mary wasn't drinking because good Catholic girls didn't do that. As I said, I think she believed everything the priests and nuns ever told her from the beginning of time to the end. And she probably took notes too because she was such a good student.

The winds of fate swirled through campus that night and sent us both, valedictorian and future All-American, to the same party, two sober bodies thrown together amid the rising blood alcohol levels and clouds of smoke surrounding us.

I was uncharacteristically subdued, skirting all the revelry thanks to my wrestling regimen. Mary was on a casual date with another football player. And she was once again wearing that winning white dress, its sleek and slim fabric clinging to her curves, the spaghetti straps slipped over her shoulders.

Somewhere amid all the alcohol, music, and the carefree college kids buzzing through another fun-filled night, I saw her for the first time.

And a thunderbolt fell from the sky.

I've never felt anything like it before or since.

She was the most beautiful woman I had ever seen. And she had a wonderful ass.

My mind, body, and soul were surging from the shockwaves. I buried those emotions as best I could—she was with someone else that night—but a feeling like that doesn't go away. The electricity interrupts your thoughts. Your emotions spiral far beyond control.

"I want to meet that girl," I finally said to Kathy, a mutual friend of Mary and me.

Maybe I didn't understand all of it then, but I was already in love. Kathy set us up on a date after Pitt's spring game my sophomore year. Naturally, Mary had been to a party or two, but she'd never seriously dated a jock before me. Thankfully, she gave me a chance.

And that's all it took for love to take root.

We talked for hours. Made a connection. And I couldn't help but notice that she brought out the best in me. When I was with her, somehow all those rugged Avella edges softened just enough to give our relationship a chance.

On one of our first dates, I walked her all the way to the doorstep of 905 Fifth Street and kissed her as gently as I could. Mary walked inside and told her mom that I was such a gentleman.

She started feeling the thunderbolt too.

On another date, I took her to a fancy place where crystal chandeliers hung from the ceiling and steaks and lobsters appeared on the plates underneath. Maybe I didn't show it much, but somewhere beneath all my toughness and testosterone was a much softer, romantic side. For Mary's sake, I let it out.

Everything clicked. We fell in love quickly, football player and cheerleader becoming the typecast couple that so many movies are built upon. Back then, neither of us could have known how long we'd last, how far we'd go, or how much we'd do.

We were too busy living in the little moments.

Full hearts. Locked eyes. Pressed lips.

The thunderbolt, the fable, the feeling that's felt so rarely that some consider it a myth, had hit us both.

And we'd never really be apart again.

Pitt

The College Days

I WAS THE KING.

At least that's what my workout buddy and future CFL star Rooster Fleming called me. The name always seemed too high and mighty for my taste—we didn't exactly have a monarchy running things down in Avella—but the nickname stuck anyway, at least with Rooster.

In Oakland, the part of Pittsburgh where the university is located, I tried staying true to my roots in Avella, with my feet firmly on the ground and my head far below the clouds. I hung around with guys on the grounds crew and some rough-and-tumble types who knew how to handle themselves on the streets.

In 1968, my sophomore football season ended after the first game, when I suffered the nasty ankle injury against UCLA. I redshirted for the rest of the year and entered 1969 as a redshirt sophomore despite Paterno's efforts to challenge the redshirt designation.

I spent some time before the 1969 season catching a break out in California. I went to a UCLA frat party and ran into Dave Dalby, the center for UCLA whom I had played well against when our teams met a year earlier, in the game that ended with my ankle injury. Dalby showed me great respect, but we were both eager to meet on the football field again. Any differences we had would be settled between the lines, in the first game of the 1969 season.

I won AP Player of the Week after an impressive performance in that game. Dalby had to wait a whole year for a rematch, when Pitt and UCLA met again in the first game of the following season.

September 19, 1970, arrived and I was frothing inside the locker room, rocking back and forth like a psych-ward patient. Dalby was getting some preseason recognition. And I couldn't wait to see him on the field.

It was game day. My junior season was about to kick off and everything was in place for a monster year. During the offseason, Pitt's PR man, Dean Billick, did a great job building the hype, feeding my name to *Sports Illustrated* and a whole bunch of other football previews. Many of them said I was the best defensive player at Pitt since Joe Schmidt, a former All-American who had a Hall of Fame career with the Detroit Lions.

Football season had finally arrived, and along with it came a perfect chance to prove I was as good as advertised. As fans filled with optimism strolled into Pitt Stadium, I had a solo camera on me and a microphone tucked under my pads. The latter was a wise ploy by Pitt's PR team to help promote me and also carry fans inside all the collisions and tackles that were about to take place.

The sun was shining on Pittsburgh. Roasting it actually, with temperatures approaching 100 degrees on the field.

Everything was about to begin.

Mary was in her cheerleading uniform. The UCLA Bruins and my rival Dave Dalby were on the opposite sideline, providing even more for my pregame fire. And underneath us all was a fresh plot of artificial turf, making Pitt one of the first stadiums in the country to have it. I had only played on that surface once before, when I hyperextended a knee and had a partial cartilage tear at West Virginia a year earlier.

Just before I headed out, our defensive coordinator, Tom Fletcher, looked at the cut-down cleats on my Riddell shoes.

"You need more traction," he said. "You should change."

I listened closely and followed orders, just as we had always been taught back home in Avella.

Even though it went against my instincts—you don't change at the last minute—I put on new shoes with thicker cleats. I hated changing equipment so close to game time. But I did it anyway.

The kickoff soared up into the sun-filled skies. Out on the field, UCLA and Dalby went on offense first. I couldn't wait to face Dalby again, this time in front of my hometown family and friends.

The first play started at about the 20 yard line and moved fast to the left. I was reading my keys at linebacker and going hard to the left to beat Dalby's cut-off block. My wrestling quickness had given me an advantage over him. The runner rushed off tackle going to the wide side of the field, racing toward the open space to my left. I was a tad behind the football—flying—and when the running back cut back, I cut in hard too.

All my weight shifted onto my left foot. And it was stuck to the turf by those tractor-trailer treads.

My knee exploded. Cartilage and ligaments were shredded. The kneecap popped out. And I'm thinking an entire season just went up in smoke.

Who knows what the microphone heard next?

I was on the ground in agony, or in medical terms, a state of shock.

"Get up! I want you," Dalby yelled. "You have to play. Get up."

Nice guy, that Dalby. Sensitive son of a bitch. He was almost crying when he realized he wouldn't get another shot at me.

Our rematch ended right then. Willie Meyers and Roger McGill, the trainers for our team, helped me hobble off the field. Gary Patterson, a lifelong friend, went in at my position. And I headed off to the locker room.

Everything I had worked toward with all those stadium steps and sweat-filled training sessions had been stolen in a single play. Dalby was pissed. And I was absolutely devastated.

"I planted my feet to get set to make the stop," I later told the *Washington Observer-Reporter*. "And I went down on my face. That was my whole season. One play."

Inside the cruel silence of the locker room, seemingly far away from the football and fanfare I had been a part of just a few minutes earlier, I asked trainer Roger McGill a question.

"You think I'll ever play with this knee again?"

"Well, one thing for sure, you sure as heck won't play without it."

Can you smile when you're in shock? I tried.

The dark cloud of that injury lingered for weeks. Doctors had to wait a while for the swelling to subside before they could even begin to operate. So, just like with my broken hand in the wrestling state finals, I could throw in the towel or try to play. I did the latter.

And it was a bad move.

It was the great comeback of Pitt vs. WVU, October 17, 1970, at Pitt Stadium. We were down 35–8 at halftime, but led by quarterback Dave Havern, we ended up winning 36–35. I only appeared in the first couple of series. My knee was strapped tight with tape and a brace. WVU coach Bobby Bowden had a pretty good team, with two big-time running backs, Bob Gresham and Jim Braxton, who both played in the pros.

An early handoff went to Braxton with Gresham leading through the hole. Coming straight at me.

Gresham went straight for my ankle. I didn't move.

That injury hurt almost as badly as the blown knee. Almost.

The doctors now had a lot of work to do.

According to the *Observer-Reporter* doctors repaired and removed the medial cartilage of my knee. In February, they took out some lateral cartilage. Wrestling was lost forever. In football, you can create schemes and cover weaknesses when there are 11 players to work with. But in wrestling, it's one-on-one, and every weakness is exposed and obvious. Any flaw is fair game. I never wrestled again. My weight fell about 30 pounds and I soon shrank down to about 198.

My athletic career was in ashes.

But a guy like me, born and raised amid the setbacks and obstacles easily found in Avella, knew how to fight back better than most everyone else.

Life had landed a punch. But I knew how to take it.

I ran. I lifted. I tore off up and down stadium steps determined to get back to where I was. I wanted to be the king again.

And I worked out harder than ever, resurrecting those dreams that seemingly died on the first play of my junior season.

I returned in time for the first game of my senior season. We beat UCLA in the Rose Bowl 29–25 and I was named Lineman of the Week after recording eight tackles and two fumble recoveries. I was in the right place at the right time but not the player I once was. Later in the year, I had 16 tackles against Syracuse and finished the season as an AP All-American.

Despite the honors, deep down I knew I wasn't the same, knew that my knees were bad, and I was a cheap imitation of the former king.

But I still had hunger in my heart, fire in my belly, and a willingness to fight for every inch.

And that was more than enough to carry me off to a career in the NFL.

Draft Day

The New Beginning

I started drinking.

What the hell else was I supposed to do? How else was I going to end the sickening avalanche of anger, anxiety, and anguish brought by the NFL Draft?

I had been thinking about this day for months—years, really—but nothing was going as expected. One team after another was passing over me. It didn't seem to matter that I was an All-American. Sure, my knee had been shredded some in college. And my ankle was bad too.

But I didn't understand why I hadn't been drafted yet.

The first round of the 1972 NFL Draft came and went without a phone call. The second round did too. And at some point that day, I grabbed a fifth of Jack Daniel's and started sipping. Then chugging. I wasn't sure when I'd want to stop.

The whiskey was at war with the rage that was building every minute. I knew I was better than some of the guys picked before me. I had played with a couple of these bozos in the North-South Shrine Game for God's sake! I was better than them. So what if my knee wasn't?

The hours passed and less and less of the caramel-colored liquid remained in the bottle, as it flowed deeper and deeper into my bloodstream.

Things would have been a lot worse if ESPN had been around then, torturing me with its television ticker, those talking heads, and all the names already attached to a team. It was one of the rare moments in my life when I felt unwanted. And I hated it.

I wanted to be left alone.

Those scars would linger for years, and I'd always advise my clients to stay far away from New York, the draft, and all the cameras that would record every second. Why subject yourself to such public scrutiny if things didn't fall your way?

Back then, I learned firsthand what it felt like. And some kid was making things worse, tying up the residence hall phone while I waited for a team to call. It wasn't like how things are now, where every player is tied to a cell phone sitting in his palm or pocket.

Back then, you needed a landline. I had a private one in my room, but I was smart enough never to give that number out to all the pro people I encountered. They would call at all hours of the night and I would lose all pretenses of privacy and sleep.

I gave everyone the number for the phone in the lobby. And when the draft arrived, I was waiting for a call on a telephone I shared with everyone on my floor. And despite repeated requests, this asshole wouldn't stop talking.

I've never been a baby or a bully, but this kid wasn't responding to polite requests. He knew exactly what he was doing.

I was waiting for a fucking call, asshole! I asked him once again to kindly free up the phone, so my call could come through whenever it might arrive.

He told me to go fuck myself.

And I went blind. The rage that had been building pick-by-pick, round-by-round, brushed up against some of that whiskey racing through my veins. I decked the kid with a single swipe, knocking him to the floor with one forearm to the head.

Even at such a heated time, why hit with a hand that could get broken? In my younger years, I hit my forearms on old junk cars before the season and this kid seemed softer than the side panels of a Model T.

Finally, the phone was free. And the asshole who had been holding it hostage was having trouble talking. He got what he deserved.

Five rounds into the draft, one fifth of Jack Daniel's later, and with the phone finally back on the cradle, the Atlanta Falcons became my life preserver, ending my ordeal by selecting me with the 119th pick.

Eventually, all the anger floated away.

Who really cared if it took so long?

It happened, right?

Ralph Cindrich, the rough-and-tumble kid from little old Avella, Pennsylvania, was an NFL player. All the anxiety and anguish disappeared. Better, brighter emotions took their place.

Joy. Satisfaction. Relief.

I did my best to let them soak in.

It was time to celebrate.

But I was already one fifth deep and I wasn't much of a drinker anyway. I think I went to bed early. There was no point in waiting up anyway.

The dream had already arrived.

Atlanta

The Falcons

REALITY STRUCK EARLY IN MY NFL CAREER.

It was 1972. I was a professional football player, under contract with the Atlanta Falcons and playing linebacker in a preseason game against the San Diego Chargers.

My first game.

Like a dumb ass, I listened to all the vets who told me to bust the wedge and barrel through San Diego's kamikaze squad of monsters on the kickoff team. I hauled ass down the field and was running right next to the kicker, who soon thought better of it and scurried off somewhere else. I crashed into five fat-ass linemen by myself, their force multiplied with their bodies lined shoulder to shoulder. I got hit so hard that Mario and the mortar shell that landed atop him came to my mind.

I came out of that collision with a lifetime ache in my upper back from a crushed disc. All from a single, solitary dumb-ass play. No problem, I suppose. It would match a lower one I got from wrestling.

Once I got myself together, I went out at linebacker.

John Hadl, San Diego's quarterback, was lined up under center just a few yards away. Hadl was an All-American halfback and quarterback at the University of Kansas, and oddly enough, wore No. 21 in the NFL. (The league would adopt a more rigid system for uniform numbers in 1973 and quarterbacks wouldn't be allowed to have anything higher than 19.)

Mike Garrett, a former Heisman Trophy winner, future Pro Bowler, and eventual athletic director at USC, was the running back. Garrett was in a split backfield, two positions ahead of me to my left. I had him one-on-one in man coverage. I was smart, but this was my first pro game and I was much more anxious than patient. It was the first play, and I needed to hit someone to settle my nerves.

Hadl seemed to be done with his cadence and was ready for the snap. Right then I took a tiny pee pee step to the left. If it was church, it would be like a fart that no one heard. But the son of a bitch Hadl made it a Broadway production. A smile stretched across his face and he looked back at Garrett, then met me in the eyes with a laugh.

This was a mismatch. He stopped his cadence and called an audible. He nodded back to Garrett again, still grinning that big-ass smile, and then looked at me one more time.

Good luck, rookie. Hold on to your ass.

I was one-on-one with a Pro Bowl back shifty enough to win the Heisman. I was completely and utterly fucked.

The ball was snapped and the play started to the left. I was sprinting as fast as I could, hoping what speed I had would be enough.

Hadl dumped the ball off to Garrett in the flat. I was closing in and bracing for a collision—*watch out, A-hole, you're dog meat!*

I had been waiting my whole life for this, about to deliver a big-time hit on a big-time back in the middle of an NFL field.

He's mine and he's dead! Just then the son of a bitch juked the opposite direction and cut back across the field, leaving tons of open yardage between the two of us.

Me? I could tell you a lot about California grass that night. If you poured some water into my mouth, we could have had a putting green. After Garrett's juke, my helmet hit the ground so hard that sod smashed into my face mask, then mouth.

I had overpursued Garrett—duh!—and now I was paying for it. My responsibility in coverage was running free, racing ahead for a decent gain, and I had no chance to tackle him. Thankfully one of my teammates did. But he was my man. And it was a total breakdown, something that had been a foreign concept in the earlier stages of my football career.

The NFL was different. It's been more than 40 years and I haven't forgotten anything about that play. I probably never will. Nothing could have reinforced my reality in the NFL more than that one play in my first preseason game. My instincts had put me in the right place to make a play, but my body didn't have a chance in hell.

In the running game, I was still a force, someone who could fill a hole and shed a blocker with the best of them. But in the NFL, you need to be good at everything, and with all my injuries I was much weaker in coverage. I was a step slow in a game that swung on inches.

"And the inches are everywhere around us. In every second, in every minute of the play."

I knew that quote was true long before I ever heard it in the movie *Any Given Sunday*. For the Falcons at least, nothing had really gone as planned.

My knees were too bad. My days were numbered. My time was borrowed.

A few months earlier, Bobby Riggle, a Falcons scout from Washington, Pennsylvania's Trinity High, had helped convince the team to pick me. But his voice didn't matter much now. Norm Van Brocklin, a talented former quarterback who became a mediocre coach wracked with brain damage was in charge of the Atlanta Falcons' roster and my future with the team.

Van Brocklin didn't think much of me and didn't care enough to soften the blow of my cut. Unless you were a vet, that's the way all cuts were. Trust me. He gave it to me straight. The Falcons released me before I ever played in a game that really mattered.

And it sucked.

The drive out of Atlanta was one of the longest car rides of my entire life. I thought about Mary, who was still my girlfriend. She maneuvered her flight attendant job to work out of Atlanta, so that we could stay close. What was she supposed to do now? Could she follow me? (She eventually did.)

And what about me? Wasn't I good enough anymore? After a childhood and collegiate career filled with success, accolades, and accomplishments, my professional tenure was starting with a heavy dose of failure.

Was I just not right for Atlanta? Was I good enough to play for anyone? Was professional football really in my future?

Somewhere deep inside, I knew I was still pretty good. Other players thought so too. As I drove out of Atlanta, a whole bunch of questions overtook the quiet car ride home.

Where would I go next? Would I get another chance? What was I supposed to do now?

The answers that finally arrived were familiar ones. And they would carry me through a few more teams, a few more towns, and a few more years in the NFL.

Nothing was over just yet. Life had landed a punch, but I had to move forward. Fight back. Get back up just as Mario would have wanted me to.

And never, ever give up.

New England

The Patriots

My NFL career wasn't dead just yet.

It was 1972 and the New England Patriots called me after I went through waivers, about a week after I was cut by Atlanta. So I was off to New England on my achy knees, chasing the dream for as long as it might last. The defensive coordinator was Tom Fletcher, the same coach from Pitt who encouraged me to change my cleats that day I blew out my knee. He didn't do me any favors at Pitt, but I sure was liking him now. He knew I could play when healthy.

Mary got transferred out of Atlanta and moved closer to me in New York City, a manageable drive from where I was playing with the Patriots.

Everywhere I looked in New England, I could see how fragile a career in football was. And I could see how hard some of the guys worked to protect it, doing every last damn thing they could to stay on the right side of the roster.

My roommate with the Patriots was Ron Acks, a linebacker from the University of Illinois who played college ball with Dick Butkus. Ron had already played four years in the league by the time we met, so he was the perfect guy to room with as a rookie. He survived Norm Van Brocklin a lot longer than I did, but he was eventually cut by Atlanta too.

Ron was a little undersized (still taller than I was), but was a good athlete who was smart and savvy, someone who always made the most of all his athletic gifts. I learned a lot from Ron in our time together and eventually passed it on to my clients when they were fighting for a spot.

Ron's thinking was that you should be nondescript if you wanted to make an NFL roster. Nod, smile, and shut the fuck up. (I always seemed to miss that last part.) He figured if you were going to stand out somewhere, it should be on the playing field. And in that case, do it every chance you got.

The other thing that made Ron an interesting roommate was that the ladies loved him. And loved him. If Casanova played linebacker for the Patriots, he would have had shaggy, side-swept hair and looked a lot like Ron Acks.

On the field, there were a lot of other guys who were just as determined to make the team. Rick Cash was a defensive lineman whose claim to fame was arriving in a trade for Fred Dryer, the football player who went on to television fame in the police drama *Hunter*. Anyway, at one practice I remember seeing Cash sprinting past me like he had just stolen a purse. Turns out, one of the coaches had called for a tackling dummy and Cash wanted to be the one who picked it up.

"The more things you can do!" he yelled to me in mid-stride.

Not surprisingly, Cash played in 28 straight regular season games for New England in his two years with the team.

The coaches on our team seemed to be up against it as well, and we needed two of them to finish the year. John Mazur, a former quarterback at Notre Dame, started the season as head coach, but went 2–7 to begin the season and resigned after a 52–0 shutout by the Miami Dolphins. He seemed like a good guy, but I never got to know him. His replacement was Phil Bengston, the defensive coordinator under Vince Lombardi, and another standup guy. But Bengston only lasted the balance of 1972, staying just long enough to start me over longtime veteran Jim Cheyensky near the end of the season. I couldn't save his job though. Phil went 1–4 to close the season and then moved upstairs, taking an easier job as director of scouting where he wouldn't have to take our talent and turn it into wins.

On my end, I played in 12 games that year on those achy knees, starting three, and surviving my first full season in the NFL.

I even had a standout game against one of the best teams in football history, the Miami Dolphins, who went undefeated in 1972 and won the Super Bowl. In a December game that we lost 37–21, I was chosen as the AP Player of the Week after an impressive performance.

But the knees were getting worse with every snap. One of the worst experiences in my life was practicing outside in the cold December of New England on hardened Astroturf, freezing my ass off, then standing in an ice tub to take the swelling down on my knees. I also tore an inner thigh muscle late in the season and had to take drugs to play in a game against Denver, something I only did once or twice in my entire career.

I had made it through the meat grinder of the NFL season, but it was hard to celebrate too much considering our team's performance. Our defense scored the fewest points in the league, and we had the worst scoring differential as well. I put that all behind me as I headed home for the offseason.

I rented a U-Haul and loaded it with lobsters and other seafood to take back to Pittsburgh. It was a lot better trip than the last time I had gone home, after being cut by the Falcons.

While I was gone, more changes arrived in New England, keeping anyone from getting too comfortable. Chuck Fairbanks, who left the University of Oklahoma in midseason just three months before a scandal broke, became the new coach of the Patriots. And Fairbanks had an old-school, in your face approach that would soon stir up some trouble on our practice fields.

In one practice, he tried to motivate defensive end Jimmy White by running over, grabbing his jersey, and trying to throw him around. That shit wasn't going to work in the NFL.

Jimmy knocked his ass back.

"I'm a grown man!" Jimmy yelled. "You don't put your hands on me."

Jimmy was gone during one of the next cut-down days. He knew exactly what we all did. It was hard as hell to play for an egomaniac.

Fairbanks would create conflict in other ways too. Heisman Trophy winner Jim Plunkett was our quarterback that year, but never seemed to be in a position to succeed. Plunk was a prince of a guy who doted on his blind parents and was one of the best pocket passers in the entire league. Naturally, Fairbanks had him running the option, which led to disastrous results until he escaped to Oakland and won a few Super Bowls with the Raiders. He and Randy Vataha were both from Stanford—which is to say they were whack jobs like everyone else from that school—but they were a lot of fun to be around in New England.

Fairbanks, however, made my life difficult on a few other fronts. His first draft pick was John Hannah, a Hall of Famer from the University of Alabama whom *Sports Illustrated* once labeled as the best offensive lineman of all time. The other first-round pick was Sam "Bam" Cunningham, a USC fullback who set a record by scoring four touchdowns in the 1973 Rose Bowl.

I had to tangle with Hannah every day in practice and earned all the bruises to prove it. I also had my share of collisions with Cunningham, who was equal parts wrecking ball and lead blocker. Somebody in the front office did a hell of a job drafting those guys.

John was the hardest hitter though. He looked like a chubby country boy, but had short hippo legs and a bend in his hips that sent you on a rocket ride every time he made contact. It was only practice, but he was the best lineman I ever faced.

Amateur wrestling had given me so many lessons in leverage that I usually held my own in collisions with offensive linemen. Hannah was different though. "Hawg," as he was nicknamed, usually got the best of me, leaving my shoulders black and blue during every day of an agonizing training camp with a rah-rah, hit-crazy coach.

That year, we played in the Hall of Fame Game, which forced our season to start even earlier. I ticked off Fairbanks big time in that game, knocking out a 49ers receiver on a route across the middle.

The referee ruled that I hit the receiver too soon and threw a 15-yard penalty flag in my direction. I suppose I was too anxious. Or maybe I just wanted to piss off Fairbanks again.

Sometime after the final cuts, before our regular season started, I got the, "Coach wants to see you in his office" line from somebody in the organization. Typically, if you made it to 4:00 p.m. EST of the final roster week, you were on the team—or at least you should be. The club owed you a game check. I got my call Friday after the Tuesday cut-down.

And the asshole Fairbanks almost seemed to be enjoying it all, taking pleasure in the pain of his players. I had just entered into a lease for the year and purchased furniture for my place. But he didn't want to see me and the feeling was mutual. I wanted out of there, far away from sick fucks like him.

I don't know why, but I don't remember anything about who I saw after getting cut.

I was out on the unemployment line once again, released by the Patriots and seeing once more why so many say the NFL really stands for "Not For Long."

But I didn't complain or disagree. I was a far cry from my collegiate self, a beat-up big man on campus, who was now playing on bad knees and borrowed time.

Bob Terpening, a scout for the Patriots who would become a good friend and eventually a general manager for the Indianapolis Colts, drove me and a couple of other players who didn't survive the cuts to the airport.

When you're knee deep in disappointment like that, it's hard to see anything positive. There was a lot of bitching that went on in that car, but not from me.

Beneath all the emotions, I was collecting exactly what I needed to be successful as an agent—knowledge, experience, and an empathy for what it's like to be a player.

Of course, I didn't know any of that then.

And my career wasn't over yet either. My next stop would send me back down south to a team in Texas that might have been one of the most interesting squads ever assembled.

In my last preseason game before getting cut, I had resembled the guy who earned Player of the Week honors a season earlier. Redskins coach George Allen took notice and made a special call on my behalf to another future Hall of Famer, Houston Oilers head coach Sid Gillman.

I'd soon find out that Sid's team was a circus troupe in sky blue shirts.

And one of the ringmasters wore a 10-gallon hat.

Houston

The Education

My head coach wore a 10-gallon hat and cowboy boots, and spilled memorable quotes nearly every time he talked. Our starting quarterback married a *Playboy* centerfold. We had a defensive end with a legendary drug habit, a gay player long before it was common in the locker room, and a receiver who made his end zone dance famous. And then there was me, clinging to the edge of the roster and doing everything I could to hold on.

Shortly after getting cut by the New England Patriots, George Allen called Sid Gillman and told him to watch my film. That favor earned me three more years in the NFL with the Houston Oilers and a few games with the Denver Broncos too.

The Oilers were one of the most interesting teams in NFL history. With my creaky knees getting worse every day, I was speeding toward life after football, and that squad gave me a healthy introduction to the wide range of personalities I would encounter as a lawyer and an agent.

My first head coach in Houston was Gillman, a future Hall of Famer who was one of the early proponents of the deep passing game. He was followed by Bum Phillips, a cowboy of sorts who just happened to coach football. He wore snakeskin boots studded with rhinestones and a hat that seemed like it was stolen from Yosemite Sam.

"There's two types of coaches," Bum once said. "Dem dat's fired and dem dat's gonna be fired."

Bum was ahead of his time in his perception of job security—but a bit old-fashioned too. When he was younger, his mom always told him not to wear a hat indoors. So when we played a game in the Astrodome he left the damn thing in the locker room.

Another one of our characters was John "the Tooz" Matuszak, a defensive end drafted with the No. 1 overall pick in 1973. Tooz was 6'8" and 280 pounds, a massive beast who fueled his body with a long list of substances that would make Keith Richards cringe. He got injections from the pituitary glands of cadavers, took steroids, popped pain pills and Quaaludes, swigged booze, and snorted a large share of blow. On top of all that, he was deep into amphetamines. Back then, guys who took a little speed were called crop dusters, and those who took more became 747s. Tooz earned the title of "John F-n Glenn." He also considered himself a warlock, and even invited me to a séance once, but I turned down the invitation. (Later in life, Tooz became famous for some Hollywood roles too, starring as Sloth in *The Goonies* before an untimely death at 38 due to what was labeled an accidental overdose.)

We had a teammate or two who were alleged to be gay. As far as I was concerned, the information was pure hearsay, but it came from older guys and others who partied on the streets. It was widely perceived and passed around the locker room, but it never became an issue with our team. All that mattered was whether the guy was a good teammate and could play ball. Michael Sam may get credit for being the first openly gay football player, but there have been dozens before him. It's just that their sexual orientations never escaped the locker room.

Our quarterback in Houston was Dante "Dan" Pastorini, a California kid who married a well-endowed *Playboy* model named June Wilkinson. June was built like a Barbie doll (44-23-35) and was given the nickname "the Bosom" by some crude magazines. We called her "the Tits" because we were more civilized.

June sat in the wives' section of the stands and often wore a pink top covered in sequins that spelled out "Big 7." Seven was Dan's number and he was rather sensitive about our antics concerning his wife.

The number-one goal of the first folks on the field, special teamers like myself, and I mean number one goal: spot June's tits. That was it.

Our buddy Dan, a good teammate and a big part of the Oilers family, was also quite touchy about locker-room comments concerning his wife. We were sensitive pricks and good guys, of course, so we understood. But how do you not honor a *Playboy* centerfold, I ask you?

"All right, you guys aren't dumb," Sid told us. "You know what's going on. I shouldn't have to say this because I know you all, and I know you all will *conduct yourselves like pros, like gentlemen.*" It's T-E-A-M, damn it!

Let's honor June, we decide, *with a heartfelt personal gift!* We had money to buy something fancy, but this would mean more, a copy of her *Playboy* picture signed from all of us. A collectible! June's centerfold was promptly hung in Dan's locker. We all contributed personal demonstrations of fine art all over it. Unfortunately, Hall of Fame coach Sid Gillman wasn't a touchy-feely guy like many of us, but he was a great teacher. This became one of Sid's teachable moments, but only because neither Dan nor he liked our artwork very much.

We didn't see Dante for a day or two after he ripped up that poster and went storming out the door. Sid came back into the locker room, smiling that grandfatherly smile of his, slowly shaking his head. This didn't look good. He didn't have to say "you dumb fucks. . . . " We were getting the picture.

Sid proceeded to kick our asses in practice, making us run until we dropped. An unhappy ending for what started out as a very nice celebration for our friend, teammate, and leader.

Our cast of characters also included Billy "White Shoes" Johnson, an electric receiver and returner who owned the end zone dance. It was his—a patented move that no one had really done before.

After Johnson scored, he'd extend an arm, raise the football high in the air, and wobble his knees back and forth, a celebration that became famous as the "Funky Chicken."

I had the assignment to block for him on the return teams. If you're not starting in the NFL, you better be able to play special teams if you want to make it. *Didn't have to play special teams in college, huh Big Time? Tough shit. You ain't on scholarship now.*

In the NFL, you do what you can to make yourself more valuable. Special teams required being brave—or perhaps insane—enough to sprint long stretches of the field and slam your body into an opponent with almost equal momentum. It was a car crash on every kickoff and punt.

"If you have no fear, you belong in a mental institution," the coaches liked to say. "Or on special teams."

It was even worse considering the NFL didn't seem to care about blown knees back then. Chop blocks (blocks below the knees) were commonplace—and our unit was notorious for them. Our Monday film sessions were fun to watch. We'd blast through our opponents' knees like a bunch of sky blue missiles, giving Johnson and his white shoes enough time to fly by toward the end zone.

Outside of special teams, I tried to survive by using my brain, learning every linebacker position and letting the coaches know when someone got hurt ahead of me. Things like that may seem unimportant, but when it came down to cut-down day, I often had a couple of allies in the coach's room.

"It's important when you're gonna be in a backup role to understand where your place is on the football team and understand how you can contribute," my linebackers coach, Larry Peccatiello, said. "As a reserve player, you have to be able to go in and play on Sunday without the same reps as a starter. You want a guy who is smart. . . . If in necessity—which comes up many times—if he has to go in on Sunday, you want him to maximize his talents, not make mistakes and not piss down his leg because he's not prepared. Ralph had all of that. He was a great person to coach."

Even with all that working in my favor, my time was still running out. Before my last year in the league, the Oilers drafted Robert Brazile, a linebacker who ran the 40 in 4.6 seconds and bench-pressed about 300 pounds.

"What's the big deal?" I once asked Peccatiello. "Take away Brazile's size and 40-yard dash and what have you got?"

"You," Peccatiello said.

He was right. I had every reason to be looking over my shoulder. My replacement was already on the roster. My knees were wrecked and I was playing Russian roulette with them every time I lined up for kick coverage. Some guys in my situation turned to steroids. You didn't have to be a Rhodes scholar to know what could go wrong there, but they made you feel like Superman, strong and fearless amid all the chaos and calamity crashing down all around you. Others let shady doctors and trainers pump them full of painkillers.

I wasn't immune—sometimes I had to get painkilling shots just to make it out to the practice field. And on top of all that, I had to get my knee drained weekly during the season.

It was pretty obvious my body was on borrowed time. I hadn't been in the league long, but I knew exactly what would happen next. Even the stars get squeezed, and I wasn't in that class. When I was with New England, the joke was Jim Plunkett had his salary cut by $20,000 after a 3–11 season. When he protested, they told him, "We could have finished last without you."

I knew my ending would involve more than a pay cut, so I tried to be proactive. I applied to the South Texas College of Law in Houston and scored an admissions meeting with the dean, Garland R. Walker.

I was in the lobby waiting for him when I heard a loud discussion inside his office. For some reason, the admissions meeting before mine got heated, escalated even further, and soon became a full-blown argument. Dean Walker threw the guy out. And I was next.

Shit.

The dean was known to be a troll. He was stoic, with a hard stare and a lukewarm demeanor that needed a hell of a lot to become friendly. You might as well forget about trying to make him smile. So I had to think of something quick.

I stuck my head inside his office and said, "How about I come back another time?"

Surprisingly, the dean broke into a big smile and a little bit later, all that tension ended with my acceptance into law school. The dean and I were quite different, but he saw past all that, and set me on my way. I owe the dean big time. I started taking night classes soon afterward, grabbing the ice packs for my knees right after football practice and heading downtown for a few hours of lectures.

It was the greatest feeling a football player nearing the end could ever find! I suddenly had a way out.

But it sure as hell wasn't easy. The South Texas College of Law was a rigorous school for people who had no other obligations—and some of them cracked under the pressure. One guy who seemed to be pretty bright tossed his pen and paper aside after just 10 minutes in an exam room.

"I'm outta here," he announced.

I never saw him again. Another student I liked asked me to borrow something like $2.45 one day. I had a habit of carrying my weekly checks in the trunk of my car and sometimes had about four or five of them stacked up, a windfall probably worth five grand. I offered the guy a lot more than the couple bucks he requested, but that was all he wanted. He was content with enough cash for a cheeseburger, some fries, a Coke, and a fresh pack of cigarettes. It reminded me just how lucky I was to play football for a living, for however long it might last.

Law school started paying immediate dividends. For starters, cocaine was everywhere in Houston at that time and some of our teammates got addicted when they were running around town after practice. But I was too busy with all my classes and readings to get trapped in any of it. I also started asking questions in class that might benefit my teammates when the time came.

"What does a team owe a player if the team doctor screws him up?"

"Can I sue a guy who hits me after the whistle and ends my career?"

Once the other Oilers knew what I was doing, they started seeking pro bono advice and always enjoyed the price. But I wouldn't be around much longer.

In 1974, Houston put me on injured reserve after I cracked a rib. The Denver Broncos picked me up to avenge an earlier feud. It was an unwritten rule that you didn't claim another team's injured player on waivers, but Gillman broke it with a Denver player and the Broncos returned the favor by picking me up when they had a chance.

I sold out my old team as soon as we played. It was what happened all the time, a common practice among teams looking for any edge that might be available to them.

My duty was to the team paying me—the Broncos. I spilled my guts on everything. I knew every last bit of Houston's defense and relayed all their schemes and signals to the Broncos. I could identify each play just by watching the Oilers line up. And since the Broncos were paying my salary that week, I was happy to provide my services.

My old coaches were plenty pissed. Pec, my former linebacker coach, gave me the finger, and fired off a barrage of F-bombs. Defensive coordinator Richie Petitbon was trying to hide behind Wade Phillips, Bum's son, while he gave the signals. They both tried to disguise their calls, but it was useless. I knew the defense too well.

Sorry, fellas!

The Broncos cut me in the next training camp, and I returned to law school before the Oilers called again.

I had one last hurrah with Houston in 1975. But sitting on my ass studying in law school the prior semester soon led to a detached hamstring, and everything was finished.

I was done, forced to start over, forced to confront a life without football for the first time since I was a Pee Wee player back in Avella. Luckily, I was a little wiser, and a little more prepared than all the others who get spit out by a league in which the average player only survives 3.6 years.

There was big money in Houston real estate and a mensch named Barry Warner helped me get a broker's license. But there was even more money in law, so I had already started on that degree too. Both of those would pay dividends in later years. I didn't know it then, but I was on a path that would lead me right back to the NFL.

And the next time, I'd climb to the top of it.

Houston Law

The Firm

THE WALLS WERE STARK WHITE.

After four years in the NFL—enough to earn a bare-bones pension from the league—my professional career was a blank slate. And my law office looked the part, a white-walled room that was as empty as my legal resume.

I started out by buying some wood furniture from a few decades back and lathered it all up with lemon oil. With a few chairs and a desk finally in place and everything smelling much better than the locker rooms of my past, I was starting to feel a little more like a lawyer.

There's something special—very American—about starting your own business. Mary's grandparents had their fruit stand in Beaver, and her Jewish relatives owned a junk business. My dad's family had a store, and my grandfather was a butcher. And my Zia Rosa (Aunt Rose) was an entrepreneur too, running a little grocery in Rochester, Pennsylvania.

I suppose there was a lot of business acumen embedded in many of my family members. Now, I was following all their footsteps, sharing the pride and the burdens of owning a business, along with the accounting, the rent payments, and everything else that came with it. The book *How to Start and Build a Law Practice*, written by Jay Foonberg and published by the American Bar Association, became my bible. Before long, the office with its wooden furniture, white walls, and lemon oil aroma was up and running.

I just needed some clients. And some work.

When I was finishing law school, I played on a softball team with a buddy of mine named Fred Joachim. Fred introduced me to Judge Frank

Price, the son of an attorney who had worked for billionaire Howard Hughes. Judge Price was not only filthy rich, IF you believed the rumors, but he was also good-looking, brilliant, and a genuinely nice guy. He was a little bit like one of my old coaches.

Sometimes, he'd provide some advice that would keep me from embarrassing myself in court. And other times, he'd find a way to loosen me up and make me laugh.

"May it please the court . . . " I remember announcing in the courtroom once.

"You never do anything to please this court," Judge Price interrupted. "Why start now?"

He scheduled my first trial in his courtroom and during it the district attorney offered an affidavit as evidence, a sworn statement that set forth proof of one fact or another. It damn sure looked official.

Judge Price looked at me and waited for my response on the affidavit. "Any objection?"

"None, your honor."

"No objection???"

The district attorney started looking at the judge.

Okay, then.

After the trial, Judge Price called me into his chamber, opened a cabinet, and pulled out a bottle of booze.

"You dumb ass," he said. "That affidavit was pure hearsay. That should have never come in."

Nothing close to that happened in the next trial. He eventually gave me some praise too, critiquing me like a coordinator evaluating my performance in game film. My legal career was a lot better because of him. An old Texan, Judge Jimmy James, helped out a lot too. James put me on my first murder case, which paid quite well thank you.

Back then I also spent some of my time working for an athletic agency in Arkansas. We represented a lot of the Razorback players, who were coached by the legendary Lou Holtz. I like Lou a lot and his Arkansas teams had a ton of talent—and a few thugs too.

I was doing some agency work on the particular day when Judge Price's secretary called.

"Judge Price would like to speak with you."

"Well, put the good judge on!"

Judge Price wanted me to represent an indigent criminal defendant. I had hoped to avoid criminals in my law career. Judge Price had other ideas.

"Thank you, Judge, but I don't think I need to do that at this time. I'm going on a recruiting trip. But I appreciate it very much. See you at the softball game . . ."

"Wait, not so fast, Tonto. I'm not asking you, I am ordering you!"

The smart and only response was "Yes your honor."

I started my criminal law career that very same day, earning a decent paycheck from the state. Lots of attorneys who are lousy at marketing stay alive by picking up cases like these.

Before long, I learned quickly that Texas has some of the best lawyers in the land. With a higher rate of capital punishment than a lot of other states, the pressure and stakes are much higher. And the cream rises to the top. I also learned that criminal law is a lot like big-time college football—everyone's lying and everyone knows it. Or at least they should.

Cops, defendants, and witnesses would stretch—or even trample—the truth almost every time they opened their mouths. And the deck was stacked against the accused, who typically couldn't pay for proper representation. Those poor bastards got stuck with rookie attorneys like me.

Early in my career, I heard legendary Texas lawyer Racehorse Haynes tell the story of what he was thinking when a case was called out in the courtroom.

"The United States of America versus Billy Joe Bob!"

"Holy shit, it's me and Billy Joe against the whole United States of America!"

One of my first criminal cases began in 1979, a trial for a woman who was accused of being involved in the murder of two nice-looking young men near Houston during the city's rodeo celebration. My client, along with a male accomplice, was riding through Texas and picked up two men.

My client and her accomplice eventually attacked the two male victims, tying up the poor guys' hands and feet like they were a pair of pigs. They placed a rope around the neck of one man, the stronger one, with each killer on opposite sides, and their feet pressed in on his head. Moments later they started pulling. The first guy fought like hell (he had some martial arts training), but it was no use. He was strangled to death a little bit later. Then, the killers took a break for some coffee and doughnuts, as the other victim awaited the awful fate that had been planned for him.

At the penalty phase of the trial, there was a large photo hidden behind a black covering. When the covering was taken off, you could see the photo, a big picture of two spent coffee cups and an empty Dunkin Donuts bag.

"These animals not only commit the first horrible act, but they take a break, come back, and . . ." the prosecutor said.

I still remember the words of one prosecutor all these years later. The second guy had been alive, tied up near his dead friend during their entire coffee break. When they returned, my client started playing with the poor guy's balls. He was crying, begging for his mother, doing everything he could to save his life.

But it was no use. They took the rope and placed it around his neck. Then, they stepped on his head and pulled. Mercifully, he died much faster, already weakened by the shock from the events he had witnessed and the trauma that had been unleashed on his body.

I had been assigned to a legal team representing the female killer, and my only goal was to keep her alive. I made every argument known to God and man.

"Killing to prove that killing is wrong is immoral. It's wrong!"

I used everything I had learned up to that point and of course, most of it was borrowed from others. I tried anything that I thought might work. And I waited.

My knees never buckled in athletic events. Nerves didn't bother me when I was on a football field surrounded by 100,000 people or on a wrestling mat with every eye in the arena awaiting my next move.

But this was different. My mouth was dry. I had no spit. If I lost here, this woman died. Even a goomba like me got that.

Worse yet, the odds weren't in my favor. They never are in these types of cases. My client had given two 28-page confessions, the first in Texas, and a second—yes, a second!—in Colorado, where she had fled with the other killer. I had no chance to win on anything except life in prison and even that would be tough. We were in the courtroom of a Texas hanging judge, Jimmy James, who always seemed eager to execute, and was even more willing this year since he was up for re-election.

As always, the deck was stacked against us. And the cards we did hold were pure shit.

Judge James and the other boys in his chambers didn't usually take kindly to Yankees like me, but they all seemed to make an exception in my case. Being a former Houston Oiler probably helped. I appreciated their respect, because it was one of the few things I had working in my favor.

With the stakes raised so high in a capital murder case, you always need to have experienced counsel working alongside you. So I was paired up with a seasoned trial attorney who had about 30 years of experience in the DA's office. Hell, he would have convicted and executed her himself. He wanted to see her die. You don't change when you've been on one side of the law for so long. And there was no question of her guilt.

None.

But my role required me to serve her best interests, so I went to work on saving her life. I did my best. I found a sleeveless dress that I thought would soften her up and help her gain sympathy in the courtroom. But that was a mistake. I had no idea that once her arms were exposed everyone would see a huge Hell's Angels tattoo.

Shit!

It was hotter than an armadillo's balls in the courtroom, but I wanted her wearing a sweater to cover up the tattoos. I also brought her a Bible, but she didn't go near it. I wanted the jury to see some kind of remorse, something that showed she was a human being capable of compassion. But she was making it almost impossible.

The only redeeming value—just one—I could find was some affection she had for her only child, a little boy she seemed to love. She wanted to see him, but I don't think she was allowed to back then.

As the trial wore on, I didn't do much except fight like hell every chance I got. Still, I'd say I lost if you scored it like a wrestling match. But in the end, the jury made an error, and the case got overturned on appeal. I learned later her male accomplice was executed in 1995, but my client escaped the first trial, and then a second one as well, with an appeal concerning her representation (something that's customary in a capital case). The state didn't want to retry her a third time and she simply received a sentence of life in prison. She survived.

I often wonder about her son and what happened to him. And I think about her own fate too, if I did her any favors by helping her spend a life in jail, locked up forever like a caged beast unfit for the outside world.

Another murderer I represented during my Texas days was freed before the trial ever went to court. The first question in any Texas murder trial that's asked is, "Did the deceased person deserve to be killed?"

If so, it's game over.

The answer in this particular case was not only a yes, but a "Hell yes!" My client must have been a gun-toting, right-wing Republican type, because he walked up to a guy, pointed his gun, and put two bullets in the guy's chest. Then, as he lay on the ground, my client put another four bullets in his body, just to be sure.

It may have seemed like another near-impossible case, but I found witnesses who said that the deceased was notorious for carrying a hook blade in his back pocket and had either used it on people before or had tried to. A lot of people were deathly afraid of him, and I don't think they were lying. The "victim" was dangerous and had a record to prove it.

He deserved to die. During the pre-trial hearing, the judge and DA agreed too.

My client walked.

After a number of cases like that, where life and death swirled around the events in question and were often determined by the outcome of the case, anything related to football, even the most hostile negotiations, would seem like mere games.

How could I be nervous staring down billionaire owners and million-dollar contracts when I had already been involved with cases that meant so much more?

I wouldn't flinch. I wanted to fight them all.

Every part of my life, from my upbringing in Avella, through my playing career and my courtroom days, had prepared me to be one of the biggest, baddest negotiators the football world had ever seen. I knew if I wasn't careful I could get my ass kicked like anyone else. But I was ready.

It was time to take on the NFL.

Adult Life

The Family Man

I THOUGHT I MIGHT LOSE HER.

It was New Year's Eve—almost 1974—and Mary and I were celebrating at a party. The ball was dropping and drinks were flowing and our relationship hit one of those tipping points that seem to arrive any time a couple considers the future.

What's it going to be? Are we in this for the long haul? Or are we just wasting our time?

I did something to piss Mary off, the specifics of which have been lost in all the years that have followed. And she flipped.

The clock struck midnight and she took a drink and poured it over my head, then stormed out of the party to illustrate her point.

She had stayed with me since we first met, followed my football career everywhere it went, and felt like I didn't appreciate all that she did. She thought I was taking her for granted.

And she was sick and tired of it.

So she took a stand, poured her drink, and waited for me to make the next move.

I thought she might be leaving for good. And that was something I couldn't accept, a fight I wasn't willing to lose.

The reality of everything that was about to wash away hit me in the next few hours, which I spent alone.

The Thunderbolt. Her love. Her laugh.

A good woman. A great ass.

I was afraid I might lose it all.

And what would I do without her?

I followed her back to where we were staying. I'd never take her for granted again. And I'd love her as long as I lived.

Mary always thought she won over my family with that drink that ended up atop my head. And she was probably right too. Every Cindrich I've ever known has always appreciated a firm backbone and a heel dug deep in the ground.

They were happy to see both from the Beaver County Junior Miss. She wasn't one to be messed with. And they loved her for that.

We soon had a huge wedding with about 400 people packed into the Fez in Aliquippa. There was a whole lamb and an entire pig and enough food for maybe a few hundred more. People laughed and drank and partied for hours.

Mary and I had our first dance as a husband and wife. And I never had to worry about losing her again. The Thunderbolt was mine forever. We went to our honeymoon in Barbados and then settled into married life and my burgeoning career as a lawyer.

Four years later, we took another unforgettable trip. In January of 1979, we flew to India through a program with Pan Am Airlines that made us carriers for orphans headed to families awaiting them in the United States.

On our first visit to the orphanage, I fell in love again. A little girl stared back at me through a pair of dark eyes, filling my entire body with warmth and softening every hard edge I had.

I'd never forget her.

We had a day off before going back to the orphanage, and Mary and I spent a night at the Taj Mahal. A full moon hung high above the white marble, casting shadows around the spires and the reflecting pool down below. Even an old linebacker like me couldn't help but catch a little bit of romance. Our son Michael was conceived that same night.

The next day, we returned to the orphanage to take the babies home to the families, freedoms, and opportunities waiting for them in the United States. There were only girls—the Indian government didn't allow the adoption of boys—and I was inseparable from that sweet baby who captivated me the first time I saw her.

Our flight home took about 30 hours, with an unscheduled stop in Turkey to pick up some refugees displaced by unrest in Iran. Eventually, our wheels touched down in America. And life opened up wide for the babies on board, the infants who were soon carried off into a country that provided almost endless possibilities.

I said goodbye to that little girl as she was passed along to the adoptive family anxiously awaiting her arrival. That family gave her a good life, lots of love, and sent us a Christmas card each of the past 34 years. Their little girl grew up and ended up serving in the army of her second country, returning to the Middle East as a soldier in Operation Enduring Freedom in Iraq. I got to meet her again in 2013.

We shared a dance and some conversation and I told her how proud I was, how blessed I felt to be a part of the life she made in America. It was a moment that makes your eyes water, even if you've seen the trenches of professional football or the war going on inside Iraq. We were both happy to share it.

And I'd soon experience some of those same feelings with children of my own. Michael, our Taj Mahal baby, was born when Mary and I were still living in Texas.

Christina was born a few years later when we returned to Pittsburgh. My career took off when my children were toddlers, but I made sure my business was a family one. Christina answered the phone and got to know many of the NFL GMs by name. Michael was invited onto the field and inside locker rooms with some of my clients, giving a growing boy a glimpse of football's greats.

It wasn't easy to balance all the egos, time commitments, and travel requirements of my business with a family life, but I always did the best I could. I stayed home on Sundays, following the family traditions and food-filled rituals of my mother, while simultaneously spurning the football games and all the extra clients and commissions they might bring. I preferred to watch the games on television instead. I always felt I gained a lot more by watching all the games at home instead of attending just one of them in person.

I figured my family was a much better investment anyway. And the dividends arrived every time I looked across the dinner table.

I'd lock eyes with the woman who gave me the Thunderbolt. I'd share a few smiles with the two little kids whom I loved more than anything.

And I'd be reminded that there were a lot of things in life more important than football, or any career that might be attached to it.

Thankfully, they were all sitting at home in front of me.

Glenn Hyde and Walt Brown

The Beginning

I NEVER THREW A PASS.

Growing up, I was always a lineman, always one of the kids doing the grunt work while the other guys got the football and all the glory that came with it.

Every once in a while, I'd convince some coach to let me run the ball, and I'd have a blast, break a few tackles, and be a beast to bring down. But before long, I was back on the line, back to where I always belonged.

I always appreciated offensive linemen. In the football world, they were the closest thing to the people I grew up with around Avella, guys who did the dirty work for little pay and even less recognition, but were reliable and rugged and happy to knock your head off if you ever went across them.

So it should have been no surprise that my niche as an agent was carved with the help of a whole lot of linemen. My career as an agent began with some marketing work for future Hall of Famer Curley Culp, a dominant defensive lineman and former amateur wrestler. I first saw Curley in the NCAA Championships, when he dropped his opponent with a crazy sort of back suplex and pinned him in the first period. Culp later became a teammate on my crazy Houston Oilers team and ate up some blockers as a nose tackle in front of me. I thought I could get Culp a gig or two and representing athletes always seemed like interesting work. I already knew a lot about it, so I gave it a shot.

Soon, I got a call from a friend to represent Glenn Hyde, a former teammate at the University of Pittsburgh who went undrafted but was hoping to find work as a free agent. Hyde was a scrappy guy who could play a number of positions—guard, tackle, nose, and special teams—and would do it all with a motor that ran like a supercharged V-8. According to the *Denver Post,* when he played for the Broncos, a former coach described his style as "hell-bent." He had his own cheering section with the team too, and a number of fans wore "Hyde's Herd" T-shirts to the games in Mile High Stadium.

"You talk about a Cinderella story," Hyde said, referring to himself. "I was too small and too slow to play in the pros, but I had a pretty good career. I got a sniff and made the most out of it. I got hooked up with coaches who believed in me. I called myself the utility infielder. I played everything pretty good, but couldn't play anything great."

Hyde was considerably undersized at 250 pounds, and he survived more on effort and savvy than anything else. He bounced around and brought me a lot of experience as an agent, including my introduction to Bill Polian, who was working with the Chicago Blitz of the United States Football League. In all, Hyde's career passed through 12 teams and three leagues (the NFL, USFL, and World Football League), giving both of us a broad perspective in the ways of professional football.

"I was a guy that never should have made it in the first place and ended up playing 15 years," said Hyde, who has beaten cancer and now lives a healthy life in Colorado. "A lot of it had to do with Ralph making the right moves at the right time and not being too greedy."

My first draft choice was Walt Brown, another Pitt Panther who was picked in the fifth round by the Detroit Lions in 1978. The Lions general manager at the time was Russ Thomas, a former player, and an old-timer who often complained about how much money the players were making.

Thomas had a championship ring that he rubbed almost constantly. And when he wasn't busy touching it, he'd stare at it or show it off. Then, he'd quickly return to rubbing it raw. The ring was so worn down that all the lettering and championship inscriptions had been rubbed off and the gold would have stripped away too if it wasn't so damn durable.

I met with Thomas to negotiate Brown's contract and hoped to loosen his grip on all the Lions' money. It wasn't an easy task. Every time I made a contract proposal, Thomas would shake his head and say no, then start rubbing his ring again and look at it just to make sure it didn't walk away.

Then, he'd go on this long, laborious speech about how much more money football players were getting now compared to his playing days. I would have preferred getting my toenails pulled out instead of sitting through his stupid lecture, but fiduciary duty required that I stick around for a few more minutes.

We didn't get the deal done that day, but we settled all the parameters a little bit later. And more importantly, I made some maneuvers so that I never had to hear Thomas's excruciating olden-days speech ever again.

Since I now had a few clients and a little bit of experience, I was starting to make a name for myself as an agent. I had started Athletes of America, Inc., a sports management firm, down in Houston in 1978. Culp, Hyde, and Brown gave me some confidence that I could make a career out of that kind of work. But the industry was much like the Wild West back then and covered in so much crap that I didn't dare jump all the way in.

One of the most infamous agents was rumored to recruit college players with fistfuls of cash and other questionable methods. Others had Mafia connections, as agents with reported ties to organized crime infiltrated the business. These boys seemed to run most of the agent business for a four-year stretch.

Two of the most notorious people rumored to have those attachments were Norby Walters and Lloyd Bloom, veterans of the entertainment industry who saw opportunity waiting in the football world and decided to wade in. Their stable of clients grew rapidly as they coerced, intimidated, and strong-armed their way toward the top of the business.

The whispers and rumors and actual evidence soon got out to other agents like me. Cars were given away. Cash payments were delivered (one player supposedly got $54,000). And there were hotel rooms stocked with drugs, liquor, and hookers, with Uncle Norby watching over it all in a bathrobe and fluffy slippers, as players and potential clients ran in and out.

Walters and Bloom quickly established a sports agency with about 50 NFL and NCAA players in its stable. And the number seemed to keep growing alongside the stories.

Kathy Clements, the wife of Notre Dame quarterback Tom Clements and an associate of Illinois-based agent Steve Zucker, was attacked by an armed intruder, stabbed and beaten unconscious by someone wearing a ski mask. According to Zucker, Bloom told Clements at the Senior Bowl that "people who don't pay their debts can have their hands broken," a reference to a client who may have owed Bloom money.

Many media outlets and journalists were scared to report what was happening behind the scenes in the agency business, but there was a ballsy reporter named Chris Mortensen working for the *Atlanta Journal-Constitution* who was willing to take it on. I handed off all the details to Mort and he dove deeply into the case. His coverage and reporting on the antics and the ensuing investigation became some of the crown jewels in an accomplished career that eventually led him to ESPN.

I made enough noise that the Mob knew my name too. At some point I got a late afternoon call.

"You're next, Cindrich."

"Yeah, you're a tough guy over the phone. Come get a piece!"

"You're dead."

"I'm armed, too."

As an avid outdoorsman, I always carried a 12-gauge turkey shotgun with three-inch shells, a pistol, and a Winchester .30-.30 saddle gun in my car. I still do. If I had some notice, I could handle myself if it came down to it. But I made sure to contact law enforcement agencies right away too. I called the head US attorney for the Western District of Pennsylvania, a guy who had worked under my brother Bob, and reported everything to the local FBI office as well.

Before long, with stories like mine and many others proliferating, the law—and something even worse—caught up to Walters and Bloom. According to the *New York Times*, a lengthy federal investigation led to the agents being tried on charges of racketeering, conspiracy, and mail fraud in 1989. During the trial, Michael Franzese, an admitted member of the Colombo crime family, testified for the prosecution, describing how he allowed the agents to use his name as a threat to keep clients from backing out of deals with the two men.

The entire ordeal prompted several states to enact laws regulating sports agents, many of which are still on the books today, even though many of them are grossly unfair.

I supported those laws at the time. I testified for them. How was I to compete against the cheating of agents and coaches with their payola out the woozoola? And how could I compete against the Mob?

But the irony of all those actions is that they now make life pretty damn difficult for agents like me. Agents have to acquire a license in every state where they recruit, which requires a good deal of time, paperwork, and money. And if the agents screw up, they are facing criminal penalties. Meanwhile, corrupt coaches and renegade boosters are known to trample ethics and just about everything else to acquire their own players, dispensing cash payouts a lot more often than most people realize. And the NCAA frequently turns a blind eye to all of it, protecting the cash cow that is college athletics while hiding behind the term "student athlete."

Four years after his own trial, Bloom was found dead in a high-priced home he was renting in Malibu. He was shot several times in the upper body. Boy had enough lead in him to be a damn good boat anchor! The crime certainly didn't seem random and ultimately never got solved.

When asked about the murder by a reporter for the *New York Times*, I told him I wasn't surprised considering the number of people Bloom probably screwed over in the course of his career.

I didn't need a dead body to realize how murky the agency waters were when I first entered the business. I was content to stay away from it and waited for conditions to improve. I had a wife and a baby at home and another on the way. I didn't want to spend all my nights in the hotels and bars where I might recruit new clients.

Plus, the agent life was hardly an assured one. Unlike baseball, where agents will often earn 5 percent of a client's guaranteed contract in a career that lasts 5 to 6 years; NFL players only average a 3- to 4-year career, and football agents can only earn a maximum of 3 percent per deal with some big-time players expecting you to take even less. Worse yet, most of the deals aren't guaranteed, so everything can evaporate in seconds. You can't make it without a number of clients and good ones too, guys who can earn second and third contracts over the course of their careers. And finding those players takes time—trips, travel, and long hours away from home. I knew those days might arrive for me someday; I just wasn't in any rush.

Once I waded in, I knew I'd have obvious advantages over my opponents. I was a former player and knew the game better than most of the general managers. I had a law degree and had argued several cases in the courtroom from tax court to divorces, a resume of legal experience that no other agent could match. In addition, I was ethical to boot, a byproduct of an old-fashioned upbringing in Avella and the famously feared backhand of my father. I knew my career would take off once I gave it some ballast.

Back then, I was happy with the few clients and legal work I already had. Back in Pittsburgh in 1981, I'd leave my law office outside the city and stop at Cip's Bar in Dormont and drink with men who really labored, guys with gnarled hands and ruddy faces who worked outdoors all year round in whatever Mother Nature might throw at them. I would slam a shot and sip a beer with them like I was just one of the guys (and maybe I was except for the suit). Then I'd head home before the buzz got big enough to get me in trouble with any authorities bigger than my wife.

It was a damn good life.

But slowly and ever so carefully, I inched closer to becoming a big-time agent, someone eager to take on the entire NFL and help carry my players all the way to the top of it.

One of my early clients was Tom Brzoza, a rookie who got me entangled with football's biggest team and an owner who was larger than life.

My next meeting was in his office.

And I wasn't about to back down.

Arthur J. Rooney

The Chief

THEY CALLED HIM THE CHIEF.

And in Pittsburgh, he was something of a god, the king of a Steelers franchise that conquered the NFL and captured four Super Bowls in the 1970s.

Arthur J. Rooney was the son of a barkeeper and a coal miner's daughter, and was raised on the rugged north side of town, with old-fashioned, Irish-Catholic values.

"My father always used to tell us boys, 'Treat everybody the way you'd like to be treated. Give them the benefit of the doubt. But never let anyone mistake kindness for weakness,'" Rooney remembered in a book written by Abby Mendelson. "He took the Golden Rule and applied it to the North Side of Pittsburgh."

The Chief founded Pittsburgh's NFL franchise in 1933 and went an entire decade without a single winning season. Football success wouldn't fully arrive until the Steel Curtain dynasty of the 1970s, when head coach Chuck Noll led Pittsburgh to eight straight playoff appearances and four Super Bowls in a six-year period. Some say those were the greatest teams in the history of the league. As a Houston Oiler, I played against them and got my ass fully kicked. The opposite sideline was filled with All-Pros and future Hall of Famers and some of the biggest names to ever play in the NFL: Mean Joe Greene. Bradshaw. Franco. Lambert. Ham. Swann. Stallworth. Blount. Webster.

All of them were a testament to the Chief, whose resolve had helped transform a mediocre team into one of the NFL's flagship franchises.

According to Gary Tuma of the *Pittsburgh Post-Gazette*, the Chief had been uniquely determined since the day he was born. He nearly drowned as a kid, surviving a close call when Pittsburgh's three rivers flooded and a canoe he was riding in flipped over in the city's Old Exposition Park. His boots filled with water. And his brother saved his life.

The Chief was a tough and athletically gifted kid—an AAU champion boxer, and a standout in both football and baseball. He earned contract offers from the Boston Red Sox and the Chicago Cubs and was offered a football scholarship to play for Knute Rockne and Notre Dame.

Art Rooney turned them all down, went to college a little closer to home, and played minor league baseball until his arm gave out, ending his athletic career.

But even then, sports would continue to dominate his life. The Chief was a huge fan of horse racing, having once won a Depression-era windfall from the Saratoga track in New York that was worth an estimated $200,000. He supposedly needed a Brinks truck to bring all the money back to Pittsburgh.

His kindness was rather legendary too. The Chief stayed grounded in his Irish-Catholic roots and supported numerous charities over the years, including orphanages overseas and many other causes closer to home. Tuma wrote that a priest once visited the Chief and supposedly asked for money to fund a new Catholic orphanage. Rooney reportedly counted out $10,000 and gave it all to the cause.

"Are these ill-gotten gains?" the priest couldn't help but wonder.

"No father," the Chief supposedly said. "I won them at the track."

In Pittsburgh, the legend of the Chief was alive and well. And it grew even bigger after his Steelers' Super Bowl wins in the 1970s (following the 1974, 1975, 1978, and 1979 seasons).

I was headed for a meeting with him toward the end of that run, although I didn't know it at the time. When I first arrived at the team offices where all those trophies were kept, I was defiant and pissed, just like when I played against Pittsburgh on the field.

I was there to collect a check for my client Tom Brzoza after a rather nasty dispute. Someone in those offices (I'm sure it wasn't the Chief) had been bad-mouthing me to recruits, members of the media, and anyone else who would listen. I didn't care or know for certain who was behind it, but I was determined to call him out if I had half a chance.

The whole ordeal started when I received a call in the fall of 1978 from Pirates manager Chuck Tanner, a big name in local sports and a friend of mine from the Pittsburgh Dapper Dan banquets. Tanner was a likeable and decent man. He lived in New Castle, Pennsylvania, and was asking for a favor. He wanted me to represent Tom Brzoza, a good kid who was a New Castle native and an All-American center at Pitt.

It was an honor to get that call, but I saw Tom as a long shot to land a consistent job in the NFL. He helped Pitt win a national championship, but he wasn't drafted until the Steelers selected him in the 11th round. The odds of an 11th-rounder making it on that team were a sucker's bet. But Brzoza never even got a chance, breaking his thumb a few weeks after the draft in an organized team workout at Three Rivers Stadium.

There were league rules prohibiting contact in the offseason, whether at Three Rivers Stadium or anywhere else. John Clayton, whose writing career earned him a spot in the Pro Football Hall of Fame, was a cub reporter in Pittsburgh then and got entangled in the events as well.

Clayton was sent to cover practice for the *Pittsburgh Press* but learned that the practice was uncharacteristically closed. He bounced around the locker room talking to a number of players and started to notice some things that were suspicious (I learned later how well Clayton's bloodhound nose was trained).

One player talked about how painful the practices were and how hard everyone was hitting. Another player had spent the weekend shirtless at the lake and was complaining about what it was like to wear shoulder pads with a sunburn. And a third player asked for Clayton's help stretching his jersey over the top of his pads.

Suddenly, all of the pieces fit together for Clayton.

Wait a minute. . . . They're not supposed to have contact in the offseason. No one should have pads on.

Clayton confirmed the violation with the league office, wrote an article about it in the newspaper, and the end result was that we were both battling the Steelers on separate fronts. Clayton's efforts got him banned from the team's facility. And I was involved because my client, Brzoza, a center, had been injured in one of those "illegal" practices and could no longer continue his career. Hell, I thought the rule itself was dumb, but it was still a violation!

I wanted the Steelers to pay up. I was roped into this thing, but my client had a legitimate complaint and I wanted to win. So my newly minted legal mind went to work and proclaimed "violation per se," which from a legal standpoint was something similar to exceeding the .08 blood alcohol threshold for drunk driving. It's inherently illegal to drive that way. The law exists for a reason and if you break it, you're guilty. There's no defense if all the procedures were appropriate, and this was a similar situation with my client breaking his thumb in what should have been a non-contact practice. Except it was a rule, not a law—no crime had been committed—but if you were to hear me, it was akin to capital murder!

Brzoza couldn't snap. He couldn't punch, couldn't jam a defensive lineman with both his hands and push him away from his body. Brzoza never got a fair shot at making the roster. I knew he was a long shot to make the team in the first place and I sure as hell didn't want this fight, but I had to do something in the best interest of my client.

Then Chuck Tanner called again and I knew he was a reliable source when it came to fairness in professional sports. I was still young, and didn't really know jack shit on that side.

"Ralph, this isn't right," Tanner said.

And he was spot on. At the same time I was picking a fight with the hometown team, Mary and I were preparing to move back to Pittsburgh. Splendid timing.

The Steelers were a legendary institution and were known hard-asses as well. (Hell, they cut Franco Harris!) They laughed at me when I requested some sort of compensation for Brzoza.

Being from Pittsburgh myself, I knew just how passionate—and maybe even insane—their fans were. I would have chosen the publicity of a street fight with the Pope over a squabble with the team.

But I had a fiduciary duty to uphold. I made my case against the Steelers with the only weapons I had available. I sent a certified letter to the team and the NFL, outlining my case. The NFL responded by offering a sledgehammer to help me pound salt, essentially echoing the

Steelers' first response. To make matters worse, the NFL Players Association wasn't powerful enough back then to take on the cause. So I utilized one of my other skills, screaming publicly to anyone who might listen. In that regard, Clayton and Vito Stellino (another talented reporter in the two-newspaper town), became my allies. But it only worked because my cause was just and my approach was honest, albeit dramatic. It also didn't hurt that both Clayton and Stellino were dogged competitors too and always fighting each other for scoops.

Back then, the NFL was the Wild West, and I thought it was that way everywhere. I relied on the press to help make my case. Meanwhile, I continued screaming that Brzoza's injury occurred during an unauthorized practice. It had cost him an opportunity to make the team and all the earnings that came with it. It wasn't fair by any standard.

After a little bit of negotiating, the Steelers and I reached a fair agreement on Brzoza's behalf. While it was a nuisance to go public in my attempt to collect, it was the only approach I had available that might work.

The NFL offices eventually got pressure from other clubs too.

Commissioner Pete Rozelle had to do something to quiet the whispers.

"What the heck Pete, are the Steelers your favorite team?"

The league ultimately enforced its rules by taking away a third-round pick from Pittsburgh as punishment. It didn't matter that tons, perhaps even all of the teams broke those non-contact rules. I had made Pittsburgh's violation public, pierced the armor of this giant, and the league had to act as it eventually did.

Now, with the benefit of a lot more wisdom and experience, I might do things differently, arguing my case in a quieter manner if I had that option. Back then, I didn't. I was advocating on behalf of my client and trying to win the argument. Over the course of my career, I'd win about 95 percent of my fights. And I always went for the knockout, no matter whom I was up against.

This time I had leveled both the Steelers and perhaps the beloved Chief too. The latter could be a mortal sin sending me off to hell. But a few others in the front office who hadn't done much by my estimation needed to be knocked down a few notches.

I was happy to have won the case against them, but was eager to collect the settlement check I secured for Brzoza and end the whole ordeal.

It was a hot, sweaty August day and I was dressed for a court appearance in a starched white shirt, dark blue suit, tie, and two gold Cross pens. I wasn't sure what I'd encounter when I got to the Steelers' office so my guard was up and I was ready—maybe even hoping—for a fight. It hadn't been that long since I wrestled.

I sat in the office sweating in my suit, staring back at the Super Bowl trophies as I waited for the receptionist to return from behind the desk. When she appeared, I called out my name loudly.

"RALPH CINDRICH. I'm here to pick up Tom Brzoza's F'n check!"

Well, everything went that way but the F'n part. The check was ready, but I still felt some animosity because I was standing in enemy territory. There were no friends waiting with a warm embrace in those back rooms.

"Mr. Cindrich," the secretary said in a soft and sweet voice. "The Chief would like to visit with you, please come back this way."

Oh SHIT! Not the Chief, anyone but the Chief!!!

She handed me the check and I fought the urge to turn around and sprint out the door. I followed my upbringing instead. I knew if I bolted, I would always regret it. I was better off facing the punishment just as I always did back as a youngster in Avella. Plus, the Chief wasn't likely to make me mow grass with a razor blade.

I braced for our meeting. The air-conditioning was on, but I was sweating profusely with the heat boiling outside and perhaps a little more waiting for me inside the Chief's office.

"The Chief wants to say hello . . ." the secretary continued.

Sure, this was going to be some hello.

Keep your mouth shut, say yes sir, no sir, and get your wise ass outta there!

One thing about tournaments, big games, and courtroom trials is that they all train you for fights later on in life. Nerves remain steady when they've been steeled before. I gathered my thoughts as I made the long walk back. I was probably the only person in Pittsburgh who didn't want to see the Chief, but there was no avoiding it now.

The secretary escorted me into his office and pointed at a seat. If you saw the play about Rooney written by my buddy Gene Collier, who helped me in the early stages of this book, the office was exactly as it appeared on stage, dimly lit and dark.

And there he was, sitting behind a desk with a lamp to one side, a chewed-up cigar jutting out the side of his mouth, a pose so familiar that it survives to this day.

The Chief.

He seemed to be squinting back at me, or maybe that was just the way his eyes looked behind the lenses of those Coke bottle glasses. I walked in, behaving like the perfect gentleman A. J. and Stella always hoped I'd become.

"Have a seat," the Chief said smiling, pointing at a chair to his left, the nearest one to the door.

He moved like he wanted to get up, but I wouldn't allow it, and leaned over for a quick handshake to keep him from standing. I couldn't have been more impressed if I were kneeling in front of Mother Teresa.

None of it was lost on me then or even now. I knew back then I would be telling people this story. I just didn't know how it would end yet.

At that time, the NFL's owners and the player's union were entangled in labor strife, as both parties struggled to reach a collective bargaining agreement. Local news stations covered the story from every angle, seeking comments from people on both sides of the conflict.

As a representative of the players, I often gave their position in on-air interviews. It was good for my agency business, allowing me to talk in language that was a little less colorful than what I employed on the football field or in negotiations. KDKA in Pittsburgh had me on constantly and I recommended Art Rooney II, the Chief's grandson, to reporters who were looking for comments from someone on the opposite side.

Art II was a young, articulate, and good-looking attorney, with a smooth delivery perfect for news reports. He was a talented lawyer with a big firm in town. There was little doubt he was on his way. I see him now at events with his beautiful wife Greta and always believe he's the type to succeed in any endeavor, whether it's law or football or speaking in a television interview.

The Chief wanted Art, his grandson, to get out of law and into the Steelers front offices sooner rather than later. Even then, the old man knew his grandson had a special combination of skills to be a force in pro football and someday become the NFL's Executive of the Year.

That turned out to be my saving grace.

"It's good seeing you," the Chief said. "How have you been? Tell me, what have you been doing?"

When the biggest, most respected voice in a city speaks, you listen well, look straight ahead into eyeglasses, and give serious answers in response. What I had to say next wouldn't be easy. I owed the Chief an apology.

I told the Chief about my current work and he asked more questions, as we discussed my college career at Pitt and my NFL days with the Houston Oilers. He made me feel important, like a good friend or a distant family member who hasn't been heard from in way too long. Maybe Joey Diven, his chauffeur and legendary bodyguard who was part of the Pitt Irish crowd I was close with, told the Chief about my work. We talked about Joey some.

It was a pleasant and enjoyable start, but finally, after a pause that extended for a couple seconds, I mustered up my strength.

"You know, Mr. Rooney, I am sorry about that," I said, referencing the Brzoza settlement that put us on opposite sides. "That cost you a draft choice."

He hesitated slightly, and pulled out his cigar that had long ago been eaten up and put it down in his ashtray. He looked me square in the eyes through his thick eyeglass frames.

"Let me ask you, did you believe what you were doing was the right thing to do?"

"Well . . . yes sir, I did."

"And did you do the best that you could do?"

Did I do the best I could do?

"Well . . . uh, hum, yes sir . . . yes sir, I did."

"Well, now, that's all that really matters, isn't it?"

He said he enjoyed seeing all those television interviews I did with his grandson. He taped them all and watched every single one of those newscasts. He called me in to thank me for getting his grandson some airtime and for not taking cheap shots in the interviews, for showing respect in the exchanges.

It turns out my beliefs about Art II being the Steelers eventual successor were spot on, perhaps better than anyone else in Pittsburgh.

The Chief and I exchanged a few more pleasantries, and our meeting ended a little bit later. Over the course of my career, I continued to piss off some of the top people in the Steelers offices, making both friends and enemies inside the organization. Kevin Colbert, Mike Tomlin, and Omar Khan, who invited me to his wedding, were always friends. Some others got crossed off my Christmas card list.

But I always knew I had an ally in the Chief. Like everyone else in town, I loved him for the man he was and everything good he brought to the city.

He even forgave Clayton too, complimenting his reporting on the Steelers practice violations and sharing a number of warm conversations with him over the years. The Chief's heart was as big as his personality.

Sadly, he died in 1988 at the age of 87. The Chief's funeral service was held in the same church where he went to mass every morning of his adult life. And the ceremony was everything you might expect, with dignitaries standing wall-to-wall, and a crowd of NFL icons parking their limos outside to pay their respects.

Those big names gathered together with small ones, ordinary people moved by his extraordinary kindness. Outside the church, a group of homeless people gathered to honor him too, shedding tears for the man who seemed to touch every single person in Pittsburgh.

I stood quietly where I was supposed to, way in the back, far behind all those big names and egos. I recited my prayers, said a solemn goodbye, gave my thanks, and made a promise to the Chief.

If I wasn't opposing his grandson or his team, I'd watch Art's back. When reporters called—and they often did—looking to dig up dirt or sling mud against the Steelers, I'd help him if I could, make his grandson aware of any impending attacks.

I think I owed the Chief that much. Like most of the people who met him, I probably gained a lot more than he did from our conversation.

All these years later, I'm still impressed by the love that he felt for his grandson. And the utter brilliance of the simple words that he spoke.

Did you do the right thing?

Was it the best you could do?

That's all that really matters, isn't it?

Mark May

The Impetus

WE WERE PERFECT FOR EACH OTHER.

I was fresh out of the courtrooms in Texas and just starting out in Pittsburgh as an agent and an attorney. I needed a client who could help me chase one of the biggest contracts in football, someone I'd be happy to fight for amid the heat and hostility of my first negotiation. I needed a name.

That guy was Mark May. Mark grew up in Oneonta, New York, and was a four-sport star in high school before blossoming into a standout offensive lineman at my alma mater, the University of Pittsburgh. May was a big guy and a big-time talent who occasionally wore a beard in college that might seem strange to those who know him best from ESPN. Back in the fall of 1980, May was an All-American, an Outland Trophy winner, and a safe bet to go in the first round of the NFL Draft that spring. He was also knee deep in the agent recruitment process and getting circled by a number of men with questionable motives.

Things were different back then. Agents didn't have to be certified and anyone could go into the business. Running back Earl Campbell may have said it best when he spoke about his own agent.

"I don't like who he be, but I like what he do."

Back then, agents had easy access to the locker rooms and practice fields and could push their agendas on players much earlier than what the NCAA allows today. Some of them suggested that May should leave school early, play in Canada, and start cashing checks and paying commissions once his freshman year was finished.

Pitt football was a different program back then too. The Panthers won a national championship in 1976, doing things the way a lot of southern football teams did, with cash payments and boundaries that occasionally got crossed. Bob Heddleston was the head of Pitt's booster club, and he orchestrated a lot of Pitt's success with meetings and clever maneuvers behind the scenes. He led Mark in my direction, but he knew I operated on the straight and narrow. In this case, that was fine with him too. Bob wanted nothing but the best possible representation for Mark.

I was it. Mark and I met in the locker room during his senior year at Pitt. Like any sensible player, Mark was looking out for himself too. I went to work on selling myself. I was an All-American, a Pitt alum, and didn't believe in bullshit. I played in the NFL and had the legal knowledge of a lawyer too. The other guys couldn't touch that.

That just so happened to be exactly what May was looking for.

"I wanted someone who had played the game, was from the University of Pittsburgh and was an attorney as well. Not necessarily in any order," May said. "He was up front and truthful. He didn't need the money, he had been financially successful and was someone who had been through what I was going through."

It was a win-win on both sides. And it probably didn't hurt that we both were avid outdoorsmen and I could provide Mark with a pond full of fish on my parents' property in Avella. Mark signed with me and never gave another agent a second thought. We were a team from then on, tied together as we faced the NFL Draft and whatever contract fight might follow it.

It's the same way today.

The Washington Redskins selected Mark with the 20th pick of the 1981 Draft, and we were soon facing a battle that could define my career. If I couldn't get Mark a fair contract—or maybe even a great one—it would be tough to recruit players in the future, especially considering I already had one strike against me because I wasn't willing—or able—to provide suitcases of cash or do other shady things to get players to sign. (When Mary and I came back to Pittsburgh, closed on our house, and furnished it, I had a total of $12,000 to my name.)

So my first negotiation was a pivotal one. Making matters worse, the Washington Redskins had general manager Bobby Beathard, who seemed to start off our negotiations by frequently pissing in my general direction.

Mark and I were content to hold out for a while and squeeze the Redskins for as many dollars as we could get before finally signing a deal. We knew what we were getting into. Holdouts are tough on all the involved parties, both mentally and physically.

And Beathard started ours off by bad-mouthing me in the press. I had encountered guys like him throughout my football career, and my coaches always advised me to play above it. Stay clean. Avoid the penalty. Well, I sure as hell tried. I stayed quiet.

Mark was doing the same as well, which was the first of many indications that he'd be an ideal client. Beathard spent his energy trying to drive us apart, by saying great things about Mark publicly and portraying me as an imbecile.

"Cindrich has backed himself into a corner, promising things he can never deliver," Beathard reportedly said. "I feel sorry for Mark May."

But as the days and weeks of the holdout piled up, and the press paid more attention to the contract impasse, Mark remained loyal, ignoring the noise as best he could. He was fishing at a friend's place in Franklin, Pennsylvania, a place so remote that he had to head into town to call me for updates on his contract. He stayed in shape the old-fashioned way, by hiking the surrounding mountains and completing repetitions of sit-ups and push-ups that would make Rocky Balboa proud. Before it was all over, he had lost something like 20 pounds.

Meanwhile, I was searching for every bit of leverage I could get. I always believed an agent's job was to maximize his client's position, grab as much leverage as possible, and then unleash it in the most beneficial manner. That role had no place for lies or exaggeration either, so I always worked to acquire realistic alternatives and then announce them as needed. I suppose my reliance on honesty might have cost me a few clients, but I never regretted it.

In this case, the Montreal Alouettes were offering Mark money to spurn the NFL entirely and play football in the Canadian League.

Back when I played, I had passed up a spot with Vancouver in the CFL because I didn't think it would help my career. But this was different and Mark was too. He had been hearing about those offers since he was a college freshman, and had resisted them all, along with whatever money they might have brought in. Now, an offer like that was exactly what we needed.

I floated the possibility that Mark might not play in the NFL at all. Maybe he'd play in Canada just like Billy "White Shoes" Johnson, my former teammate, and many other NFL talents did. And Bill Putnam, a former executive with the Alouettes, spoke publicly to confirm it (I was never wild about the CFL though, because back then the Canadian dollar was only worth about 82 cents of a US one). Putnam announced that his team was actively pursuing May, and that both Mark and I seemed receptive to his overtures. It also helped that veteran tackle Terry Hermeling told the Redskins he was planning to retire.

Game. Set. Match.

In our first real fight, Mark and I had Beathard by his beanbags. After proclaiming for weeks that he wasn't concerned about Mark's holdout, Beathard seemingly reversed course, and sat down with me as soon as the news came in from Montreal. We hammered out the agreement following three hours of negotiations. The contract was drawn up in Washington and flown to Pittsburgh where May signed it before boarding a plane for the Redskins' training camp in Carlisle, Pennsylvania.

Mark's deal was worth $650,000 over four years, a very good rookie salary at that time. It was also reported that his holdout had earned an extra $100,000 from the Redskins. According to the *Washington Post*, Beathard was forced to abandon his rigid bargaining stance in order to get May into camp and prevent him from playing in Canada.

But Mark's comments after he signed his deal tore apart my smokescreen.

"I kept Montreal very low-key and very much in the back of my mind," he said. "All I really ever wanted to do was play with the Redskins. Montreal came, but my main concern was reaching an agreement with the Redskins," Mark told the national sources.

Even if Beathard knew he had been manipulated, I tried to pad his reputation in the press, as I always did after winning a fight with a football executive.

"The timing was just right," I told the media after his holdout ended. "They wanted Mark in camp and we wanted to get this settled. Those are important reasons."

Everything worked out just fine for Mark and me in our first contract war. He was making good money, and the team was soon thriving under head coach Joe Gibbs. Gibbs started building his football team up front with Mark and fellow Pitt Panther Russ Grimm, who was taken two rounds after Mark in the 1981 Draft. The Redskins' offensive linemen became known as "The Hogs," and they led the team to Super Bowl victories in 1982 and 1987.

By then, Mark and I had moved well past a partnership and had become family. Even though I'd occasionally piss him off and I sometimes considered him a pain in my ass, we worked through our faults. We were perfect for each other. We might scream or shout or hang up on each other hundreds of times, but in the end, one of us would always call back. We'd make peace. And move forward again.

Our relationship went well beyond football. Mark's mom had died at childbirth and his father was killed in a terrible accident, so I always tried to be his big brother, filling any voids that might have existed under the surface. He returned the favor for my own kids, who loved seeing him every summer when we stopped at his place on our way to the Jersey Shore.

When he won his second Super Bowl in Washington, he, along with some of my media friends, got my son Michael and me back into the locker room after the game, allowing us to feel the thrill of victory with the Redskins. Michael was only a few feet away when the Lombardi Trophy was handed out, a lifetime memory made possible by Mark. And when Mark got hitched in Hawaii, keeping his promise to get married there if he ever made the Pro Bowl, I was his best man.

We're brothers. And fighters too.

Mark's second contract in Washington came up just as the USFL was getting off the ground. I made noise about him signing with the Tampa Bay Bandits and the team even sent him a plane so he could fly to watch their practice. Mark played his supporting role as he always did, stayed loyal, and let the leverage build. In the end, we negotiated a better contract because of it.

A similar pattern followed in San Diego, where Mark signed after he left Washington, allowing me to battle my good buddy Beathard again, who was now working in the Chargers' front office.

After San Diego, Mark finished his career with the Cardinals and his old Redskins offensive line coach, Joe Bugel, a friend and former coach of mine. In his last contract, Mark made sure I negotiated a number of incentives that were equal parts painful and profitable.

"If I changed positions in a game, I got a $1,500 bonus. I had one game where I played all five positions," May said. "That season, I had different incentives if I played 75, 80, 85, 90, 95, or 100 percent of the snaps. I was the only one who played every one of them. It was worth like $200,000 extra."

My mensch mentors over the years had nothing on Mark May in business. Trust me.

Mark still remembers when he went into Cardinals executive Larry Wilson's office and saw him calculating the incentives he had earned that season. Wilson was fully pissed and visibly steamed, like he'd been chewing on an oil filter all day.

"[When we were negotiating], I'd say, 'Just talk to Ralph.' And they'd say something like, 'Fucking Cindrich.' But it was never Ralph, it was me. Ralph would sometimes advise me to sign. He'd say, 'Mark, I think it's a fair deal.' But I'd say, 'Can you go get me this? If you can get me this, I think I'll be happy.'"

What a pain in the ass!

I loved him.

Mark followed a successful playing career with an equally productive one in the media, where he works at ESPN as one of the network's top college football analysts. I've negotiated all his contracts, incentives included.

As funny as it sounds, I suppose our relationship is a lot like a good marriage. Things aren't always easy, but there's enough love and respect present to make everything work. One style complements another. We've made money outside of football too, with some video stores near Pittsburgh that left us with a surplus of money and perhaps a thousand VHS and Beta tapes in Mark's house. I often joked that he wouldn't give up the pornographic ones.

My first victories as an NFL agent were won with Mark. He was an early indicator of the success I'd experience with offensive linemen, the loyal, hard-hat and lunch-pail types who would become the core of my agency. Bill Fralic, another talented lineman from my alma mater, would follow a few years later.

And his contract battle might have been the craziest one of them all.

Bill Fralic Sr.

The Father

ONE OF THOSE SLICK, SMOOTH, SWEET-TALKING AGENTS WASN'T GOING to work. Bill Fralic Sr. wanted someone with a steel backbone. And brass balls.

Fralic Sr. forged a birth certificate to enlist in the Army early and got shipped off to the South Pacific before he ever turned 18. He lied his way into the Korean War and ended up inches away from an explosive that almost killed him, his bleeding slowed and his life saved by about four feet of snow and frigid subzero temperatures.

He survived the whole thing. Then, he collected a Bronze Star and two Purple Hearts and headed back to Pittsburgh, where he spent his entire career in a steel mill, fighting the higher-ups as a union chief and fathering a child who was so good at football that he'd never have to entertain such work.

Bill Fralic Jr.—or Billy according to his family—was the youngest of three boys who were engineered to play football. His father initiated mandatory weight-training sessions three days a week once each boy turned 12. And his reasoning was a lot more sound than you might expect.

Fralic Sr. dropped out of high school and wanted something better than mill work for his own kids. But he knew a steel worker's salary wasn't enough to pay tuition bills for all three boys. Football would have to do that.

"My oldest boy, Michael, I took him downstairs and I said, 'Look at this.' I had a big piece of rubber, which I covered with a rug so when they dropped the weights it wouldn't crack the cement. I had two sets of weights, enough stuff that two guys could be workin' out at the same time. I told Michael, 'You're 12 years old Michael, and now, from here on in, you're liftin' weights. I'm gonna quit workin' 4-to-12 (shifts) and work daylights so I can make sure you're doin' what you're supposed to. On Monday, Wednesday, and Friday, you're comin' down here and you're trainin'. You don't have to wersh the truck, you don't have to wersh your mother's car, you don't have to help me paint, you don't have to cut the grass, you don't have to do nothin'.'

"'But you've got to lift weights and you've got to play football. When football season's over you can wrestle or you can play basketball.'

"When Joe was 12, I took Joe down, told him the same damn thing. Only one I didn't have to tell the same damn thing to was Billy. When he saw what the weight lifting was doin' to his brothers, he was tryin' to do it when he was 8 years old."

The legend of Bill Fralic Jr. began in that basement. Billy started training earlier than his brothers—and all his peers too—and quickly grew to epic proportions. When he was 11, his father tried to sign him up for the Morningside Bulldogs, a teenage football team in the city of Pittsburgh. The rules required all players to be at least 13. They initially told him no.

"Well," Bill Sr. said, "will you just look at him?"

Billy walked in behind him.

"You know what?" the team official said. "We just changed the rules."

In Little League baseball, some players were so afraid of Billy they refused to bat when he pitched. Others had their parents intercede instead.

By the time Billy turned 12, his father's weight training regimen had helped him bulk up to 210 pounds and he was 6'2" and a half. And the same plan paid off for his older brothers too. Michael earned a football scholarship to the University of South Carolina and Joe earned one to Marshall University in West Virginia.

Billy was rapidly ascending to even bigger things.

"When Edgewater Steel was doin' good, the ambition of 90 percent of the guys I knew was to get their kids jobs in Edgewater. That was the best thing they could hope for. When they'd say, 'What are your kids gonna do?' or whatever, I'd say, 'My kids are goin' to college; they're not gonna have to work in here.'

"They used to laugh at me. 'You got three kids that's gonna go to college?' They laughed."

"I figured it was the only way they could all go to college. Maybe if I'd had one kid or maybe two I could have sent them, but three, no way."

And so, Bill Sr. built football players in much the same way that other men reconstruct old cars in their garage. And the youngest son was a masterpiece, a physical freak who was stronger than his steel-working father by the time he turned 13.

Billy became the first sophomore to letter in football at Penn Hills, a storied program on the east side of Pittsburgh. As a junior, he won the heavyweight wrestling championship in a league that comprised all of western Pennsylvania. And as a senior, he was named Mr. Football USA, an honor usually reserved for the splashier skill-position types, like Herschel Walker, Eric Dickerson, and Marcus Allen, the players who preceded Fralic's selection.

When Billy arrived at the University of Pittsburgh, head coach Jackie Sherrill said he was the only offensive lineman he'd ever seen who was able to start the day he arrived.

"I haven't seen a better offensive lineman as a player or as a coach," another Pitt coach, Foge Fazio, said. "I can't believe anybody can be better than Bill."

Fralic became a three-time All-American and twice finished inside the top 10 in voting for the Heisman Trophy. He's also believed to be the first player to have his pancake blocks recorded in college. According to the University of Pittsburgh, the school's sports information department started tracking Fralic's pancakes—blocks that put an opponent flat on his back—in order to quantify his physical prowess.

In fact, Fralic seemed so focused and so successful in football that a reporter from the campus newspaper once asked if he even cared about anything else, if he had a single hobby outside the sport.

Fralic quickly rattled off three of them—playing golf, screwing girls, and drinking beer. Do those count?

Billy was a campus legend before he ever left college, a fact that was reinforced when Pitt retired his jersey (No. 72) during a halftime ceremony at his final home game.

The athletic beast built in the Fralic basement had validated his father's higher education plans, but there was a lot of football left to be played. Billy was a guaranteed top-five pick in the 1985 NFL Draft and that brought new challenges in Fralic Sr.'s eyes.

First of all, he wanted an agent for his son who had both ethics and guts, someone who could get a good contract without screwing over everyone in the process. Fralic Sr. had felt the heat of negotiations as a union president in the steel mills. He knew the bargaining table was no place for cowards. Or crooks.

Secondly, he was worried his son would burn through whatever money he might earn in the NFL. He needed an agent who could protect his financial future.

I soon became the man for both jobs.

Fralic Sr. was a fan of amateur wrestling and knew my name from my days on the mat down in Avella. He trusted my toughness, my ties to Pitt, and everything else I might provide. He hand-picked me to represent his son.

And as the 1985 NFL Draft approached, I had two tasks as far as Bill Sr. was concerned.

Get his son lots of money now. And get him some more for later too.

Neither of those things would be easy.

To pull it off, I would need a professional wrestler, a cooler of beer, and something that had never been done in NFL history.

The legend of Bill Fralic was about to grow even bigger.

Bill Fralic Jr.

The Phenom

His contract was covered in blood before it ever got signed.

And I suppose that's a fitting metaphor for everything that happened before Bill Fralic became an Atlanta Falcon and one of the best-paid players in the entire league. If I wasn't there to witness it all, I probably wouldn't believe it myself. It was one hell of a ride, a bumpy road filled with huge potholes and giant pains in the ass.

It all began with the 1985 NFL Draft. Having been through the draft and all the ensuing negotiations with Mark May and a few of my other clients, I was eager to take on the NFL owners again.

And I wanted a knockout.

The first part of our battle began with the Minnesota Vikings. Buffalo had the No. 1 pick and had long ago settled on Virginia Tech's Bruce Smith, a cat-quick defensive end who would become a cornerstone of the franchise and a Hall of Famer. The Vikings wanted Fralic at No. 2.

But the feeling wasn't mutual.

Billy wanted to play somewhere warm and that sure as hell wasn't in Minnesota, even if they had a dome over the field keeping all the bad weather out. Worse yet, the Vikings were notoriously cheap, led by a bunch of Ebenezer Scrooge types controlling the team's contract dollars.

Their general manager was Mike Lynn, who was a lot more of a businessman and bean counter than a football guy. Lynn made his riches running movie theaters, while other GMs were watching film and spending endless hours in scouting departments. Agents and players always tried to avoid getting drafted by Lynn and his tight-fisted team, but were rarely successful. Lynn would draft whomever he wanted and would sit on the poor bastard until he broke.

"You want to hold out? Not play? Join your daddy in the steel mill? Okay by me."

But in my case, I was an attorney with oratory skills sharpened by bitter courtroom battles, so I had no problem telling Lynn how it was going to be. If he drafted Billy, he'd only see him in a wrestling ring and his cheap ass might even get fired as a result.

Leading up to the draft, I spoke so loudly and so often about Billy's desire to play somewhere other than Minnesota that anyone with half an ear knew about it.

"It's a prison sentence, not a draft selection," I said, certain that my words would make their way to the Twin Cities.

My stance was also strengthened by Mark May's holdout a few years back and the smear campaign Redskins GM Bobby Beathard employed during that entire ordeal. Beathard said I would do anything to get my players more money, moving them to the CFL or any other league with a bigger check. I couldn't buy that type of PR. As Muhammad Ali once said, "Everyone is afraid of a crazy man." And I was certifiably insane when it came to protecting my clients.

Unlike some other agents, I had brass balls and wasn't beholden to every last dollar I could get from my clients. So Lynn had to be fearful of what might happen if he chose Fralic. Perhaps he'd waste his selection entirely. Our game of chicken continued into draft day and I hoped like hell that Lynn would back down.

The draft began and Bruce Smith went No. 1 to Buffalo as expected. As the second pick approached, Mel Kiper Jr, who had just joined ESPN's draft coverage a year earlier, started talking with fellow analysts Chris Berman and Bob Ley about all my charades.

"We'll see what an impact Ralph Cindrich has on this draft right away. I think Minnesota wanted Fralic. I know, you talk about Indianapolis, they would have taken Al Toon [another client] but Cindrich wrote a letter to [Colts owner Bob] Irsay stating that he didn't want Toon to play with the Colts. Same with Minnesota. So we'll see if those teams shy away from Fralic and Toon. We will see if Cindrich has a direct impact on the draft."

Truth be told, using a few choice words, I actually left a screw-you-and-your-owner message in Indy for my old friend Bob Terpening, who was working in the Colts front office, telling him not to draft Toon. Terp passed the message onto Irsay, so the Colts got the same warning with Toon that I sent to Minnesota on Fralic's behalf.

Don't take my client! Bad shit will happen!

In the simplest sense, we were all playing a poker game. And I won both hands.

"With the second pick in the 1985 Draft, the Atlanta Falcons select Bill Fralic."

Minnesota traded the second pick to Atlanta and Indianapolis ended up skipping over Al Toon too, leaving him for the Jets at No. 10. I had gotten both of my players to more desirable destinations by manipulating the draft.

But there was no time to pat myself on the back.

Rookie contracts weren't easy to begin with, and I had an even greater challenge thanks to Fralic's father.

"Ralph, I love my son, but I know the son of a bitch," I remember Fralic Sr. saying. "He will spend every dime he gets his hands on. You have to make sure he has some money for the future too so he can take care of himself."

And so the fight with the Falcons was about to get bigger than all the others in the draft, with those two separate funds I had to fill with money.

One for now. And another one for later.

Good luck, Ralph.

The Falcons general manager at the time was Tom Braatz, a former NFL linebacker like myself who was a straight shooter. I always enjoyed his honesty and still have a ton of respect for him.

But negotiations are never easy, even if there are good people on the other side. On our end, Billy stayed out of the negotiations, but I kept his father, seasoned by the contract battles at Edgewater Steel, plugged in throughout the process. We discussed everything as a team, but he was a bit too close to his son to have completely independent judgment. I led the way, but Bill Sr. was a great teacher, never overstepping his boundaries, instead offering encouragement: "You're doing great, Ralph. That's the way I'd do it if I could."

In contract battles, if you don't have the trust of the people close to the clients, you'll lose every time. If a single person goes soft, it's impossible to maintain a hard line. Thankfully, when I talked with Bill Sr. I always felt like Superman afterwards. And his son trusted all of us to take care of him.

"I wasn't really concerned with it," Billy remembers. "I had a good agent; he kept me in the loop. I was just busy getting ready for football. I knew it would all be taken care of. At that time, typically, there was a holdout by the top picks. I wasn't really worried about that either."

"My parents were very influential in the process, mainly my dad. He has a mind of his own. I knew that. But I knew he was very close to Ralph. Through most of my professional career, I found that it's better to focus on what the hell you're doing at the time. I was very happy to let all of them handle it."

Our negotiations began and both sides tried to grab onto whatever leverage we could find. Then, the holdout dragged on. Someone could have cracked. But Billy was steadfast and Bill Sr. was supportive too, even as I shot holes in some of his shitty ideas.

"I got this idea," Bill Sr. said to me. "You're gonna tell 'em that Billy has decided he doesn't wanna play football and that he's gonna go over to Europe and do some other kind of shit."

Any football league that paid players legitimate money over in Europe was playing something we Yankees called soccer. And Billy Fralic wasn't fucking Pelé.

"You want me to tell Tom Braatz and these other guys I'm dealing with, the Atlanta Falcons, you want me to tell them this?"

"Yeah."

"Bill, are you out of your mind?" I said. "I don't work in a steel mill. I don't make anything for a living that you can touch. All I've got to make my money is my skill and my reputation. I'm no liar. People have to know they can believe what I say!"

Fralic looked at me like he was about to say something important.

"I'll tell ya what, Ralph; I'm not sure I can trust a guy who won't lie."

"Say that again," I said.

He did.

Fralic Sr. was actually making a lot of sense, but I never wanted to make lying a part of my business. It was too easy to get trapped—and I'm too stupid to remember a bunch of lies anyway. I had tried them before back in Avella and got caught every time, earning a bunch of backhands and bruises as soon as A.J. found out. So as an agent, I never really believed in bullshit or bluffs. I much preferred legitimate alternatives. That way you at least had a contingency plan while you held onto your balls and waited to see what a team would do next.

In 1985, as we were battling the Falcons, the USFL was at war with the NFL, throwing enough money around to steal players like Herschel Walker, Reggie White, and Steve Young from the more established league. Billy clearly belonged in the NFL, but we had no problem flirting with the competition, even flying down to a meet with John Bassett, the owner of the Tampa Bay Bandits and an affluent heir to big-time Canadian whisky.

We were out on a yacht in the bay outside of Tampa, meeting with head coach Steve Spurrier (whom I always liked because he didn't believe in bullshit), and visiting with football assistant Tim Ruskell, who later became a GM. My family even joined us on the trip and my kids, Michael and Christina, thought Tampa Bay was a pretty damn good place, just in case the opinions of pre-teens held any weight in negotiations. Although I didn't believe the USFL was the best option for Billy, it gave us a little bit of leverage, but it wasn't enough just yet. The next thing we needed in our negotiations was a nest egg that would take care of Billy if he somehow blew through all the money I was about to secure in his contract. For that, I needed some help.

No one ever had much money growing up in Avella, and I sure as hell wasn't Warren Buffett, so I needed someone to teach me a little bit about annuities, trusts, and all the other financial tools that could safeguard Billy's economic future. And I had to study, to learn enough about all these complicated instruments to get them down on paper when it came time to write a contract. If anything was the least bit shaky, the NFL would toss aside everything I had worked so hard to acquire.

There was a guy in Pittsburgh who helped me find the perfect solution. The fund was called a rabbi trust and it was included in IRS regulations, even if it was not officially approved. According to David Bruckman in the *CPA Journal*, a rabbi trust is a deferred compensation plan that essentially safeguards future incomes or wages an employer owes one of its workers. It got its name from a synagogue that implemented the idea to pay one of its rabbis. And it was exactly what we needed for Billy Fralic. God bless that mensch and all the others who always seemed to show up in my life when I needed them.

Now, I just needed to get someone to agree to all this in a contract, which sure as hell wouldn't be easy since it had never been done before. If you haven't noticed, the NFL is not at the forefront of change. It was a landmark deal, an absolute game changer if everything would get approved.

But we still had a lot of other things to settle. As the holdout wore on, the pressure piled up in negotiations because of the draft's slotting process, in which teams pay rookies a salary that falls between the players picked before and after them. With Bill Fralic, the No. 2 pick, still unsigned, a lot of other deals were stuck in the mud, waiting for our deal to help establish market values.

The Falcons slowly increased their offer. Ever wait for an IRS check? It was excruciating, but our holdout went on—it had to—way past the deadline for Fralic's report to rookie camp. Soon afterward, Bill Sr. showed the only weakness I had ever seen from the son of a bitch. It was a lesson I held onto forever.

His son was inches away from a fortune, but we never knew that. You never do. And the old man was sick. All his hard work, his plans, his dreams, his bravado as a good father were coming to fruition. There were millions sitting on the table—more than any of the Fralics ever dreamed of—so why should he risk it for a few more dollars?

Fralic Sr. had just undergone back surgery and was still out of sorts, a shell of his tough, steel mill, self.

"There was only one time I faltered," Fralic Sr. said. "Ralph calls me up and tells me what's going on, and I said, 'Maybe we ought to just forget it and take the contract.'

"He [Ralph] said, 'No, we're not gonna do that.'

"I called him back a little bit later, and told him, 'You're right.'"

I learned a lot from that incident. One, if you're sick or ill like ole Bill, find a hole and burrow to the bottom of it. Rest. Come out strong. Think of Jackie Gleason in *The Hustler*. Eat, clean your body, clean your mind, and come back renewed. This was a momentary lapse for one of the toughest, strongest, men I've ever been around. Bill Sr. was my rock. He was the only one who could control his son—and Billy was in the words of his nurturing father "a wild fuck." Most importantly, Bill Sr. believed in everything I said. I needed him.

Thankfully, the conditions cleared up quickly. Bill Sr. soon came back to his senses. And at some point in the process, Billy told me if he wasn't a pro football player, he'd want to make a career out of professional wrestling. And with his size and experience as an amateur wrestler (Billy's high school record was 99–6, even though he wrestled older and more experienced heavyweights early in his high school career), it wasn't impossible to imagine all of it actually happening. In fact, with the right conditions, cobbled together with one of my connections, we just might get a little more leverage with the Atlanta Falcons.

The World Wrestling Federation was riding a wave of popularity in 1985, fresh off a huge event held in Madison Square Garden called Wrestlemania I. Money was pouring in, and the sport—if you could call it that—was going mainstream, with people like Muhammad Ali, Mr. T., and Cyndi Lauper making appearances at the first Wrestlemania. Fralic could fit in alongside Hulk Hogan, Andre the Giant, and the Iron Sheik. And with all the attention he would bring to the WWF after a star-studded career in college football, he could make some good money. It was an option, not quite as lucrative as the NFL, but at least something resembling a legitimate alternative.

I wanted to confirm all that with someone who knew a lot more about wrestling than I did. That plan would become our reality if negotiations broke down, so I had to be certain of it. And that's where Bruno Sammartino came in.

According to Chris Togneri in the *Pittsburgh Tribune Review*, Bruno was a skinny kid starved by World War II in Nazi-occupied Italy who found weightlifting after he arrived in America. Before long, he was built like a block of marble from his home country and became a headliner in pro wrestling, starring in televised programs aired by Studio Wrestling in Pittsburgh and later the WWF, which is now known as World Wrestling Entertainment (WWE). Before his career had ended, Bruno had become the longest-reigning champion in WWE history, with a tenure that stretched a total of 11 years overall.

I met him back when I went to Pitt, and we would make appearances together at the school for the blind. Bruno was always gracious with his time and the kids loved the muscle-bound teddy bear. This time around, I hoped he'd help me transform Billy into a pro wrestling superstar. Or at the very least, create the illusion of it.

The only problem was that Bruno didn't want any part of it. Underneath the rise of professional wrestling, there was a lot of ugly stuff going on.

"I was appalled by wrestling," he said. "It just wasn't the drugs; it was all the changes. I felt like Vince McMahon Jr. wasn't interested in wrestling; he was interested in what he called entertainment. They started having these beautiful-looking girls on and there was always some kind of nudity. The vulgarity, it was embarrassing. The profanity, you know we've all used it at some time, but there's a time and a place."

I understood completely. I never really dropped F-bombs myself until I played in the pros. Local historian Bill Cavarsan from Avella even stopped me once and said he had never heard me swear.

So I could sympathize with Bruno's desire to protect Billy from everything that poisoned professional wrestling. Bruno and I settled on a makeshift compromise. He would agree to train Fralic as a wrestler, but only if Billy promised that he would never actually go through with it. Was this a contract or what?

"Listen to your guy with the Falcons," Bruno told me. "See what you can work out."

A few days later, our holdout intensified even further and I floated the possibility of Fralic as a professional wrestler, telling Tom Braatz that he might earn a six-figure salary with all that rasslin'. But Braatz wasn't really buying it, saying that pro wrestlers didn't get the signing bonus that pro football players did.

He was absolutely right and even I knew he had a point. Playing football was THE option that had to get done. I just needed some theatrics to give us more leverage in the tug-of-war that was taking place.

Since we were going nowhere on the telephone, I asked Braatz about a meeting in Pittsburgh. I had big plans. My reconnaissance said he loved to fish and drink beer.

Who didn't?

Braatz was actually with the Falcons when they drafted me back in 1972. He was a Wisconsin guy, and like most everyone else from that state, a genuinely honest, solid, salt-of-the-earth person. He also enjoyed adult beverages and was an All-Pro beer drinker who was tough mentally, physically, and stubborn as hell. He was a freakin' Wisconsin German, a rough-and-tumble type who could drink all day and get himself back in choirboy form a few hours later!

As an agent, you had to be careful with the drinkers though. Negotiators—the old pros—liked to take you out to dinner and get the drinks flowing (more on your end than theirs) and make sure you had everything you could ever want. The entire time, they'd talk about how the contract could work and would certainly swing the numbers in their favor if you fell for it.

Braatz invited me out for drinks about a dozen times, but I always said no. Instead, I lured him to my own turf with the promise of fishing, one of his other loves. And of course, there would be some drinking too.

I had Braatz meet us at the office of my brother Bob's downtown law firm, a nice place with floor-to-ceiling windows and a good view of the Steel City. Bob had been the US attorney for the Western District of Pennsylvania and a federal judge too. His office was the perfect setting for a performance.

Bruno Sammartino would be waiting inside when Braatz arrived. I had seats assigned and everything else choreographed like one of Bruno's matches.

Bruno and Billy Fralic Jr. would be sitting across from each other like old friends, or perhaps even tag-team partners. When Braatz came in,

Bruno would say goodbye, play it cool, and walk right past Braatz with a nod, making the most of our negotiating ploy.

Braatz would undoubtedly recognize him. And he'd have to wonder.

Why was Fralic all chummy with the WWF champion? Is he really going to wrestle? Hell, if I lose our No. 2 draft pick, I'm f'n history.

After Braatz showed up, I'd load coolers of Iron City beer and some Pepto Bismol that I had stashed to help keep me sober. We would drive out to my parents' farm outside Avella for a full day of drinking and fishing. Perhaps I'd even turn the tables on Braatz, getting Billy a deal with the rabbi trust included, finalizing the figures between chugs of beer and casts of the line.

Braatz finally arrived, Bruno exited, and the seed had been planted. Professional wrestling was an option. Maybe it wasn't the best one, but it was a legitimate alternative, and one that we had just made public.

See Tom? Billy could easily make six figures in wrestling. And he could do it right now.

"Well, you about ready to go fishing?" I asked Braatz.

He was out of the chair before I finished the sentence. About an hour later, we had some Iron City beers in one hand and a fishing rod in the other, discussing what a phenom like Bill Fralic Jr. was worth in a league finally recognizing the importance of offensive linemen. The tension floated away amid the beer suds in hand and blue water below us. The Pepto Bismol had long ago settled into my stomach, a preemptive strike against whatever Braatz may have had planned next.

The beers kept going down and our conversation was becoming more serious as we got closer to a deal. At some point, I grabbed my briefcase and contract tables to make sure I hadn't lost my mind. It seemed I was still on track with what I had targeted for Billy's contract. But in reality, what I was acquiring was even better than expected. All I had to do was get it down on paper.

It was time to work out the details. I had a big-time Iron City buzz and was drafting an agreement on tablet paper that had to hit all the parameters of an extremely sophisticated contract. All this was happening at a pond with fishing poles in the water. Not surprisingly, I lost track of my lines. Somehow, when I wasn't watching, a trout took my bait. Braatz got reeled in too.

Billy was about to receive a signing bonus of $575,000 and a salary of $175,000, which was fully insured for the next four years. The Falcons would make a loan of $500,000 available instantly and would add performance incentives to the contract that could exceed $30,000.

My first goal of getting Billy all that money up front was taken care of. But the biggest prize was the rabbi trust, a landmark contract that was unprecedented (both before and after) in the NFL.

In accordance with the rabbi trust, Billy would receive a 40-year guaranteed annuity of $150,000 annually, which meant $6 million total. If he died somewhere short of that 40-year window, his estate would receive the balance of the money. If he lived longer than 40 years, he'd continue to receive $150,000 every January 1st. If the Falcons went bankrupt, the league would be on the hook for all that money.

With everything included, Billy's contract was worth a total of $7.7 million in 1981. Bruce Smith, the No. 1 pick who signed with my friend Bill Polian and the Buffalo Bills, got a contract worth just $2.8 million.

To be honest, the riches of that rabbi trust were rather preposterous, and the league should have never let the deal get approved. It was a multi-page maneuver that guaranteed money far beyond Billy's playing years. The league office should have voided it, but for some reason, they never did.

So Billy was rich, both now and far into the future.

Before we quit fishing that day, I pulled out the trout that took the bait, reality providing the perfect metaphor for our negotiation. And when I pulled the hook away, a few drops of blood fell on the paperwork below my feet.

That crimson-stained paperwork would become the basis for Billy's contract. It was earned with blood, even if it belonged to a fish. And I suppose the Iron City Golden Lager probably deserves a little credit too. "About 14 Iron Cities later," was Braatz's count, according to Gary Tuma of the *Pittsburgh Post-Gazette*.

We signed everything soon afterward, ending the holdout about five days into Billy's first training camp. Fralic Jr. received his signing bonus and sent a check for $300,000 back to his parents. He told them to pay off their house, buy a new car, and maybe get a new mink coat and a Rolex for his mother. Perhaps his steel-working father would want a Rolex too.

Fralic Sr. made sure his wife got a watch. For the first time since we met, he blew off my advice and went straight to the most prestigious jeweler in town and laid down the cash for some jewelry. He didn't want a deal from the jeweler. He had plenty of cash. His buddies from the mill would never be able to afford anything like that.

Fralic's mom eventually sent Bruno a fruit basket too.

"It was as big as this damn table," said Fralic Sr, who was sitting behind a large table in a luxury condo that was acquired by having a very rich son. "I mean she went ape shit."

Billy made four Pro Bowls and played in the NFL for eight years, earning even more money than what was negotiated in that initial contract. He also became a successful businessman after football, by starting a lucrative insurance firm that provides coverage for semis. And even with all those profits, he also continues to get paid from the rabbi trust every year, earning $150,000 every January from that contract he signed back in 1985.

In the end, Billy's contract was easily the biggest victory I'd ever gotten as an agent—one of the biggest in NFL history too.

It was the knockout I had been hoping for.

But there was no time to celebrate. My other client Al Toon, who was picked just a few spots later, was still unsigned.

And his holdout with the Jets would last much longer.

Al Toon

The Jet

AL TOON DROVE A DATSUN.

He bought it with the earnings from his first real job, turning his wages at a local dairy into the best vehicle that his money could afford. And that old car spoke volumes about the guy who would become my second top 10 pick in the 1985 Draft. Al was substance over style, fundamentals over flash, and a welcome departure from all the me-first guys who line up at wide receiver, perhaps the biggest diva position in all of football.

Al was a two-sport star at Wisconsin, which seemed to have an assembly line of high-character guys. He was a two-time All-American in the triple jump and so gifted in the event that he actually hoped to be an Olympian before a pulled hamstring in trials forced him to focus solely on football.

I met Al through Larry Milak, another Wisconsin alum and one of my old teammates with the Atlanta Falcons. Back then, I learned a lesson from Larry that I never forgot, a message I passed along to my clients every time I had a chance. When you can get to a team's facility ahead of everyone else, you do it. Larry got down to Atlanta early in his first year with the Falcons and by the time the rest of the rookies arrived, he was a lot like a veteran, having learned everyone's name and established better relationships with the older players than all the others who came behind him.

Larry was just a smart, savvy guy who knew the game and went on to business success after football, getting involved with some Burger King franchises that became a lucrative investment. He was also friends with

Al and worked as his advisor through the agent recruitment process. Larry introduced Al to me after talking with Ron Acks, who was my roommate during my playing days with the New England Patriots. Ron gave me a good recommendation and let it be known that I was an agent who could be trusted, a valued commodity in an industry often filled with urchins.

Al went into the process quite cautiously too, being careful not to get pulled in by a crooked agent who could send his career sideways. After our first meeting, it became clear that all of the involved parties were playing it straight. Even though Al was certain to be a high pick and some other agents might have offered him cash, neither he nor Larry wanted a single cent.

"I love this kid," Larry said. "He trusts me and I trust you to take care of him."

It was that simple. Al and Larry trusted my integrity and my credentials, and before long I had signed on to be Al's agent.

We were friends from the first handshake.

It was a warm feeling I had been lucky enough to encounter once before, when I became a fast friend in my first meeting with Mark May.

This time around, I was actually somewhat surprised to sign such a high-profile client without any previous connections to Al or Wisconsin. But with the draft approaching, and with both Al and Bill Fralic headed for the top 10, there was no reason to waste time celebrating my good fortune.

Draft day arrived and Fralic went No. 2 to the Atlanta Falcons. We thought Green Bay might pick Al at No. 7 and even spent some time trying to get the Broncos to trade up for him, because Denver was an attractive destination with John Elway already in place at quarterback.

But in the end, my gut feeling was that he'd get drafted by the New York Jets. Their player personnel director, Mike Hickey, subconsciously used the term "no-brainer" when talking about Al, so I knew there was serious interest inside the team's headquarters.

Sure enough, the Jets selected Al with the 10th pick in the 1985 Draft. The draft fell smack dab on Al's 22nd birthday. My gift was getting to work with one of football's most tight-fisted teams.

I wanted to get Al out of New York, but he didn't want any part of it. So I went into negotiations with Jets president Steve Gutman, who was a good, decent human being everywhere else, but a complete pain in the ass when it came to dollars and cents. Gutman never seemed to get pressured to finalize his deals by the Jets ownership or the New York media for that matter (at least until I got involved), and without that pressure, he was content to keep a close grip on the team's money, paying more attention to profit margins than the players on the field.

Our negotiation was going nowhere fast so somewhere in the process I shifted my focus to another contract involving Al. Al and his fiancée Jane were getting married soon, and most sensible agents encourage their clients to sign prenuptial agreements aimed at protecting the player's money in case the relationship goes awry.

"Well, Al, it's time to talk about a prenuptial agreement as we discussed," I said.

"What do you think about it?" Al said to his bride-to-be.

"I don't like it!" Jane said.

Okay, then, that settled it. But Al and Jane never needed that agreement anyway. They've been happily married ever since, with decades of marriage and four accomplished kids who are now finding their own success.

While I waited for the Jets to give Al a reasonable offer, I negotiated deals for my other clients in the 1985 Draft. Nick Haden was a guard from McKees Rocks just south of Pittsburgh who played at Penn State. He had a reckless spirit and a hilarious wit, something that often came out when he spoke to reporters.

"That's the way I grew up," Haden once told the *Philadelphia Inquirer*, when trying to explain his physical style of football. "Even back then, if we didn't win the game, at least we were going to kick their butts and take their women. We had problems with the women, though. They beat us up. That gives you an idea of the kind of women we had around."

Ah, Pittsburgh! Where men are men and so are the women!

Haden was drafted by the Raiders and their personnel director was Ron Wolf, a great guy who was also one of the worst negotiators I ever came across. In terms of football, though, Wolf was a Hall of Fame mind much like Bill Polian.

In our first conversation, I threw out completely outlandish contract numbers for Nick that should have been quickly swept aside. Ron should have laughed at me. Instead, he offered to investigate my contract offer. God bless him.

Anyway, Haden eventually signed a more reasonable deal and Bill Fralic followed a little later, with all the theatrics that I already mentioned. That left me with Al and the New York Jets, who didn't seem to be in much of a hurry, even as Al's holdout extended deep into training camp.

August wore on, the regular season approached, and the pressure began piling up as people started to wonder if Al would ever get signed. Reporters started calling me at all hours. Team officials kept in close contact as well. I was on vacation in San Diego during one negotiation and made my wife corral our kids in the bathroom and had them sit on the floor while I talked outside in the bedroom. With so much big money at stake, I couldn't afford any distractions. Plus, the bathrooms were pretty nice in San Diego.

Anyway, the Jets still failed to deliver, offering a contract that according to the *New York Times* was less than the deal signed by the second receiver taken in the draft (Al was the first). And yes, I fed that reporter the information. Just a part of a day's work as an agent. I loved the relationships I've had with media over the years. They know I respect them. You win over the media, you win the war, particularly in New York.

I wasn't going to accept a deal like that and Al held tight throughout the whole thing, keeping himself occupied with cardio workouts and an extended vacation with his fiancée aboard a pontoon boat in the waters of Wisconsin.

With the regular season just a few days away and the pressure nearing a fever pitch, we squeezed the team in an interview with the *New York Times*.

"In fairness to me and the Jets, I would like permission to seek a trade," Toon said in his first interview with the *Times* since the holdout began.

Gutman had no choice but to increase his offer. He came to Pittsburgh and after some more back-and-forth negotiations, we finally settled on some contract numbers that seemed reasonable. I told him I wanted to speak to my client and his wife. Steve asked me where he could get a haircut. Now, Steve was a nice Jewish guy from New York, so I suppose my next trick was a dirty one. But I figured a little divine intervention might help seal our deal.

I sent him across the street to Brother Richard, the barber.

The funny thing about Brother Richard is that he's often more sidewalk preacher than hair stylist, and is prone to talking about Jesus, God, the Holy Spirit, and redemption, every time he snips a strand of hair. You sit in his chair as he stares at himself in the mirror, clippers in one hand, scissors in the other, trying to control his gestures and the sharp implements at his side, as he sends up fervent and impassioned PRAISE TO THE LAWD!!!

Brother Richard might cut your entire head of hair without looking at you once. He's more mesmerized by his sermon and his reflection. All the while, you're trapped in the chair, dodging the things in his hands that might impale you and hoping like hell that your haircut will be halfway decent.

After a couple of visits myself, I put an end to all those theatrics. I grabbed Brother Richard by the collar.

"Richard, brother, I'm down here. My hair is right here. I only want you looking at my hair!"

My Jewish friend Steve was going to love him. Perhaps Brother Richard would help him repent for his contractual sins.

He eventually came back with his hair cut.

"You never said to me he was a Jesus guy," Gutman said.

"You never asked."

Brother Richard couldn't convert Steve, but we got a contract done and Gutman got his ass on the first flight back to New York.

Al missed the first week of the season and was the last first-round pick to sign that year, but his contract was better than those signed by some players picked three or four spots ahead of him. And in his very first game he validated the deal, with his first NFL reception going for 50 yards. Before the season ended, he recorded a 10-catch game against the Miami Dolphins, broke the Jets' rookie receiving record, and ultimately earned a spot on the NFL's All-Rookie Team.

Al never got a new car after signing his rookie contract, so his old Datsun sat at the team facility throughout that first season. When the year was over, he figured he would drive off in the car and give it away to his sister back home. He left team headquarters early in the morning and hit the George Washington Bridge right around rush hour. His transmission died moments later. Semis swerved to avoid him, and surely some New York birdies went flying by his window.

Somehow, he made it to the airport. And he eventually bought a new car too, saying goodbye to the Datsun that delivered him to the NFL.

Over the years, he became one of the league's best wide receivers, fearless across the middle and explosive in the air. He was named the AFC's Offensive Player of the Year in 1986 and led the entire league in receptions in 1988. He received two more contracts over the course of his career and became a cornerstone of the Jets franchise, earning three Pro Bowl berths and being selected as the team's MVP three straight seasons.

But his courage on crossing routes and his tremendous toughness probably accelerated the end of his career. I always bitched at Al because his dedication to the team and his determination to succeed led him to cast aside his own personal safety. According to William C. Rhoden of the *New York Times*, Toon had nine concussions during his eight-year career with the Jets. One of the worst hits was in a game against the Steelers, when safety Thomas Everett knocked him out cold, followed by linebacker Greg Lloyd celebrating by pounding the ground three times like it was a professional wrestling pinfall. Lloyd's outrageous antics would have received a 15-yard penalty, a hefty fine, and maybe even an ejection in today's head-conscious culture. Back then, Toon's best revenge was to recover quickly—and he always did.

The final hit came in a game against Denver in 1992. We sent Al to a team of neurologists soon afterward, including one who worked with Muhammad Ali, who was already showing some signs of brain damage from his own head trauma earned inside the ring. All of the doctors were unanimous. Al had to hang it up.

"My priority was my kids and my wife and what my life would be like in 20 or 30 years," Al said.

Toon retired in a tear-filled press conference in the middle of the 1992 season.

But the cruel thing about professional sports is that it often lures players back in, even when they're long past their prime or in Al's case, better served by staying away.

Al briefly considered a comeback after a touch-football game during Pro Bowl week when he was chosen as the team MVP.

Maybe if he played somewhere warm.... Maybe if the team didn't play on Astroturf...

I knew Al was starting to get serious, so I contacted my good buddy Steve Gutman again.

"Steve, I have a bit of a problem that I need to talk with you about. Al is considering a comeback."

A lot of guys would have rushed Al right back to the field, especially considering his immense talent and the little that was known about concussions.

But I don't think Steve even let me finish. He cared more about Al's health than any benefit that might involve the Jets.

"He's not going to play. We have his rights. He retired with us. He's not playing."

Steve Gutman was a good man. Maybe some of Brother Richard's sermon sunk in.

With Gutman stonewalling any comeback, Al eventually returned to a clear conscience too. With his history of concussions, Al had decided to pay six figures for disability insurance during his last contract, protecting himself in case of an injury just like this one. That policy kicked in now, covering a lot of the contract dollars that would be lost with an early retirement.

So everything was set. Money wasn't going to cloud his mind either. His priority was his kids, his wife, and the next three decades of life.

His retirement would stand.

The emotional words delivered at the press conference back in 1992 would be his last as a player. Some of them were the perfect summation of Al, a guy who always seemed to find the perfect balance between faith, family, and football.

"I remember being in the hospital the night my son, Nicholas, was born," Al said in his retirement speech, according to Al Harvin of the *New York Times*. "I got very little sleep that night and then went and caught 13 passes against Indianapolis."

Al's sparkling career had met its end.

But that baby boy would soon grow up.

And with the crazy way the world turns around, football, Al, and baby Nicholas would bring us all back together soon.

Paul Gruber

The Cornerstone

I LOVED REPRESENTING GUYS FROM WISCONSIN.

Something special happened to the football players up there seasoned amid the beer, brats, and bitter weather of Badger country. They were humble, hardworking, high-character guys—a lot like the work boots and blue-collar crowd I grew up with on the fields and farms of Avella.

Reliable above all else. Steady on routes across the middle and stable on the edges of your offensive line. They were also tough as hell, which worked out perfectly since we were fighting together for every dollar we could get.

I signed Wisconsin wideout Al Toon in 1985 and he held firm through an extended contract war with the New York Jets. Paul Gruber followed three years later. And it wasn't long before we found some fights of our own.

Paul had a good bit of his home state buried inside his 6'5", 290-pound frame. He grew up in Sauk City, a small town tucked into the banks of the Wisconsin River, and only went 25 miles south for college, to the University of Wisconsin in Madison. That school was made for him.

Paul had brown hair and All-American looks, like an oversized leading man in Hollywood. He was John Wayne with a football helmet and 50 more pounds.

He played offensive tackle with a combination of size and speed that got the scouts so excited there might have been some movement between their legs. And Gruber did everything the right way too, staying away from steroids, pills, and all the other illegal drugs. Paul's body was built like an Amish barn, with a lot of skill and a steady stream of hard work.

Paul ran the 40-yard dash below 4.8 seconds as a junior, but quietly suffered a high, microscopic, and hard-to-detect tear in his groin sometime during his senior season. It was a potentially career-ending injury and had ruined things for some other players. Gruber was cleared to play through it as long as he could tolerate the pain, but it kept him from sprinting downfield. If he did, his groin would pop and the leg attached would become useless.

With draft workouts approaching—and the 40-yard dash being the centerpiece of them—the injury could have cost him millions.

That's because there's nothing fair about the NFL Draft and the process that precedes it. Every inch of your client and his character is poked, prodded, and analyzed by every single team in the NFL. The slightest flaw in any area—even the rumors of one—can ruin a player's prospects and wreck his future earnings in the draft, which typically reduces compensation for each ensuing pick.

As an attorney, your duty is to always operate in the best interests of your client, to protect him or her. It's the same as an agent. If you have a weakness, you don't expose it or announce it. You do everything you can do to protect your client, but you don't lie. If there is a problem beyond your own expertise, you go to an expert. In Paul's case, it was a doctor who said the injury was no problem, Paul would recover just fine.

So with all that in mind, I was obligated to keep Paul's injury from overshadowing all his other assets as a draft prospect. Otherwise, some teams might skip over him on draft day and his first professional contract would be diminished as a result.

Paul and I decided to skip the sprint at the combine, figuring the dash Paul ran as a junior would buy us time. A lot of players back then skipped the 40-yard dash at the combine. The consensus said it was a slow track and that belief was usually reinforced when times were compared to other surfaces.

One of the accepted tenets of the NFL is that you have to do two exercises above all the others if you hope to get drafted. One of them is a 40-yard-dash, a drill that goes all the way back to legendary coach Paul Brown, who estimated that distance as a rough equivalent of what was needed for punt coverage. After running two 40-yard dashes, at some point you'll have to bench press 225 pounds as many times as you can. Skip either of these exercises and you're flushing a whole bunch of money down the toilet—and perhaps every chance you have of getting drafted along with it.

You have to lift. And you have to run. And you have to pass a physical too.

Gruber was going to have trouble with two out of three, so I had to get creative. One of the first things I did was schedule a private workout for Paul at a date I pushed to the limit—the last time period possible. There was no room for a make-up date if this one didn't work. We didn't know the exact condition of Paul's groin, but we hoped it might have a reasonable chance to heal by then. We felt pretty confident that he could complete all the other exercises without much difficulty, but the 40-yard dash and all the explosive muscle movements it required would still pose a problem.

A typical pro day workout usually begins with the 40-yard dash, but we couldn't risk that. If Paul re-aggravated his injury at the beginning of his workout, the rest of it would be ruined, with Paul limping around and moving poorly through all the drills that could make him millions.

We had a decision to make—or at least I did. I was in charge of the workout and was supposed to know a few things. I did know that skipping the 40-yard dash completely would cost us in terms of both dollars and draft position. Paul could plummet down the draft board and get drafted in a later round by a team run by dickheads. Or even worse, perhaps he might not even get picked at all. I decided that we would do all the other drills first and get them out of the way before we got to the dash. And once Paul ran that, I could meet him at the finish line and scurry him off the field before anyone might realize he was hurt.

Even if the ending went awry, we at least would have all those other drills to hang our draft status on. I set the plan in motion and hoped like hell that it would work.

Paul's pro day arrived and almost all of the scouts were in attendance, proof positive that he might be a high pick if everything went according to our plan. All the other drills and exercises, which didn't require the muscle explosion or exertion of a 40-yard dash, were flawless. Paul worked out for about two hours, displaying the kind of size, quick feet, and conditioning needed to be an elite NFL tackle and a top 10 pick in the draft. No one seemed to know there was anything other than perfectly working muscles pumping inside of him. The head coaches present seemed happy as hell.

After all the other exercises were finished, I pulled Paul over to the side while he was bent over sucking air. Not many people could handle all those drills without a break. I asked Paul if he could still make it through one 40-yard dash to finish things off.

Paul was sweating profusely in a gray Wisconsin workout shirt. It was a hot, sunny, spring day and Paul was on Astroturf, which is always several degrees hotter than the actual temperature.

Could he still do it? Hell, most offensive linemen are done midway through this type of solo workout. Not many people could keep going. There were no breaks, no huddles, and no other players to give him a breather.

Paul wasn't sure if he could still run—and I wasn't either—but he was willing to try. We both were betting on his toughness, but was it even worth it? Maybe there was too much at stake. I made a decision on the fly and was going to skip the run completely.

"Okay boys, listen up!" I announced with a clap like I was the commissioner of the league. "It's time to call it quits. Thanks a lot, we're heading in."

We almost made it.

"Hey, wait a minute!" some jagoff scout from the Jets yelled. "Not so fast. We need a 40."

I was already pissed at the Jets. Al Toon's negotiations had gotten ugly at times, and I didn't want another client going anywhere near New York. The Jets didn't seem interested in winning and had a lot of mediocre teams that served as pretty strong evidence.

Al Toon was enough. I didn't want Paul Gruber going there too.

But that jagoff scout seemed to garner some support for his request, getting other personnel people talking and nodding in agreement.

Now, there was no decision on my next move. I had no choice.

"Let me talk to Paul," I said aloud, M.F.-ing everyone else under my breath.

I leaned into Paul's ear and whispered.

"Can you run just one? All we need is one, that's it. I'll get you off the field. Rest a little while I go back and let them know."

"I don't know, but I can try," Paul said.

He ended up running a 4.95 40-yard dash, slower than the 4.7 something he ran when fully healthy, but it was plenty respectable for a top offensive line prospect, especially at the end of such a long, hard, solo workout. I draped my arm around his sweaty shoulders as soon as he crossed the finish line. And we promptly headed off to the locker room, with Paul dragging his leg behind him and me on the other side trying to cover it with my body as much as possible.

"Hey, we need another 40!" the same Jets scout yelled.

"Get it from your momma, jagoff! He's done," I yelled back.

Did I mention that the Jets pissed me off?

Acrimony aside, Paul's performance was outstanding. Coaches were still buzzing about his combination of conditioning, size, and speed. Our plotting and scheming had worked perfectly. His injury had been hidden enough to avoid any glaring red flags.

"When I was a junior, I had run pretty well," Gruber says now, his pro day and NFL career both complete. "I was pretty consistently around 4.8 seconds in the 40. We chose not to run at the combine since I had run as a junior for the scouts. But we had a tryout day at Wisconsin after the combine and had to manage that [injury] situation. We did all the football drills and everything and I knew if I ran a 40, I was in good shape. I ran it, but I don't recall how."

"It all worked out," Gruber said. "My draft stock kept improving as I got closer to the draft."

All those maneuvers just led us out of one fight and directly into another. Paul was now in position to be a top 10 pick in the 1988 draft. But his groin was still injured and no one, including the doctor who examined him, knew exactly how bad it really was. Paul didn't. I sure as hell didn't. But I did know for a top gun, high draft choice, it was the equal of a death sentence.

Meanwhile, I still wanted to get him drafted as highly as possible, for the best contract we could get.

We made it within hours of the draft and no one had seemed to hear anything about Gruber's injury. Then, Ron Wolf of the Oakland Raiders called. Wolf worked under Raiders owner Al Davis and played a key role in Oakland's war room during the draft. Ron and I were pretty good friends.

"Big Al loves this guy on draft day," Wolf said. "But tell me about this inner thigh injury he has."

How the heck did he find out? I had to think of something to say. And I had to do it fast.

I told the truth. "I'm not a medical doctor, Ron," I said.

Others might say I sometimes come off like one.

I couldn't tell Wolf about the injury or my client might spiral down the draft board. And I couldn't lie either because any misinformation you provide has a way of hanging around, staining you and your clients far into the future. And I wasn't a friggin doctor. I didn't know at that time that Paul wouldn't miss a play for 12 years! I was told that a microscopic tear in your inner thigh could end your career without adequate time to heal.

I gave Wolf the name and telephone number of Gruber's doctor, considered by most to be one of the best in the area.

"Ron, we go back some," I said.

But actually our relationship only went back to Nick Haden's contract in 1985. Wolf wasn't a great negotiator, but he knew football. And he knew about as much medicine as I did.

"You rely on the doctor, Ron."

The Wisconsin guy was well respected and later went to work down in Mobile with legendary sports surgeon James Andrews. Ron called the doctor, then called me back a little bit later. It was late in the evening—my kids had finished dinner and were off to bed. Wolf was chomping on an apple.

"We're going to be taking your boy at the No. 6 pick tomorrow," Wolf said.

Perfect. The Raiders were our stopgap at No. 6, but Paul and I knew he might get drafted even earlier. The Tampa Bay Buccaneers had just picked Vinny Testaverde a year before and were considering putting Gruber on the line to protect him. They were two picks ahead of the Raiders at No. 4.

Draft day arrived and we were watching at my house as usual. I always advised my clients to stay away from the coverage and cameras in New York. There was a lot more risk than reward by being there, and it certainly wouldn't help if your client slipped. All the anxiety would be broadcast nationwide. I'm sure Brady Quinn and Aaron Rodgers would have much rather been at home when they plummeted instead of in the fish bowl that was the draft's green room.

Fortunately, that never happened with Paul. In 1988, Aundray Bruce, a defensive end, went first to the Falcons. Neil Smith went next to the Chiefs and Bennie Blades followed to the Lions. The Tampa Bay Buccaneers selected Paul with the No. 4 pick.

A big celebration ensued in my house with both of my kids ecstatic that Paul had landed in the same state as Mickey Mouse.

"Now we're going to Disney World!" Michael, eight, and Christina, six, screamed.

Clearly, we had done something right with all of our pre-draft scheming. But the drama wouldn't end there.

I had no intention of letting Paul attend minicamp. I never had any of my top guys attend. It was flat-out dumb. Nothing was guaranteed in the event of an injury.

Back then, missing minicamp was easy, not only because of the injury concerns, but also because you could insist on an injury guarantee for your client and many teams would refuse to grant one.

Problem solved. Voilà! An instant holdout.

In Paul's case it made no sense to practice without being fully protected in the event of injury, so we were happy to hold out. Paul could not afford to have his groin pop before he signed a contract.

He wanted to play and he wanted the best contract he could get. For me, I had to protect him on the business side of things. The delicate balance of all those factors made the next four months more interesting. It was rumored that Buccaneers coach Ray Perkins had wanted a wide receiver in the draft and had reportedly claimed that he'd rather sleep on nails than draft an offensive lineman early. He believed offensive linemen were almost interchangeable, unimportant players who weren't worthy of a high pick. He had used six different left tackles in the previous season.

And that philosophy might have explained his team's poor performance. The Buccaneers went 4–11 in 1987.

I held Paul out of the team's minicamp and the corresponding workouts as I fought for a contract. The war was underway. On the opposite side, the Buccaneers had a tough negotiator named Phil Krueger. Krueger had a coaching career that spanned more than 25 years and he was equal parts grizzled and gruff in negotiations. I called him PT Boat Commander Kruger. Tampa Bay's owner, Hugh Culverhouse, was also on the league's finance committee and management council, two groups that hoped to keep salaries down all across the league.

On our end, Paul kept a low profile, never once speaking to the media. But he couldn't help but hear the whispers from some people he knew. They thought he was crazy for not rushing to collect all that money on the table.

"That [holdout] was a lot more stressful than the draft process was for me and my wife," Gruber said. "If I feel like I'm right, I kind of stick to my guns. . . . We just stayed back in Wisconsin for a month or whatever, but it was kind of weird. Everyone thought I was crazy. Friends from college and high school, they're kind of going, 'You're nuts.' That was more stressful, not knowing what the potential outcome was. You're a 23-year-old kid turning down a lot of money."

I was in a tough spot too. Agents are expected to secure lucrative deals for their clients, and any time there's a holdout, that pressure is amplified. If I didn't deliver for Paul, it would be a lot harder to get clients in the future. But I knew I had the winning hand. I knew absolutely the old man, Culverhouse, would cave. It was leverage, not enormous by any means but significant nonetheless.

A negotiating point you have to learn is that if you remain unrealistically high or low, and your client busts, you're screwed in about every direction you could possibly imagine. And none of them are good.

As Paul's holdout dragged on, Perkins helped our negotiating stance by actually calling left tackle a skill position, saying that it was needed to prevent linebackers like Lawrence Taylor from terrorizing your prized quarterback. Our camp stayed quiet as we squeezed the team as best we could.

Ralph's fighting spirit
evident at a young age
CINDRICH FAMILY
COLLECTION

Ralph—Avella High
School Football
CINDRICH FAMILY
COLLECTION

Ralph—flying
nun! COURTESY OF
THE UNIVERSITY OF
PITTSBURGH

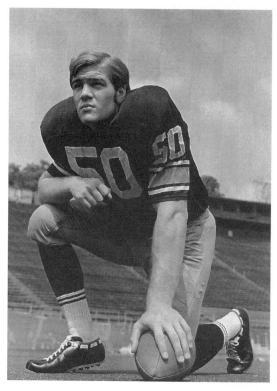

Ralph—Pitt
Football COURTESY OF THE
UNIVERSITY OF PITTSBURGH

Ralph—Pitt Football
COURTESY OF THE
UNIVERSITY OF
PITTSBURGH

Get out of my way!
COURTESY OF THE
UNIVERSITY OF PITTSBURGH

Ralph—Eastern Champ
in wrestling at Pitt
COURTESY OF THE
UNIVERSITY OF PITTSBURGH

Ralph, putting on his best smile
CINDRICH FAMILY COLLECTION

Ralph with brothers and sisters, (standing left to right) Ron, Ralph, Bob; (seated left to right) Rebecca, Rita   CINDRICH FAMILY COLLECTION

(Left to right) Courtney Cindrich (Michael's wife), Mark May, Mary Cindrich, Ralph Cindrich, Christina Cindrich, and Michael Cindrich at Ralph's induction into the Western Pennsylvania Sports Hall of Fame   CINDRICH FAMILY COLLECTION

Ralph as young attorney, when the Mob gave him a call   CINDRICH FAMILY
COLLECTION

NEW ENGLAND PATRIOTS FOOTBALL CLUB, INC.

The New England Patriots Football Club, Inc. hereby employs

<u>Ralph Edward Cindrich</u>   , Player, on the so-called

Taxi Squad as said term is used in Professional Football.

The Player will receive a weekly salary of <u>Four hundred</u>

<u>dollars ($400.)</u>   so long as he is employed by the

Club commencing with the first League game of the 1972 regular

season.

The Player agrees to abide by all rules and regulations of the

National Football League. The Player agrees to keep himself

in good physical condition and to play when requested by the

Head Coach of the Club and may be dismissed by the Head Coach

in his discretion at any time.

If Ralph Cindrich is activated
in 1972 season, player agrees   NEW ENGLAND PATRIOTS FOOTBALL CLUB, INC.
to sign 1972 contract at base
of $21,000. plus a $2,000 bonus
for making the 40 man squad.
                                       By _____
                                          UPTON BELL, General Manager   Date

                                          _____ 9/8/72
                                          RALPH EDWARD CINDRICH   Date

                                          R.D. #2, Avella, Pa. 15312
                                          Player's Address

                                          _____587-3434 (412)_____

Contract with New England Patriots   CINDRICH FAMILY COLLECTION

Mary as Junior Miss Beaver County   CINDRICH FAMILY COLLECTION

(Left to right) Mark May, Ralph, and Lou Holtz at Mark's charity event to raise money for Catskill Area Hospice and Palliative Care   CINDRICH FAMILY COLLECTION

Zach Strief with (foreground, l-r) Ralph's nieces Marlo and Paige
Postufka, nephew Luke Postufka, and Luke's friend Austin Rees
COURTESY OF THE POSTUFKA FAMILY

Nick Toon with (l-r) Paige, Marlo, Austin, and Luke   COURTESY OF THE
POSTUFKA FAMILY

Tensions rose. Rumors circulated that the Buccaneers had hired former FBI agents to find Gruber in the woods of Wisconsin. They never did. And each day, Paul's groin got stronger, bringing him closer and closer to peak performance.

The holdout stretched deeper into summer and then into training camp, and the pressure kept building. Finally, the Buccaneers cracked. Our gambles had once again paid dividends. As my old coach and client, Richie Petitbon used to say, "I hate to gamble, but I love to bet!" Tampa Bay had to break. The team lost the No. 1 pick in the entire draft, Bo Jackson, just two years before when he decided to play baseball instead. There was zero chance that would happen again. No franchise could withstand that.

Culverhouse caved and told PT Commander to get the deal done. I sensed his break coming in our first conversation and I thought to myself while I listened to him.

"Fuck you, jagoff. You want to play hardball, remain too high, and try to break us? I'm not moving, asshole."

And yes, yes I did, absolutely enjoy beating his ass on the contract. He called me a prick with his cronies for a number of years.

Thank you very much, Mr. Culverhouse. Paybacks are a bitch.

In the end, Tampa Bay signed Paul for five years and $3.8 million, the richest contract ever for an offensive lineman. The *Sporting News* called it "the best news for linemen since they were allowed to extend their arms." The deal was better than the one given to the No. 1 pick that year, Aundray Bruce, and also better than the one just given to Anthony Munoz, a veteran tackle who was viewed as the best NFL player at his position.

Not surprisingly, some people on the management council and finance committee were furious with Culverhouse, calling the contract the worst deal in the history of the league. According to *Sports Illustrated*, Gruber's deal was "an instant revolution" that "changed the future for the NFL's grunts." Agents could translate that to mean it was the best contract in NFL history at that time.

"Gruber's five-year, $3.8 million deal with the Tampa Bay Buccaneers was the most significant contract for any rookie this year," Vito Stellino wrote in the *Sporting News*. "It was the best contract ever signed by an offensive lineman and likely will start a new salary spiral at the position.

Gruber will average $760,000 at a position where $500,000 used to be the top of the scale. It also set a precedent that an offensive lineman can be paid commensurately with the top defensive players."

The only downside of the contract was that Paul was going to be a marked man in training camp. Here was this rookie, a guy who hadn't been to a single practice or played a single down in the NFL, making more money than anyone else at his position. Anywhere. Some of the players were going to be pissed.

Having been in training camp myself, I knew what would happen next. And all these years later, Paul still remembers the advice I gave him.

"I remember [Ralph] telling me, 'Someone's gonna test you,'" Gruber recalls. "'The first guy that tests you, beat the fuck out of him and don't stop. If you stop, everyone's gonna fuck with you. Kick his ass.'"

Sure enough, early in training camp, defensive lineman Harry Swayne took Gruber on. Fights happen almost every day in training camp, but for a rookie, the first one matters the most. With my advice still fresh in his mind, Gruber and Swayne traded punches like it was a football fight to the death. Perhaps it should have been no surprise that Swayne, another client, ended up as an offensive lineman and became a pretty good one at that. He now works in the Ravens front office.

When their fight ended, Paul had gained enough respect to keep future challengers at bay. All was quiet on the offensive front.

But peace is short lived in the NFL. Before long, Paul was approaching the end of his rookie contract, which meant that another battle was brewing. Gruber had played well and didn't miss a single start during his first five seasons in the league, despite playing for some dismal teams. The Buccaneers had won just 24 games in that same stretch and never once had a winning record. Gruber was one of the few bright spots in an otherwise hopeless abyss.

Not surprisingly, Paul was ready to move on. We refused every contract offer from the Buccaneers, hoping to force a trade. At the time, I was representing a lot of Pro Bowl players with whom Paul was friendly, but the success they experienced on the field was foreign to him.

The Raiders were interested—just as they were on draft day—but time was running out. We had pushed Paul's holdout to the eve of the trading deadline.

Raiders owner Al Davis tried to use that timing to his advantage. An hour before the trading deadline, Davis offered Paul a one-year, $1.4 million deal. The Raiders figured Paul had to either sign their low-ball offer or return to his former team. And they figured that last bridge was already burned, considering Gruber had a growing family that would include three kids, his house was already on the market, and he had spent the last several weeks exchanging media bombs with the Buccaneers' executives.

"Take it or leave it," Al Davis told me.

"I could, Al," I said in response. "But I'd rather tongue my 70-year-old fifth grade teacher. And he was ugly."

I was spurning the Raiders, but didn't have a backup plan just yet. Or a better contract offer either. I went to work and drafted a letter to the league that bought us another 20 hours. Since this was 1993, the first year for free agency and the franchise tag, league officials didn't really know what to do next either. So I decided to make up the rules as I went along.

I called Buccaneers general manager Rich McKay, a good guy I had grown to like, and told him I thought I could get Paul back on the team if there was a better contract offer available. Rich and I settled on a one-year deal worth $2.4 million, a million more than what the Raiders had offered just a few hours earlier.

"Cindrich made two creative moves that bought another 20 hours. He produced a letter to the NFL that indicated the Bucs legally nixed a one-year tender offer option, which brought the NFL office into the mess and put the deal in jeopardy if no contract with the Raiders could be reached. In the end, the ploys (employed by Cindrich) allowed Gruber to turn the Raiders down and sign a $2.4 million a year deal with the Bucs," wrote Fred Edelstein of the *Edelstein Pro Football Letter.*

Paul was headed back to his old team, but not before a few final moments of chaos. After his house had been sitting quietly on the market for weeks, a real estate broker called Gruber at 10:00 p.m. that same night, happy to announce, "I have an offer on your house."

That house thing would have to get settled. And there was also the business of making nice with the Buccaneers and Culverhouse, who was certainly pissed about all the bad press he'd received in the previous months.

Paul had a peacemaking meeting with McKay and Culverhouse scheduled for the next day so they all could make amends and Paul could finally sign his contract. Before he did, I gave him one last piece of advice.

"Just don't fuck this thing up."

Paul couldn't help himself. He was still pissed.

"We just went at each other," Gruber recalls. "It was a long drawn-out, two-hour meeting. At one point, Rich had walked out and called Ralph [and told him it wasn't going very well]. . . . Everyone expected me to just apologize, but we both just got everything off our chest."

Eventually, the two parties, player and owner, ran out of fire and foul language and found a way to move forward.

The deal was done. Paul and I had teamed up to beat the Buccaneers twice, getting two contracts we both could be proud of. With this second one in 1993, we were continuing a trend that was taking off across the entire league. Linemen, who had been lagging behind in both fame and fortune for years, were finally starting to cash in. Outside of the quarterbacks, top-flight offensive linemen were getting some of the most lucrative deals in the early days of free agency. And left tackles like Paul were proving to be the most valuable. The term "blind side" became popular as people recognized the importance of protecting the back end of all those right-handed quarterbacks.

That acknowledgement, coupled with the advent of free agency, made my negotiations extremely profitable. There was finally more money on the table for all those grunts on the offensive line. You just had to be willing to fight for it.

Paul and I had no problem with that.

Bill Polian

The Worthy Adversary

BILL POLIAN WAS ONE OF THE BRIGHTEST MINDS IN FOOTBALL.

He had paid dues almost everywhere, starting as a scout for the Kansas City Chiefs and climbing upward from there, moving on to the USFL and all the way into Canada, where he won the CFL's Grey Cup with Winnipeg and Montreal.

Polian became the general manager of the Buffalo Bills in 1986 and soon built the team into a perennial powerhouse, acquiring a number of Hall of Fame players who would take the team to four straight Super Bowls. In his office overlooking Ralph Wilson Stadium, he chomped popcorn, chain smoked, and found great football players in the same film where others missed them completely.

Will Wolford was a prime example. Many general managers thought Will could only play guard—if anything in the NFL. But Bill believed Wolford had enough athleticism and skills to move out to left tackle, a position many believe is the most important one on the offensive line.

There were several other players on the Bills with similar stories, guys who had potential that it seemed like only Polian could see. Wild Bill was damn good at his job, the wizard behind the curtain of Buffalo's success. Later, he'd turn Carolina and Indianapolis into consistent winners, building a resume that recently earned a yellow blazer and a bronze bust in the Pro Football Hall of Fame. Congratulations, my friend!

But I should also note that Polian had a penchant for pissing people off. He was sandpaper tough and somewhat short-tempered too, prone to outbursts that I suppose would align with the Irish stereotype.

Mike Duberstein of the NFLPA would sometimes call and ask me to advise other agents who had to work with him. As if I knew what to do. Bill wasn't exactly easygoing.

But I respected the hell out of him and liked him a lot too. And since I was also prone to pissing people off, dropping a flurry of four-letter words on people who deserved it, and mentioning that their mothers might have serviced an entire company of marines, who was I to judge?

All was fair in love and negotiations.

My history with Bill went all the way back to 1977 and the USFL's Chicago Blitz, when we negotiated a contract for my client Glenn "Lumpy" Hyde. And somewhere between all the bad words we often exchanged, there was a mutual appreciation for what each of us did.

"I always respected the fact that [Ralph] had been a player and a good player, that's what makes him different," Polian said. "He knew what the players went through, knew what the game was about and knew what was important and what wasn't important. He understood what my job was both from a financial standpoint and a team standpoint. We're both football people. You could reach a point in a negotiating session where you weren't going anywhere.... And we had a lot of common ground that we could go to if we ran into loggerheads."

With Bill being one of the best—especially with a rather limited budget—team builders out there, and me being one of the ... ah ... humblest negotiators in the business, we often ran into disagreements: big-ass ones to be exact.

One of them arrived in the negotiations for Kent Hull and Will Wolford. It just so happened that both players, two critical pieces of the Buffalo offensive line, had contracts that expired at the same time. I took advantage of that.

Joint holdouts were almost unheard of in pro sports. The only other one we knew about involved Don Drysdale and Sandy Koufax in 1966, two legendary pitchers for the Los Angeles Dodgers.

Naturally, I tried a similar tactic with two offensive linemen.

Bill and I had a meeting sometime early in the summer, before a lot of the league executives went on vacation. And I wanted him to know I meant business. I suppose you could say we were at loggerheads.

"Ralph came in and was really aggressive and combative," Polian remembers. "We had argued with one another before, but he was never terribly combative. Man, it was a different Ralph. . . . The meeting ended quickly and poorly and we got nowhere. I was a little taken aback by it—that normally wasn't his style. It upset me a little bit. The more I thought about it, I said, 'I think I get this.' Ralph is gonna be obstreperous here, because he wants us to understand they're serious about it."

The message got through. So Polian checked in with Buffalo's offensive line coach, Jim Ringo.

"I told Ringo that Ralph came in and banged the table and he was pretty combative," Polian said. "I think he's serious about it."

Ringo said, "Good, they [Hull and Wolford] don't need the first part of training camp and they don't need the first preseason games."

Ringo knew my guys would show up in shape and be ready to play whenever they arrived. He planned to get some of the backups more practice time and playing reps while the starters were out. He was close with those guys. We weren't sweating it.

With one party agreeable, Polian then had the unpleasant task of talking with Bills owner Ralph Wilson. He had to tell him that two terrific offensive linemen on his suddenly blossoming team were holding out together. And they probably wouldn't be signing anytime soon.

"Who do they think they are, Drysdale and Koufax?" Wilson wondered.

"I said, 'Well, yeah,'" Polian recalls.

"We're not gonna negotiate two for one, this is crazy," Wilson said.

Polian said he'd keep negotiating. He also let it be known that the team couldn't force either player to switch agents, not that they would anyway. They were stuck with me and all my tactics.

"This is ridiculous," Wilson said.

The owner stormed off to the Wimbledon tennis tournament in England. And the holdout dragged on. July became August.

"Ralph would come in and we'd meet and make no headway," Polian said. "We'd haggle and argue and spend some time swapping theories. It was business as usual. I was trying to create an atmosphere that was civil, but it was clear I wasn't gonna budge. I'd report to Ringo and he'd say, 'It's not time, let Ralph sit there for a while.' We kind of danced this dance for a while."

The stalemate finally broke in my favor. I knew it would eventually. Negotiations are mostly a matter of leverage and I had a lot more in this particular case. The regular season was about to start and the Bills were going to be good. They couldn't afford to have two of their best players out of action. And my position got even better when the team struggled in one of their final preseason games.

Ringo went to Polian and said it was time to bring the guys in. Polian went back to Wilson and laid it all out, including the dollar amounts that he thought were needed to get both deals done.

Wilson was still pissed. He didn't like giving out the money both players were about to get. And he didn't like that Hull and Wolford had banded together in the first place. But what else could he do? He ultimately opened up his pocketbook.

"He [Wilson] said, all right, it's too much, and we're never gonna have one of these tandem holdouts again, but go ahead," Polian remembers. "I did my best to indicate that I was doing it under complete duress. I had a gun pointed at my head by Ralph and a gun pointed at my head by Mr. Wilson. I figured someone was gonna pull the trigger if we didn't get them [the deals] done."

"I don't think there's ever been a tandem holdout again."

In the end, everyone won. Hull and Wolford signed lucrative new deals and the Bills team built by Polian kept winning games, becoming the best team in the AFC for a number of years. But before long, another stalemate arrived in the negotiations for Shane Conlan. And this one almost ended up in punches.

Shane grew up in Frewsburg, New York, about 70 miles from Buffalo, and went to college at Penn State, where he helped to solidify the school's reputation as "Linebacker U." Joe Pa had me frozen out at Penn State—only a few agents were approved by the coach—and I never got a chance to represent Shane the first time around.

Shane's first agent was State College approved by Joe Pa, meaning he was willing to work within the parameters Joe established for his program.

But the agent couldn't get everything done on his own, so I took over on the second go-around. Shane wanted and deserved big dollars, which pissed off Wild Bill completely. The first agent had gotten fired and now Polian had to deal with me again in Shane's negotiation.

Fast forward to our fateful phone call. It was summer. I was sitting on the back deck of our house in Mount Lebanon, a quaint, quiet, sidewalk-lined suburb on the south side of Pittsburgh. Our neighborhood was filled with houses from around 1910 and was home to a whole bunch of respectable people who kept reasonable hours and shared polite courtesies in the community.

I was about to ruin all that.

Behind our house was a deck where I could enjoy a good summer night and a few puffs from a fine cigar. Below the deck was a valley that dropped off about 40 feet with a small stream meandering through it. Every once in a while, I'd walk my hunting dogs down into the valley and over the stream on a bridge I built. It was a nice piece of property, and I always enjoyed my time out back.

But I never realized that the valley provided perfect acoustic conditions to carry a voice or two throughout the whole neighborhood, transporting conversations to anyone within a couple hundred yards. Maybe I knew that. Or maybe I just couldn't control my big mouth.

And I was calling Bill Polian, who must have been on the back end of a bad day, which was certainly understandable. Bill hated every single day that he had to deal with agents. He went right after me, apparently upset that I had been brought in as a negotiator on Conlan's behalf. I really didn't know why he was so mad. Maybe it was some type of Irish thing?

I gave it right back.

"YOU MOFO!" I yelled. "DON'T YOU EVER TALK TO ME THAT WAY, OR I'LL KICK YOUR F-ING ASS."

See kids, this is why you go to law school. Become a professional. Learn how to speak properly.

We were only a few minutes in and the foul language and four-letter words were already overflowing, spilling down into the valley below and flooding all the neighboring homes that just happened to have a window open. There were a lot of them too—the air-conditioning wasn't very good in what few old houses had it.

I suppose it's safe to say that my neighbor Sally learned a few new phrases that night—or at least heard a few she didn't appreciate—courtesy of yours truly. But unlike all the after-school tutors who might supplement their Mount Lebanon incomes with a little French or Latin instruction, I never charged for my language lessons.

I'm not sure if it was my language that night or her Christmas cookies that I criticized, but Sally quit talking to me soon afterward.

Does this mean I don't get any more cookies?

The bigger problem was that Polian pissed me off so badly that I couldn't sleep. I got maybe an hour if that—and started thinking about Polian as soon as I woke up.

I called his secretary and booked a plane ticket to Buffalo early that morning. I flew to New York, drove right to Ralph Wilson Stadium, and stormed straight into Polian's office.

There were rumors that Polian had sometimes challenged other agents to line up across from him in a three-point stance. This reportedly happened with an agent negotiating for Jim Kelly, and I prayed that Polian might try the same thing with me. I wanted to crush him.

I was looking for a fight, maybe even expecting one. I leaned over his desk and stared him straight in the eyes.

"If you ever fucking talk to me that way again I'll beat the living fuck out of you! YOU UNDERSTAND ME?"

I was in a rage, shivering with anticipation, and hoping he'd try something—anything—so I could pounce on him like a primordial beast. He even burps, I swing.

But there's not a single flinch. And all these years later, I'm very grateful for that.

I turned around, grabbed his door on my way out, and slammed the hell out of it, just so he and everyone around knew I was still pissed. I drove right back to the airport—feeling a lot better, thank you very much—and flew home. The tensions eventually eased, the deal got done, and I drove up there to sign it.

Bill and I went out for a beer. We made peace.

He said something like, "We've been friends for a long time, let's never let what happened, happen again. Let's agree to disagree."

Fine by me. I had seven or eight clients in Buffalo and we'd have to negotiate again before too long.

Bill and I were back to being friends.

"You forget those things quickly, they were never personal," Polian said. "We all have a selective memory. When there are rough spots or combative moments, you tend to move on."

We both did our best to forgive and forget. But then Polian ended up in Indianapolis and I was making Tarik Glenn the highest-paid left tackle in the league. And I had Jeff Saturday too.

He was swearing at me again.

And I wasn't about to take it.

Sally better shut her windows.

Steve Bono

The Veteran

STEVE BONO AND I SHARED SIMILAR ROOTS.

We were Pennsylvania boys anchored by old-fashioned values. There were blue collars in our bloodlines and tradesmen on our family trees. Everywhere we looked, there were people willing to roll up their sleeves, stick their hands in the grime, and pour themselves into the pursuit of an honest day's work.

That hard-hat mentality hung in the air like a heavy mist in our hometowns. I grew up around the mines, mills, and farms of Avella, a rough-and-tumble town about 30 miles outside of Pittsburgh. Steve was from the opposite end of the state in Norristown, a working-class suburb roughly 20 miles west of Philadelphia. Bono's father, Biagio, was a tool and die maker. His son was a two-sport star.

After graduating from Norristown High, Steve traded coasts and went to college at UCLA, where he excelled in both football and baseball, as a quarterback and a catcher. The Minnesota Vikings drafted him in the sixth round of the 1985 NFL Draft.

Bono's first agents were Dennis "Go Go" Gilbert and Mike Trope. Gilbert reportedly got his first client when he was still in law school, after he saw Nebraska running back Johnny Rodgers on TV and rode an impulse onto an airplane and flew all the way to Lincoln to recruit him. But Gilbert would become best known for his big-name baseball clients (Barry Bonds, Jose Canseco, George Brett). And neither he, nor Trope, who seemed to work behind the scenes, were very involved with Bono.

"I had them for my initial contract," Bono remembers. "They sent me a bill and then just disappeared. I never heard from them again."

Bono was looking for better representation and a high school friend led him to Cindrich and Co. before the end of his rookie season. Steve appeared in just two games during his first two years in the league and was cut by the Vikings after the 1986 season. The Pittsburgh Steelers claimed him on waivers, but cut him again before the next season began. His options were dwindling. His NFL career seemed to be running out of sand. But a second chance arrived when the NFL players went on strike in 1987.

Bono suddenly had a chance to play again—but only if he was willing to walk across a picket line. That sure as hell wasn't easy for someone sympathetic to the working class, someone whose father was a tool and die maker and a longtime member of a machinists' union.

His friendships made it tough too. Bono was good buddies with many of the players on strike, including his roommate at the time and all the quarterbacks he had just split reps with in Steelers camp.

It was a mess for me too. Some of the players I represented were on the front lines of the strike, sitting out games and surrendering their wages until their demands were satisfied. How the hell could I help their owners by getting one of them a quarterback?

The NFLPA, the union representing the football players, had made it clear that any agent with a client crossing the lines would be a marked man of sorts. And that would make it difficult to recruit clients in the future among other things.

But on the other side was Steve, who was running out of opportunities and needed to kick-start his career in the worst possible way. In the end, it was an easy decision for me, a duty owed to the client. My personal obligation was to serve the best interests of Bono. Ethical agents shouldn't be thinking about other relationships or future earnings or even their career when they consider the client sitting in front of them. I advised Steve to cross the lines and play. His career may have depended on it.

If he were my son, I would advise him to go out and earn a spot any way he could.

That test came up a number of times in my career and it never failed me.

If he were my own son, what would I do?

Interestingly enough, Steve's father, the card-carrying union member, also happened to be picketing at the same time. But he echoed my opinion.

"They were on strike at the same time," Steve said, recalling his father's advice. "I didn't wanna disrespect him and his fellow union mates, but he's the one that kind of said, 'We're fighting for a quarter more an hour and better health benefits.'" (Football players' salaries are obviously completely different.) "'You have to go and prove yourself individually. This is an opportunity and it doesn't really have to do with anything going on with a union.'"

"I had been cut," Steve added. "To me, that was probably my final decision point. If I was on the roster, it would have been harder to cross union lines."

All three of us (Bono, his father, and me) were in agreement. Steve crossed the picket lines and started three games for the Steelers before the strike ended that year. One of Bono's top targets was receiver John Stallworth, who was one of many big-name players who also crossed the lines that year according to *Sports Illustrated*'s Peter King. During that three-week strike, Bono went 2–1 with five touchdowns and a modest 76.3 rating, but the long-term effects of that experience are impossible to quantify.

Before 1987, his career was on the ropes, quite possibly nearing its end. But after those three games, Steve's career stretched on for 12 more seasons, millions more in contract dollars, and two Super Bowl wins with San Francisco.

It's hard to imagine that could have happened any other way.

After the strike season and another one in Pittsburgh, the San Francisco 49ers signed Steve as a backup for two future Hall of Famers. Steve Young and Joe Montana, a good friend and fellow Pennsylvanian, were both ahead of Bono on the depth chart. Montana had led the 49ers to Super Bowl victories in both 1988 and 1989. Young was the heir apparent, a talented player who was the No. 1 pick in the supplemental draft after the USFL fell apart. With those two ahead of him, Bono didn't get another chance to start until 1991 when both Young and Montana were injured.

With the headliners sidelined, Bono revived his career once again, going 5–1 to close out the 1991 season and finishing the year with the fourth highest passer rating in the league. After that, he returned to a backup role for two more seasons behind Young (Montana had signed with Kansas City). Then, the craziness began.

It was time for "Bones" to move on. He deserved a raise. And a chance to start somewhere else.

Naturally, the Chiefs, who had some people I didn't like sitting in their front office, were very interested. Fortunately, head coach Marty Schottenheimer, who went to Fort Cherry High School just a few miles from Avella, covered up any front office flaws on the field and the Chiefs were an attractive destination for Bono. Steve's buddy, Joe Montana, was already there and would be headed off to retirement soon, leaving a clear path to the starting position. Plus, it was the same system he had success with in San Francisco. And you don't take success in the NFL for granted.

What happened next was one of the more creative personnel maneuvers in NFL history. And it was mostly a one-man show. San Francisco president Carmen Policy was a maestro at finding loopholes within the league rules. We all watched in awe as Policy worked his magic. To this day I don't know how the hell he did it, and many of the other parties have said the same.

The 49ers released Bono after he refused to take a 50 percent pay cut. San Francisco later re-signed Steve before trading him to Kansas City for a future draft pick. Then the Chiefs signed Bono to a two-year, $2.5 million deal.

In reality, Steve's release, re-signing, and trade were all part of an elaborate plan reminiscent of *Ocean's Eleven*. Carmen Policy ended up with the draft pick he finessed, and we also received a new contract for Steve in a system he knew well with the Chiefs. Carmen the Magnificent ran the whole show and no one else got wise to his intricate plans. There were rules among thieves. He outmaneuvered the NFL.

Of course it didn't happen without one final hitch. Just as all the obstacles were being cleared and the trade was finally taking shape, the 1994 NFL Draft began. The draft is always crazy for an agent anyway, with all the egos and futures constantly cresting and falling, but in the middle of this one, Pete Carroll, then the coach of the New York Jets, called Bono unannounced.

"Steve, if you agree to take a pay cut," Carroll said, "we'll trade for you right now."

Fucking Jets. They always kept things interesting. But I was a fan of Pete Carroll. Thankfully, Steve called me and we nixed the whole thing (wrong scheme, wrong place, WRONG organization) and I didn't have to deal with that insanity again. Steve's trade to Kansas City eventually went through, but success didn't arrive right away.

Steve missed the offseason workouts in Kansas City and joined the team later in the summer. He struggled a bit with the transition in culture, philosophies, and personnel en route to a 0–2 record as a starter that year.

But Bono rebounded just as he always did a year later. He led the Chiefs to a 13–3 record in 1995, threw for 3,121 yards, 21 touchdowns, and was selected to the only Pro Bowl of his career. He also set a record at that time for the longest touchdown run by a quarterback, with a 73-yard bootleg against the Cardinals. That play still survives even today, a grainy, 23-second clip with more than 42,000 views hanging on amid all the fresher, flashier ones available on YouTube.

In 1996, Bono went 8–5 in his 13 starts with Kansas City and then moved on to Green Bay, St. Louis, and Carolina before retiring at the end of the 1999 season. The career that arrived at a crossroads in 1987 had followed the right path and motored on for another dozen years in the NFL.

Our partnership was a fruitful one. Over the years, Steve and I built our relationship—and our success—on the simple things that surrounded us growing up.

Hard work. Commitment. Conversation. Cocktails. Fish sandwiches. Family.

Those humble ingredients filtered from generations past worked just fine for us in the NFL.

But not everyone in the league operated the same way. Some people favored glitz and glamour, sparkle and shine. One of them was Jerry Jones, an oil tycoon and burgeoning billionaire who bought the Dallas Cowboys in 1989.

Jones believed in everything big. He was outspoken and brash and occasionally trampled upon old-fashioned ideals on his quest to push everything over the top.

My next fight would take me to his doorstep.

And it was going to be a doozy.

Herschel Walker

The Headliner

It was the biggest trade in NFL history.

And I was thrown right into the middle of it, a hired gun brought in to negotiate the terms.

But I had an awards dinner to attend that was honoring my dad. And my son's Pop Warner team, the Mount Lebanon Raiders, had practice and a game. Those millionaire owners would have to wait. At least for a little bit.

"What do I tell Jerry Jones?" one of the guys working on the trade asked me. "Jerry has a plane ready to leave at 6:00 a.m."

"Just tell him that the plane is going to run out of fuel. Dunno. Don't really give a flip. I'm not going to be there tomorrow. Jerry didn't call and ask me if I could be there. I don't live by his schedule. I JUST CAN'T BE THERE!"

What was the rush?

In the interim, I coached my son Michael's practice.

I'm sorry, was something important about to happen?

"Keep your head up, bury your face in the numbers, and blast through the ball carrier, kids! Your jockstrap will take care of everything else."

I got pulled into the trade by Peter Johnson of the International Management Group. I had recently joined IMG, the powerful sports marketing and management firm, as president of the football division, which was going after the growing fortunes stacking up around the football world. One of my first assignments with the company arrived after a panic-stricken call from the higher-ups.

Herschel Walker, one of the firm's biggest producers, is about to get traded to the NFL's Arctic team and he doesn't want any part of it. What the hell are we supposed to do???

Johnson was a former player who headed up IMG's team sports division and a legendary schmoozer, someone whose charm and charisma kept clients from leaving the firm for the other agents who were always trying to steal them away. He was a team guy loyal to IMG and his talents were too good to be wasted solely on football, so they spread him out quite a bit.

Peter knew how to recruit players and maintain relationships, but had no patience for the NFL way of negotiating. When I was thrown in, received the file, and read it, a lot had already gone down. It was pretty clear the parties were going to part. It was just on whose terms and when.

One of the football people involved was Jerry Jones, the well-known owner of the Dallas Cowboys. Jones was raised in Arkansas and played college football there, but his personality was always a better fit across the border. Jerry was a Texas typecast, full of big talk, bigger ideas, and a massive fortune made in the oil business.

He backed up all the big talk. He knew the game of football and knew big business even better, with billion dollars of assets to prove it.

Jones paid an estimated $140 million for the Cowboys—America's Team—in 1989 and then planned to trade their best player, Herschel Walker, just a few months after taking over.

Who would do something like that? Jerry!

Herschel started out on the other end of life, growing up dirt-poor and a bit disadvantaged amid his seven siblings and the red roads of Wrightsville, Georgia. He was an overweight and somewhat insecure kid before shedding a few pounds and growing into one of the biggest names in football. In high school, Walker reportedly started a daily regimen of 1,000 push-ups and 2,000 sit-ups to transform his physique, and eventually became a 6'1", 220-pound wrecking ball at running back, a player who carried his tiny school to a state title and rushed for 86 touchdowns in a single high school season.

He was a legend before he ever arrived in college, but he somehow became even bigger there, the Paul Bunyan of the peach trees, with athletic exploits that seemed to blur fact and fiction. Herschel led the University of Georgia to a national championship in 1980 and finished among the top three in voting for the Heisman Trophy every year he was in school. He won the award in 1982, finishing the season with 1,841 total yards from scrimmage and 17 touchdowns. He was a marketing monster for whatever professional team would get him and perhaps one of the greatest players in the history of college football.

"As a sophomore in college, he was already an NFL player," a pro scout once said. "All you had to do was give him the ball four times. He'd gain a yard, three yards, one yard, then break one for 60 yards."

Walker left college after his junior season to play with the USFL's New Jersey Generals. The upstart league stole Herschel and some other high-profile players because they paid handsomely, let certain guys pick their teams, and also accepted players a year earlier than what the NFL allowed. In three seasons with the USFL, Walker won the rushing title twice and finished 1985 with 2,411 yards rushing in 18 games, an eye-popping total that became a professional football record.

Dallas drafted his rights that same year and when the USFL folded, one of football's biggest stars got one on his silver helmet too.

But Dallas, with new coach Jimmy Johnson, a shrewd and sharp man whom I nearly fought a few years later, was going nowhere fast in 1989. Walker was the team's biggest asset and Johnson thought it made sense to trade him immediately, giving up on the current season for the promise of future years. One thing about the great coaches, they're riverboat gamblers. And they believe like hell in themselves.

"We had Herschel, and after him we had nobody," Dave Shula, the Cowboys' offensive coordinator reportedly said at the time.

Jerry Jones wanted to make a deal.

The Cowboys had made their intentions to trade Herschel widely known, hoping to create a bidding war among potential partners. Minnesota and Mike Lynn, my old friend from the Bill Fralic days, offered the Cowboys the best deal before the agents got involved. Lynn was a bottom-line, dollars and cents guy who made a ton of money in the movie theater business years prior to being hired by the Vikings. But everything he directed on the football field seemed to get piss-poor reviews. He was a prick in negotiations too—indifferent, callous, and cruel when he had the upper hand, which was always the case because free agency hadn't arrived yet.

Lynn and the Vikings desperately needed a spark. Minnesota had been mediocre in recent years and a name like Herschel would look good atop the team's marquee.

We have Herschel Walker! And we stink. But we have Herschel Walker!

The Cleveland Browns were also rumored to be interested, but my old friend Ernie Accorsi, a Pennsylvania native and a skilled personnel guy who was once the Browns' GM, said the interest was overblown. Perhaps the Cowboys manufactured all of it to drive up the price.

So Minnesota was it.

Herschel wanted a new contract, but he was happy with the Cowboys and didn't want to leave for the miserable weather in Minnesota. In Dallas, Herschel had a mansion, some expensive cars, and family members in town to watch him, in a luxury box provided by the team.

Most everyone in Dallas working on the trade figured Herschel's feelings really didn't matter. They usually don't give a damn in the front office and fans believe that players get paid so much that who really cares if a millionaire is forced to move?

Herschel didn't have a no-trade clause that might keep him around anyway. He was under contract and was supposed to honor it, no matter what team he played for.

Jerry Jones, who's always been a shrewd businessman and a marketing genius, made sure to seize the moment, mentioning the trade and some of the players involved to the assembled media who were already in Dallas for a league meeting. Jerry always loved an open microphone and anyone who might improve his publicity.

Whether it was inexperience, overconfidence, or Jerry's "I don't give a damn" approach, his words helped my cause. Suddenly, I had more leverage than anyone realized.

Herschel had some power in the process that everyone was overlooking. He could threaten to retire, I said. If he refused to play, the whole deal fell apart, and the players who were already rumored to be involved were poisoned, something I was happy to mention to anyone with ears.

Back in my playing days, I remembered when the Washington Redskins traded five players to my Houston Oilers for just one, safety Kenny Houston, who became a Hall of Famer. Defensive back Jeff Severson, a teammate who arrived in the trade, often seemed to be bitter about it, as if his contribution was only worth one-fifth of Houston's. I clearly remember him and the other guys smirking when it was mentioned that it was a five-for-one deal.

But that experience showed me how being involved in a trade—or even being rumored to be in one—could flip the delicate balance in a football locker room upside down.

When I finally spoke with Jerry Jones, I laid it on pretty thick. And that's damn hard to do with Jerry.

"You know, Jerry, damn shame if we don't make a deal. Wow, the number of guys who will be pissed! I can't imagine them all even wanting to play for their teams anymore. You? I had this Oilers teammate, Jeff Severson, and he . . ."

The wheels had to be spinning in his head. He was a player once. He knew.

In the NFL, a player typically has three choices in response to any contract issue or transaction—play, retire, or breach the contract and press for something else. Believe it or not, I never had a single breach of contract or a holdout if I worked on the previous contract. I figured the war had to be worth something, and going back on one contract would ruin all your efforts in those that came after it. Plus, I was ethical damn it. Back in Avella, I got an ass-beating or two that taught me to tell the truth and honor my word.

But in the case of Herschel Walker's trade, my ethical test didn't apply. I didn't negotiate Herschel's first contract. And furthermore, I was employed by IMG to serve his best interests, making his needs more important than those of the other parties involved in the trade. It was also clear that the relationship of Herschel Walker and the Dallas Cowboys was dead. Buried.

So the strategy was pretty clear. I had to announce publicly—and loudly—that Herschel wasn't really interested in playing for Minnesota. "[Lynn] better come up with something [money]," I told *USA Today* at the time. Walker's $900,000 contract, which would escalate to $1 million the following year, didn't include a no-trade clause. "But he's in a position to say I'm not going to do it."

I was at the poker table, but I had no hand to play. I was hoping to monetize the uncertainty of whether Herschel would accept his trade to Minnesota. Of course, he would eventually accept the deal, but it didn't hurt to drag things out for our own benefit and see what we might be able to get in the meantime.

Underneath our public posture, we all knew it made the most sense for Herschel to keep playing. He still had some prime earning years left in a profession that didn't give you many to begin with. If he really retired and didn't complete the terms of his contract, he'd actually lose money, considering he'd be required to surrender a portion of his last signing bonus.

There was too much to lose if Herschel hung it up. He had to keep playing. The trade had to go through. We all knew that privately.

But publicly, we played a different game. We told anyone with a television camera or a reporter's notebook that Herschel really loved it in Dallas, he was happy there, and maybe he wouldn't ever want to leave, all of which was true. Maybe he would retire. But then again, maybe, just maybe, if there was a little more money, and possibly some other perks too. . . .

As the teams finalized all the players, picks, and other terms of the trade, I kept slow-playing our position to maximize its benefits. Time can be your best friend or your greatest enemy depending which side you're on.

I figured Dallas would be in a rush to seal the deal, set to receive a collection of players and picks that would help redefine the franchise. The Cowboys were the football equivalent of a hound dog in heat. I wasn't as sure about Minnesota and my BFF Mike Lynn. So I kept working them both as best I could, trying to keep the deal alive and also acquire the best possible compensation for Herschel.

Eventually, everything fell into place. With my schedule finally cleared, I got on a plane and flew down to Dallas to help sign off on the biggest trade in NFL history. We made it official on October 13, 1989, my son's birthday. And surprisingly, I met Herschel for the first time there. Since Herschel was a big moneymaker for IMG, the company shielded him from all other agents—even their own—in fear that one might steal him away. The whole deal from start to finish only took 48 hours, but we profited from every one of those hours that we delayed it.

In all, a total of 18 players and picks were involved in the two-team trade, a seismic shift that would form the future of the NFL. No other NFL owner makes this deal, and no doubt Jerry Jones received grief from the other owners, but it led to the Cowboys becoming Super Bowl champions.

And all of our maneuvers got Herschel concessions from both sides, including an unheard of exit bonus from the Cowboys worth more than a million, and a package from the Vikings that gave him a furnished home in Minneapolis, a new Mercedes-Benz, 10 first-class airline tickets for the duration of his contract, and bonus clauses that could be worth another $375,000.

Peter actually walked him through the entire list of perks, and I went on my way. In all, I spoke maybe two or three sentences with Herschel. I was the textbook definition of a hired gun.

Herschel played three pretty productive seasons for the Vikings and the team improved somewhat, but the trade terms were almost impossible to live up to. Minnesota fans called the deal "Lynn's Folly," a transaction that looked even worse when compared with the Cowboys' performance afterward.

Dallas used the trade as ammunition for a complete overhaul of the team's roster, building a dynasty that won Super Bowls in 1992, 1993, and 1995. In addition, the team turned one of the draft picks it received into Emmitt Smith, a running back who was even better than his predecessor, a player who would eventually become a staple of the franchise and the NFL's all-time leading rusher.

In the end, Herschel got more money, the Cowboys got a few trophies, and the only one who might have been worse off was my old friend Mike Lynn.

Poor Mike had been fleeced.

Me, I was just doing my job. And I was continuing to ascend as an agent, grateful for all the good fortune and blessings I'd found. The NFL was thriving too, headed toward a financial boom with new networks, bloated television contracts, and other revenues padding the pockets of GMs like Lynn, who was rumored to have a financial interest in the Vikings.

There was more money to be had, and everyone wanted a piece of it. So players and owners were taking up arms all across the league, with agents like me deeply entrenched in the middle.

Down in Miami an especially bitter war was already underway.

I'd land right in the thick of it, a battle that would soon become the longest holdout in Dolphins history.

Did I ever mention I loved a good fight?

This one wouldn't disappoint.

John Offerdahl

The Gridiron Griller

Toughness. Tenacity. Pride.

The same intangibles that took John Offerdahl far beyond his own expectations, sending him into the NFL and the Pro Bowl five times, made him a monster in negotiations. He wasn't going to flinch. And his best attributes weren't going away anytime soon.

Three years into Offerdahl's career, Joe Robbie, the Dolphins' abrasive owner, picked a fight by all accounts breaching a verbal contract that was set in place by his son Mike a few years earlier with another agent. The ensuing struggle became the longest holdout in Dolphins history, a contract war that would be Robbie's last before his untimely death a few months later.

My old friend Bob Terpening, the former Indianapolis GM and Patriots executive who drove me to the airport after I was cut, blamed me for Robbie's demise (he blamed me for the deaths of Bob Irsay and Hugh Culverhouse too). Most everyone else believed it was a respiratory problem and a long-running illness.

But I suppose John and I probably added to his stress.

John's story began in Fort Atkinson, Wisconsin, a town between Madison and Milwaukee on a bend in the Rock River. Offerdahl had four older sisters and joked that he often wore their hand-me-downs growing up, an upbringing that wasn't exactly a fast track to the testosterone-filled trenches of professional football. He weighed 185 pounds coming out of high school and only got a half scholarship to Western Michigan, a Mid-American Conference (MAC) school in Kalamazoo that was Division I-AA at the time.

But John made such an impression on head coach Jack Harbaugh (the father of John and Jim) and some other coaches in camp that he earned a full scholarship and a starting spot at linebacker before the season ever began. He ended up setting the MAC record for career tackles (694) and led the conference in that same category his final three seasons. But even with all that success, he wasn't one of those players who sped through college always staring at the NFL up ahead. In fact, if it weren't for a college coach who made him realize that he had an NFL future, he might have quit football entirely, a little burnt out by the grind of it all.

Instead, John refocused and finished his career strong, earning a trip to the East-West Shrine Game and the Senior Bowl in Alabama as well, where he ended up with a starting spot. Offerdahl had a huge game in Mobile and on a fourth-and-one play at the goal line, he stuffed all-everything tailback Bo Jackson, the future Tecmo Bowl stars colliding without any help from a cartridge or controllers.

John shot up the draft board and suddenly had to treat pro football as a profession, locating an agent to help him handle the process. He worked with his dad, an accountant with an analytical mind, to help him narrow the field down to myself and IMG's Peter Johnson (I wasn't with IMG yet). They ultimately picked Peter, whom I liked quite a bit when he wasn't complaining about the beatings I gave him on the racquetball court.

"Ralph was right there, my dad and I just made the decision to go with IMG at the last second," Offerdahl said.

A few months later, John was drafted with the 52nd pick in the 1986 Draft, the first Miami selection that year since the team traded its first-rounder to acquire Pitt linebacker Hugh Green.

Soon after the draft, Peter started negotiating John's rookie contract. Johnson was trying to get John a deal that fit the draft slot, a middle ground between the amount paid to the players selected before and after him.

But Joe Robbie was already applying the squeeze.

According to Jeremy Lang of the *Orlando Sun-Sentinel*, Robbie was "a hard-nosed, impulsive, tempestuous businessman who never backed away from a battle." And in John's first contract, he was certainly holding true to form.

Robbie was born on July 7, 1916, in Sisseton, South Dakota, just a few miles from the Minnesota border, to a Lebanese father and an Irish mother. He grew up during the Great Depression and served through 45 months and five invasions in the South Pacific with the US Navy during World War II. He earned a Bronze Star before he came home and then went on to college and a lucrative career in law and politics.

He bought the Dolphins' franchise in 1965 and hired Don Shula five years later, a head coach who would lead the team to an undefeated season and a Super Bowl in 1972, and then a Super Bowl repeat in 1973. His other major victory was building the stadium that bore his name with about $110 million in private funds, clearing all the obstacles and collecting enough finances to get it done. Joe Robbie Stadium opened in 1987, and it still stands today as the renamed Sun Life Stadium. But all that business success wasn't won with a pantywaist personality.

"He is the toughest man, pound for pound, I have ever met in football," said Norris Anderson, a longtime columnist for *Football News*.

But Joe Robbie would soon meet his match with another Midwest kid from the middle of Wisconsin.

"We knew it was gonna be tough when he [Robbie] called me the stubborn Norwegian," Offerdahl said. "He clearly knew I would probably be a man of conviction."

Offerdahl held out during his rookie training camp while Johnson kept working on acquiring a fair deal. Weeks passed. The pressure built, with Shula, who was still head coach, talking to the media about his disappointment and all the time that John was missing. Both sides finally found a middle ground, with the Dolphins offering a three-year deal that was in line with the market.

But when John went to sign it, a curveball arrived too. The contract had a team option for a fourth year, with a modest raise that wasn't previously discussed.

Both Peter and John balked, unsure if they should accept it. But they ultimately relented, only because Mike Robbie, Joe's son and a good guy and friend, promised that the team would renegotiate the deal after three years.

It was a verbal contract, sealed with the dubious certainty a handshake provided.

And even though he was a few weeks late, he caught up quickly, using his intellect and all those other intangibles to earn a starting spot as a rookie. He appeared in 15 games and was named the NFL's Rookie of the Year in 1986 and a starter for the AFC's Pro Bowl team as well.

In his second year, he tore a bicep in the preseason and missed three games in the strike-shortened season of 1987. But he returned in time to impress again, playing in nine games and earning a second Pro Bowl berth. He followed that year with a full 16-game season and his third-straight Pro Bowl selection.

"Offerdahl has done a heck of a job," Coach Shula told the *Sun-Sentinel* after the Pro Bowl selection in 1988. "He`s been healthy and he`s been consistent. He has to be one of the finest inside linebackers in the NFL."

After the Pro Bowl, Offerdahl's initial three-year contract had expired and John was due for a big raise. He was grossly underpaid, a three-time Pro Bowler who was only the 28th best-paid player on his team. Furthermore, he had satisfied all the performance triggers to clear out the contingencies. It was time for Miami to pay him as promised.

But with Mike Robbie no longer there, Joe Robbie and the Dolphins didn't live up to the verbal agreement with Mike. They thought he should play for the team option that was signed under false pretenses during his rookie deal. And the Dolphins' first long-term offer was far below market value. Furthermore, they refused to negotiate again until John reported to camp, which would have weakened his own bargaining position.

So John had no other choice. He was headed for a holdout, a victim of a verbal contract that was about as reliable as a piece of one-ply toilet paper in a diarrhea clinic.

This time around, I was now in place as his agent, through my involvement with IMG's newly formed football division. And I knew John wouldn't crumble under the heat of our negotiations, giving us a chance to get what we wanted in the end. But no one expects to go that long in a holdout, and very few have ever done it.

John would be the exception.

"You're starting with somebody who takes a lot of pride in his work," John said. "You come to the game with some elements: one a hard head, a determination, a grittiness about yourself, a tenacity, those are things that are hard to turn off in other parts."

So with John dug in on one side, tough as tarpaper Joe Robbie on the other, and an agent from rough-and-tumble Avella in the middle, this contract war had the potential to be an epic one.

And it didn't disappoint. Training camp and the preseason both went by without any sign of a ceasefire. One day bled into another. John and his wife were laying low up the beach in Stuart, making their initial plans for a bagel cafe business that would bring profits long after football had ended.

The season began and both sides traded occasional volleys in the media. The Dolphins went 1–3 in their first four games, turning up the heat on everyone involved. Joe Robbie took a lot of shots. John got a couple too. The hardest part for Offerdahl was hearing the whispers, having people wonder if he was committed to the team or completely crazy for turning all that money down.

In reality, he was fully committed—it killed him to be away—and absolutely sane too, but he was exercising the only option players could use in protest. Before free agency, there was nothing other than a holdout to keep the owners honest.

Players had to protect themselves in any way they could. So John held firm through the whole damn thing, even when his holdout approached three months, the regular season hit Week 6 (the Dolphins had improved to 3–3) and the NFL trading deadline drew closer. The Dolphins were adamant that John wouldn't be traded. Something else would have to stop the standoff, which could have continued forever.

John and his wife went back up north not far from where they went to college and prepared for life without football.

But Robbie and the Dolphins finally backed down after 81 days, sending out a compromise in the form of a one-year contract that could get John back on the field now with a modest raise as well. Before training camp started, the team wanted John to play under the option finagled in his first contract, a deal worth just over $200,000. After his holdout, he signed a pro-rated deal for $500,000 that, even after the deductions for the practices and games he missed (six), would pay him more for 10 games than he would have received playing the full season with the original salary.

We won. In the end, it was all a numbers game, and it set us up to get John paid the way he deserved to be, like the best linebacker in the league.

That damn Norwegian gave the players a rare victory over the people in power. I played my part too, but it was John's persistence, principles, courage, and conviction that really swung the tide. We were perhaps the only people who ever beat Joe Robbie.

Once he returned to the field, John earned his money just as he always did. He was even selected for his fourth-straight Pro Bowl, despite appearing in only 10 games. And once his one-year contract expired, he signed a four-year deal worth an estimated $4 million that made him the highest-paid linebacker in the league. That deal kept him in Miami until his retirement in 1994.

But John's story didn't stop there. Like many of the clients I represented, he found success after football, selling off a chain of bagel stores that he first opened in 1990. I read his business proposal at the time and thought he was wasting his time in football. He was a business genius and this was after being a pre-med major in college. Maybe I shouldn't have been encouraging him to bury his head in ball carriers.

John now owns and operates Offerdahl's Cafe Grill, a chain of seven fast-casual restaurants in the Florida area that offer a variety of fresh-grilled meats (steak, chicken, shrimp, salmon) in addition to a plethora of other options.

He calls himself the Gridiron Griller, a nickname that blends both areas of his expertise.

But I always knew him best as that damn Norwegian, the guy who dug in deep against Joe Robbie, scoring a victory for the players in an arena where they lost all too often.

Fortunately, there was more help coming from a courtroom. Other players would soon have a weapon that Offerdahl never did.

Free agency would soon arrive.

And when it did, I was going to turn the NFL upside down.

Will Wolford

The Trendsetter

THINGS WERE ABOUT TO CHANGE.

In September of 1992, a jury of eight women ruled in favor of eight football players who sued the NFL over the league's restrictive salary system. According to Thomas George of the *New York Times*, the jury ruled that the NFL's Plan B free agency was a violation of federal antitrust laws and rendered it illegal.

Plan B free agency had allowed teams to prevent 37 players on the roster each year from negotiating with other teams, keeping them from earning their true value on the open market. Four of the players in the lawsuit received damages that in total would exceed $1.6 million.

"This is a total and huge victory," Jim Quinn, the players' lead counsel, told the *Times*. "For the rest of the players, liability has been found; the only issue is how much damages they get. We are not trying to blow up the world or look for the destruction of professional sports."

The decision wasn't going to destroy professional football, but it sure as hell was going to shake things up. Before the verdict, most players were bound to the teams that drafted them (which is why I always tried to obtain the best possible landing spots for my clients). Trades were rare. Player movement was minimal, with many guys starting and ending their careers in the same city. But once 1993 arrived, capitalism would reign in the NFL. Except for a few players who could be restricted by franchise or transition tags, which both locked in players for one year at averages based on their position, my clients would have open access to all the other teams. And some of those teams might be willing to spend big.

It gave me an abundance of leverage that I had never known. All I needed was a client near the end of his contract and a chance to use it.

Will Wolford was just that.

Wolford was a Kentucky native who played offensive tackle at about 6'5" and almost 300 pounds but had the light feet of a ballroom dancer. As a kid, he played basketball and jumped rope for hours on end, building the athleticism that would make him a valuable commodity in a league leaning more heavily on athletic linemen who were nimble protectors in the passing game.

Will was smart enough to attend Vanderbilt, a rigorous school where academics still mattered, and agents started swarming him after his senior season, smitten by his size and talent. Fortunately, Wolford's dad was deeply involved in the process.

Moe Wolford was also oversized, a former football player who owned a bar and could smell bullshit a hundred yards away. During the recruiting process, he saw right through many of my peers and pushed Will toward me.

"I was very lucky that my father was there step for step. He was a real good judge of character," Wolford said. "There were a couple of guys we whittled it down to. I liked a lot of the guys who pursued me and some of them would offer some things that weren't legal or ethical. Ralph never approached that line.... As a young kid, I wasn't sure [though]. I gravitated toward the guy that supposedly offered me a racehorse and lived on a ranch in Dallas. Ralph was an attorney. A former player. He was a very consistent, class guy. You make a lot of decisions in life and you talk about one that was a great decision for me. That was it."

I love Will too.

He was drafted with the 20th pick in the 1986 draft by the Buffalo Bills and general manager Bill Polian, who had a knack for building championship teams and seeing talent where others might have missed it. Soon after that, I went to war with Bill, a frequent opponent who was prone to craziness and curse words and might threaten to kick your ass if you crossed him. He was a man of my own ilk. Despite our legendary battles, we always somehow found friendship again once the deal got done.

After perhaps a few four-letter words from both Bill and me, Will signed a contract better than some players in the top 10. He went to work at left tackle on a Buffalo team that was loaded with talent (including Hall of Famers Jim Kelly, Thurman Thomas, and Andre Reed) and used a hurry-up, pass-heavy offense typical of today's game. With Will as a bookend protecting Kelly's blind side, the Bills became an AFC dynasty, making it to four straight Super Bowls. In one of them, Wolford neutralized Giants linebacker Lawrence Taylor, a destructive force who was the most feared pass rusher in the entire league.

After the fourth Super Bowl loss, things were blowing up in Buffalo and Bill Polian was taking the hit. Loyalty went out the window when John Butler took over for him. It made sense for Will and me to consider other teams.

Fortunately, Will was fresh off a Pro Bowl season and entering his prime at the same time he was hitting the open market. Free agency gave us access to any team that was interested. And I was certain I could make him a whole bunch of money.

"It was the perfect storm to land a nice contract," Wolford said.

But things can change quickly in the NFL. They sure did for us. The Bills placed a transition tag on Will, one of the few remaining weapons teams had to keep their players from rushing out of town. That gave Buffalo a chance to match any offer Will might get somewhere else.

Suddenly, all those teams that were interested in Will were staring at a roadblock right in front of their face. Buffalo could end up nixing all their efforts. Why would teams disturb their salary structure and perhaps piss off some of the current players by chasing after one they might never get? They might be better off going after a less risky proposition, even if it was a less talented one.

Will and I were in trouble. That free agent windfall we had envisioned was in serious jeopardy. I had to maneuver the system somehow and find some sort of loophole that could get Will a contract that wouldn't be wiped out by Buffalo in the end. And the only way that could happen was to find a hole in the collective bargaining agreement that no one had ever found. The end result was the infamous "poison pill" clause that made its way into contracts all around the league. I was the godfather of it. I knew the collective bargaining agreement well enough to devise the maneuver and had also found some teams willing to play along.

Four or five teams were interested in Will, and the Colts were open to both spending money and my creative ideas. Indianapolis agreed to pay Will $7.65 million over three years. It was more money than any offensive lineman had ever been paid by a decent margin. But more importantly, the Colts accepted a clause I added to Will's contract that guaranteed he was always the highest-paid player on their offense, the "poison pill" that was about to become famous.

In Buffalo's case, that pill made the contract impossible to match.

How could the Bills even consider the same deal? They had Jim Kelly and Thurman Thomas, two headliners making a ton of money. There was no way they could guarantee that Will's salary would always be the biggest one with the stars they had on their team. They were done for—if the league would let my little end-around stand.

"The NFL didn't like the idea of any player having a clause in his contract guaranteeing him more money than his teammates, and it made noises about voiding the deal," Michael Lewis wrote in his book *The Blind Side*. "That's when Ralph Cindrich went on the warpath. He asked, pointedly, if the league would have the same reservations if the clause had been in some quarterback's contract. He accused the league, in the pages of the *New York Times*, of 'discrimination against offensive linemen.'"

I always had a way with words, especially when a reporter might help me scream mine from the mountaintop. Not surprisingly, the NFL let the deal slide, but only after saying "no such deal would be permitted in the future." And there were a couple of boys—attorneys, actually—in the league office who were none too happy.

The end result was better than anything Will or I or really any other offensive lineman might have ever envisioned. A year earlier, Will would have been happy to stay in Buffalo for a salary of about $1.25 million per year. I sold him on patience and the promise of the open market. Fortunately, I was right. Five teams were bidding on Will, with four of them offering more than $2 million per year.

Those unknown grunts up front were finally getting a fair share of the NFL's increasing riches. And with free agency giving everyone access to the open market, left tackles like Will were getting rewarded handsomely.

Paul Gruber provided even more proof. That same offseason, Gruber, another left-tackle client who rocked the NFL with his first deal, signed a second with the Tampa Bay Buccaneers worth $9.65 million over four years.

Teams were starting to recognize that guys like Gruber and Wolford were worth every penny. They protected the back side and blind eyes of the right-armed quarterbacks who were somewhat oblivious to what was happening behind them. In the hierarchy of the NFL, quarterbacks were viewed as the most valuable assets, and left tackles owned the most responsibility in terms of protecting them. So it just made good business sense to pay for a great one.

Before 1993 was over, nine of the 28 franchise players tagged by NFL teams were left tackles. The term "blind side" became popular as the position seemed to gain more prestige and importance. The buzzword flourished in football circles and then soon sailed well beyond them, as Lewis's book became a bestseller and a movie version starring Sandra Bullock reportedly made more than $300 million.

Left tackles would never become as famous as the big-name quarterbacks they protected, but as Will proved, it was finally possible for them to make more money. Will's contract guaranteed he would be the highest-paid player on the Colts offense for the entire three years of his deal. He'd make more money than the team's quarterback, running back, or anyone else that might be signed during that stretch. But of course, there was one last obstacle, as there always seems to be in deals like this.

In his final physical before signing the contract with the Colts, the team found a torn left rotator cuff. As fate would have it, it's likely the injury occurred when Will was playing defense, when he tackled a Giants player after an interception in the Super Bowl.

Suddenly, the entire landmark contract was in limbo.

"I was scared to death," Will remembers. "I figured that one [the Colts] would rescind their offer and they would walk away and everyone else would walk away too. I thought I'd have to head back to Buffalo and take whatever they offered."

In the end, I used my remaining leverage (or the pretense of it) to ease the Colts' fears, and convinced them to simply add another option year if Will missed significant time. It all got worked out.

The contract was signed. The signing bonus was secured.

In the very first year of free agency, we attacked the salary structure of the entire league and raised the market rate for those warriors on the offensive line.

It was a fight I would continue for my entire career.

And it was only just beginning.

NFL vs. Cindrich

The Suits

I'VE ALWAYS LOVED RAILROADS.

Growing up around the coal mines in Avella, we had trains coming and going constantly, carrying their hauls and capturing my imagination every time they rolled past. I have good memories of crossing the tracks as a kid and turning my cleats toward the practice field.

I knew what a railroad job was like too—I'd seen plenty of 'em back home. But this one was far different from anything I had ever heard about. This time, I was tied to the tracks. And the railroad was about to arrive.

It was September 10, 1999.

Officially, it was RE: White vs. NFL (Deposition of Ralph E. Cindrich, Esq.). But screw the deposition stuff. It was a street fight. And I was up against the strongest cartel in the world—or something like that—some pretty rich and powerful bastards in the NFL.

I'm writing from my state of mind at the time—and I get pissed off every time I go back to it, all the anger and angst of years past returning in full force.

I had been fighting all my life so I guess you could say I was prepared for the big shots of the NFL, even though I wasn't exactly an eager participant. And I learned a little something from every ass-beating I ever got too.

I threw around a tough-ass kid from Burgettstown like a rag doll in a one-on-one rumble at an Avella fair. A few months later, "never back down Ralph" was coerced into fighting in a Burgettstown bathroom full of his older buddies. I got my ass fully kicked—kneed in the nuts, and some other face-dirty stuff you didn't do on the playground. And except for getting sucker punched at the Greek Club in Oakland during my Pitt years, I've always taken precautions so shit like that didn't happen again.

In the World According to Ralph, you don't win a street fight boxing, wrestling, or playing by any rules. You have to get a knockout or neutralize the enemy early on. You need a plan. You always need a plan.

I wanted no part of this particular fight, but it showed up unannounced on my doorstep.

Will Wolford played out his landmark "blind side" contract with the Colts and that deal pissed off the NFL royally. The league didn't like the creative "poison pill" clause I added that made him the highest-paid player on the offense for the entire term of his contract. And they probably didn't like that I threatened to sue them for discrimination if they didn't let the clause stand.

I had stepped on their toes. And those suits don't get nice when you piss them off.

I was a marked man.

Suddenly, Will became a free agent again too, when the Colts rescinded a transition tag that would have kept him on their roster. Losing the tag was actually perfect for us, because we were back to the open market again and I already had a target in mind.

I always held the Pittsburgh Steelers in high regard for many of my clients. I knew the organization well and had a number of players who had great success there.

In Will's case, Pittsburgh had a power running game and needed a new guard. Head coach Bill Cowher was a pretty good friend. We were both from the Pittsburgh area and had similar experiences in the pros, two smart guys who knew how to stick to a roster, so we got along pretty well.

It wasn't always that way though.

A few years earlier, I inadvertently disclosed the extent of a player's injury to a writer before one of Cowher's weekly press conferences. It ruined the uncertainty Cowher was hoping to exploit heading into his next game.

Coaches are anal that way. And some of that stuff is bull crap because everyone knows you can't keep information like that quiet. But they never expect an outsider to make it public. And the coach with the legendary chin was fully pissed.

As always, I was ready to fight. Everyone knew my client wouldn't play. I called Cowher and missed him, and anxiously awaited a return call from the coach. When it arrived, I was ready to go after him. But the entire ordeal was defused in seconds.

"Ralph, I'm glad you called," Cowher said. "I wanted to let you know that what you released upset us, our football plan, and our total layout for the game. I didn't want them to know who to practice for."

It was all about football and the smooth son of a bitch was explaining it to me.

"Sorry coach, I was just trying to clarify things for Ed Bouchette [a friend and football reporter with the *Pittsburgh Post-Gazette*]. It won't happen again."

I always remembered that conversation, and never again was I so arrogant. Cowher and I made a quick peace, setting the framework for a solid relationship we'd maintain for years. That was the way I operated with most teams and coaches. He was a good coach and I got along with most of the good ones. The few exceptions were jagoffs, and I've always been happy to point them out.

As Wolford planned for his final foray into free agency—this was it for him—I saw a lot of positives in Pittsburgh. For one, Cowher was in control. He took care of his players by not beating them up too much outside of games. Future Hall of Famer Dermontti Dawson was the center and he helped average players around him perform well enough to make Pro Bowls. And Will was still light years beyond average, even in his later years. They would both benefit from playing together. It was a lot like the situation Will enjoyed in Buffalo, when he played on the same line as Kent Hull, a legendary center who died way too soon.

This was likely Will's last contract, so we had to be smart about a number of the decisions we'd make. For one, Will only wanted to play guard, where his busted shoulders wouldn't be as exposed to the speed and space defenders had on the edge. He already had surgery on his shoulder—one that almost jeopardized his deal in Indy—and rotator cuff repairs were a lot more messy back then. Playing guard in Pittsburgh seemed like a perfect fit.

But I also knew Cowher was a pragmatic bastard (like every other frickin coach) who would value Will's experience if anyone got injured at left tackle.

I thought like coaches. I understood and even loved that part of their job. The good ones talk to guys the same way young men speak to their sweethearts in the back seats of their high school cars. They'll say just about anything to get what they want.

We both knew Will could get moved out to his old position in no time. With his injuries, and his age, facing bull rushers on the outside and needing full extension of his arms, it was quite a bit to ask. So I wanted to make sure Will got paid what he was supposed to if he got bumped out to tackle.

Will was a big-time offensive lineman and his previous contract—along with Paul Gruber's as well—helped establish left tackle as a premium position, one of the most lucrative spots on the entire team. So if he played there, he deserved a better salary.

I put in escalators that could reach another half million dollars if Will played a certain percentage of snaps at left tackle. Cowher and Dan Ferens, the Steelers negotiator, who was a shrewd accountant and a good friend, of course agreed.

The contract got done.

It seemed like a good deal for both parties involved. I had my problems, you have yours. Mine wasn't the Steelers' salary cap. But unbeknownst to me, Cowher called in Will after one practice and talked him into signing a new contract without those left-tackle provisions.

Why did Will sign it? Because it helped the team and Cowher is like that smooth-talking kid in the back seat with his girlfriend.

"We're not moving you to left tackle, you know that," Cowher told Will. "But if we do, we'll honor that agreement and pay you those provisions. Right now, it's killing us cap wise. We need the room. And you're not playing there. We're wasting it."

It's what any good football coach and his money guy would do. It was football-wise and right for his team. But the problem was that oral agreement to pay him if he moved out to left tackle triggered a provision in the recently settled collective bargaining agreement.

No oral agreements were allowed that circumvented the salary cap. Those provisions were inserted solely for the protection of the league's competitive balance—a few measures to prevent teams from cheating. And of course, prevent unscrupulous agents from working with the teams to circumvent the cap. The penalties for such conduct were hefty and were created with teams in mind.

But labor boss Gene Upshaw, who only had an agent or two he liked, arranged it so the agents operated "at the leisure of the NFLPA." Thus, agents were required to sign NFL contracts so as to comply with all the provisions of the contract and CBA, which gave the NFLPA a measure of control over agents like me.

I obviously didn't agree to Will's new deal, which was signed without my knowledge or my signature. I didn't even know about it. Everyone knew if they included me, I would muck up their agreement. And I did. You couldn't have my signature or agreement without those provisions.

Will wasn't ignorant of what he agreed to either. He was a smart guy from Vanderbilt whose wife, Jude, was an attorney. And he was an old vet on top of that, someone who had been through it all before and had seen some shenanigans among his NFL peers.

But Will was a team player above all else and he believed in helping Cowher, hoping that his willingness to change his contract might help the team win a few more games.

Will and I had worked together so much I couldn't be upset that he didn't consult me before he signed. In a way, it was the right thing to do and it was the rules—not Will—that were screwed up. But I was hell bent on taking on someone if the modified contract cost Will money.

In all my years as an agent, nothing like this had ever happened before, so I confirmed everything in writing. I requested a written memorandum from the Steelers, copied to the NFL, NFLPA, and the team as well. I didn't want the address but I would have copied God if I could have. I made it clear Will had signed the last agreement entirely on his own.

But somehow, I was suddenly the one who came under attack. The case was coming to Pittsburgh—and essentially involved charges of fraud. Even Upshaw thought it was a railroad job by the league. My name and words were all over the document. And for someone who built his career on the strength of a reputation, this was just about the worst thing I could have envisioned.

"You [Cindrich] had an oral side agreement with the Steelers outside of the actual contract where they would pay him in direct violation of the CBA."

"You piece of shit." They didn't say that but it sure felt like they did.

Along with the Steelers, which meant the NFL's Dan Rooney, architect of the CBA, they charged that I had agreed silently to something not present in the contract. The Steelers would be the last team to pay bills from a slush fund. I witnessed Dan Rooney verbally throttling a young Omar Khan, the team's cap specialist and my buddy, at a Super Bowl party for renting a limo instead of a regular rental car.

"You will ruin my reputation!" Rooney screamed.

The charges the NFL was trying to get me on were "screw you" provisions for agents and dirty clubs who cheated—people who played around with money in a way that a player would get paid by the team without the amount counting against the cap. The charges were the equivalent of fraud within the collective bargaining agreement, the contract between the league and the players.

If anyone made a silent agreement to pay Will with provisions that were not in the contract, it was a violation.

My signature was not on that contract. I never knew of or agreed to take out those provisions. When I learned of the new contract from Will, I confirmed what he related as his understanding and included an addendum to be signed.

But that wasn't the real issue. I had so many major contracts, so many holdouts, had pissed off so many GMs, and had so many crazy provisions, that the NFL came after me saying I had knowingly violated the league's new collective bargaining agreement.

It was all chicken shit. My feelings were hurt. League officials were threatening me with a fine approaching a half million dollars.

"Come on down, Ralph! And what's his prize, Larry? Not one! BUT TWO—YES, TWO—$250,000 fines!"

I got a subpoena to attend a deposition in Pittsburgh in my offices. And at least seven—count 'em, Ralph, seven!—NFL and NFLPA attorneys would be present along with a bunch of representatives from other parts of the organization who came along for the show. Al Capone never drew such attention.

"Hey, what are you doing today?" "Well, come with me. We're going to cut the balls off that prick Cindrich."

It was the legal equivalent of an ambush, and I had every reason to be worried. My agency was doing well financially, but this could be a crippling blow. The fine, if it stood up, was to be paid with after-tax dollars.

"Excuse me, mind if I pay this with my credit card so I can get the points?"

The league's lawyers had no qualms about delivering it either, considering they had just given a $250,000 fine to fellow agent Leigh Steinberg for his alleged shenanigans with Carmen Policy and the San Francisco 49ers. I had dealt with Carmen, and well, Carmen could spin a story.

Will and I were quite different. But as I said, I was in a street fight with a cartel made up of billionaires coming after me with unlimited resources.

The best course of action as always was to be honest, prepare for the upcoming battle as best I could, and then unleash a few guerrilla tactics of my own. This wasn't a fair fight and everyone knew it

The first step was with the NFLPA and its counsel, who made it clear he wasn't representing me but the process. Gene Upshaw never treated veteran players like me the same as the ones who arrived during his tenure. I didn't exchange Christmas cards with him.

The attorney in the NFL proceedings for the NFLPA, David Fehr, from Churchill, Pennsylvania, prepped me for the deposition and did a masterful job in the little time he had, something like an hour or so before the proceedings. All these years later, I can still remember his advice.

"Stop," he kept saying. "Answer only the question. Stop. If you're unsure, here's your answer: 'I don't know.' Then shut up."

"Don't volunteer anything. Answer the question only if you know the answer. Then ..."

When we were both finished, I asked David for a moment of candor from one lawyer to another. All the henchmen were waiting for me in the adjoining conference room behind the pocket doors of my old Victorian building.

"Prick to prick," I said. "What are my chances of skating in this case?" His reply:

"Just answer the question!", which didn't translate to "Go get 'em, Ralph, you're going to kick their asses."

The odds were not in my favor. But they rarely were for people from Avella—and I had already stomped on a lot of them along my way.

Before this all began, I made plans for my own counterattack in the proceedings and waited in the weeds for the enemy. I've lost fights in my lifetime, but win or lose I learned from all of them, and always went down swinging. And I sure as hell wasn't going to change my approach with these NFL jerks.

My office was a perfect setting for a showdown. There should have been tumbleweeds bouncing around that dark green building with the wide front porch.

The NFL entourage showed up in power suits, pressed shirts, and shined shoes. The lead attorney was a smug, smart-ass, preppy-looking prick from Harvard Law School, a lawyer dead set on hitting me with at least a $250,000 fine.

The other league lawyers strolled in too, arrogance and egotism spilling out almost everywhere in their wake. I had the pocket doors open that connect my conference room and my private office. Chairs were set up and waiting for their arrival. I arranged every one of those chairs carefully. If I didn't win this case, I might as well get used to moving furniture around anyway.

The proceedings were about to begin. About 20 lawyers and witnesses were crammed into the confines of my offices. The Steelers' attorney, my neighbor and friend, Mike Manzo—RIP—was one of them, but all he could confirm was that Dan Rooney never knew of an oral agreement to pay Will outside his contract.

Rooney was in the clear. I was essentially on my own. The tension spiked. It was a John Grisham book unfolding live. And I feared it was a lynching.

I took my seat and invited the opposing lawyer to do the same on the opposite side—a special one set up right across from me. Because I really liked him. The hired stenographer was seated to my right. The shades were arranged nicely so the sun hit the NFL attorneys in their faces. Beautiful day, huh?

Finally, the lead attorney sat down and we locked eyes, prick to prick. Mine were on fire.

Bring it, you preppy little asshole.

I wanted to send my fist into his face and knock him clear across the crowded room. I remember that feeling as clearly today as I did then. I didn't belong in the middle of this fraud case. But this battle was won with brains, not brawn. And maybe a little cunning too.

We moved past the preliminary questions that everyone knew the answers to, and went on to the other details that would determine the case. It was a long deposition and it reached a point where the lead counsel asked a critical question at the heart of the case, a question meant to entrap me.

I was more than ready but also moving like molasses, taking my time when reciting things as simple as my birthdate and address, being every bit as deliberate as instructed.

As slow as I possibly could.

I was going home to sleep in my own bed that night, unlike those assholes whose flight plans were shot because I extended the meeting. When you read a deposition, you don't see or know how fast or slow it's moving. You learn in other cases where things are taped not to be so slow. Somewhere in the middle of it all, the attorney smirked again.

"Aha! A gotcha question, Cindrich!"

He looked around at his colleagues, leapfrogging confidence and landing in the middle of arrogance. He put his hands forward then crossed them a bit. Then, a little smugly, he leaned back in that chair to show a little more dominance.

His seat swayed backward, his balance was upset, gravity was too, and he eventually reached the point of no return.

He was going down. Hard.

Only his seat pants and the soles of his feet were fully visible in the air. He and his chair flipped backwards into the fireplace. There was chaos and commotion in the office as his colleagues jumped from their chairs and rushed to his rescue.

"Who the hell put that chair in here?" was the pissed look I gave but kept quiet.

They all knew. As soon as the lead attorney gathered himself, I waited—out of courtesy—for his now fucked-up eyes to clear so he could see the smirk on my face.

My opinion?

It was game over.

The counsel eventually regrouped and we resumed our proceedings.

But the outcome was already settled.

Ralph 1, Pricks 0.

As the deposition ended, all the lawyers, aggravation, and potential fines were about to expire too. Honestly now, as a defense, I can say I tried to fix that chair.

My body is busted up all over, but my hands are as smooth as a baby's ass. My favorite words to my wife Mary are "hire someone." Get them to do it. I guess I'll never get confused with an Amish craftsman!

Will's testimony was also critical to my case. The word was the player could get fined too but mostly, if he cooperated, he could participate or even receive the fine money assessed to me. But there's a nice percentage of players who would sell their sister for a few bucks—let alone $250,000. Will corroborated and confirmed absolutely everything that I said. When we all walked away, the league simply had no choice but to drop the case.

This bullshit cost me a lot of time, money, and worry for my wife. But I won the case.

And just as I suspected, Will was indeed moved out to tackle when injuries hit the Steelers offensive line that season. Steelers' owner Dan Rooney paid the salary escalator that was in the original contract and then self-reported his actions to the league office, since that incentive wasn't technically included in Will's current contract. The NFL responded by taking away a third-round pick from Pittsburgh, the second time I'd been involved with a case that caused the Steelers to lose a pick (Brzoza was the other instance).

With all the legal entanglements out of my way, I could refocus my energies on the players who were making my career. Guys like Will were about the best clients an agent could hope for—talented on the field, tough in negotiations, and trustworthy in everything that they did.

Those qualities, coupled with the advent of free agency, were helping us change the game. The linemen who had long been held back by a system that undervalued their contributions were cashing in, producing fame and fortune far beyond football.

Things had indeed changed.

Football would never be the same.

Kent Hull

The Heartbeat

THE KICK WENT WIDE RIGHT.

Legions of fans can still see it flying through the air, an image still ingrained in football's consciousness a few decades after it happened.

I saw it all live, seated in the stands of Super Bowl XXV, supporting my clients on the Buffalo Bills, the NFL team that had my largest collection of players: Kent Hull, Will Wolford, and several other important Bills players.

It was the fourth quarter of an old-school, smash-mouth game controlled by the New York Giants, who set a Super Bowl record for time of possession by holding the ball for more than 40 minutes.

The Giants were leading 20–19. But Jim Kelly and the Bills' up-tempo offense got the ball back with just over two minutes to go. They still had a chance.

Kelly started the drive by scrambling for eight yards. Two more scrambles, two completed passes, and a Thurman Thomas run moved the ball past midfield. Thomas ran again and Kelly spiked the ball at the Giants' 29-yard line.

There were eight seconds left to play. Buffalo was only down by one.

We all know what happened next. Bills kicker Scott Norwood went out for a 47-yard field goal—nothing near a chip shot—a kick that would decide the outcome of football's biggest game. The Bills were holding hands on their sideline. Giants players seemed to be locked in prayer on the other. I held my breath in the stands.

The snap went back, the hold went down, and the kick went up, wide right as fate would have it, a wretched heartbreak sailing through the Super Bowl sky.

Norwood missed it by about a yard. He slumped his shoulders and hung his helmet and sidled off the field. After the game, he faced all the cameras and answered all the questions, even those that didn't have an easy answer.

What happened? Why? How does it feel?

There wasn't a man in America who felt worse than Scott Norwood that night. Or anyone who felt as lonely either.

Fortunately, Norwood had my client Kent Hull as a teammate. Hull was the Bills center and the backbone of the team, a leader and a mauler who was a driving force behind Buffalo's success and all that offensive prowess behind him.

As Hull was heading out of the losing locker room, he noticed that Norwood was still there, sitting in his uniform.

Hull walked over. And as the story relayed in the *New York Times* goes, his words were something like this.

Let me tell you something. It's not all on you. If everyone else had done our jobs better—myself included—that field goal could have been kicked from a lot closer than 47 yards. Now go get in the shower. . . .

Hull waited for Norwood to get showered and dressed. They walked out of the locker room together, facing whatever waited for them outside as teammates.

"If you had to look at one person that was respected or looked upon for an encouraging word or looked upon as a guy that could pull the team together, you didn't have to look any further than No. 67," quarterback Jim Kelly once said in an interview with Buffalo's WGRZ station. "He was the heartbeat of the Buffalo Bills. The guy that was our true leader was Kent Hull."

Hull was raised in Greenwood, Mississippi, and eventually grew beyond a love of basketball and a skinny frame suited for the sport to play college football for four years at Mississippi State. He earned four varsity letters there, and his college coach once said he was as tough as a two-bit steak.

But off the field, Kent was one of the kindest men you might ever meet.

"He was the kind of guy that if he had 20 bucks, you had 20 bucks," Hull's college roommate, Mike McEnany told the Associated Press. "And he was an amazing football player, but he never felt comfortable talking about it. He wanted to talk about you. He was the kind of guy that everyone wants their son to be like when they grow up."

After college, Hull signed with the USFL and Donald Trump's New Jersey Generals, helping teammate Herschel Walker to a pair of rushing titles and a single-season rushing record. The USFL folded soon afterward, and surprisingly enough, Kelly and Hull signed with Buffalo on the same day in 1986. Kelly got picked up in a limo, Hull in an old equipment van.

"The way I like to describe it is, Jim rode in on a limo and I rode in on a load of pumpkins," Hull once said, according to a 2011 article in the *Buffalo News*.

However they arrived, Kelly, Hull, and Wolford helped revitalize a Bills franchise that had gone 2–14 the year before. During their time together in Buffalo, the Bills employed a high-powered, no-huddle offense, with Hull making line calls almost instantly and snapping the ball in seconds to keep defenses on their heels.

"If Jim was the star of the no-huddle, center Kent Hull was its unsung hero," Steve Tasker wrote in his book, *Steve Tasker's Tales from the Buffalo Bills*. "Besides identifying defensive formations and making the appropriate calls for the offensive line, Kent would also shake off certain calls Jim might make. It was kind of like a catcher advising a pitcher about what he should throw. I remember several occasions when Jim would call a play at the line, and Kent would turn his head around and give Jim this 'You can't run this play, you idiot' look, and Jim would change the call."

Kelly and Hull were the best of friends, but Kent was close to guys all across the locker room, on both offense and defense. I met Kent through Will Wolford, his teammate on the offensive line.

General manager Bill Polian had stocked Buffalo's roster with some of the best talent in league history. There were Hall of Famers and Pro Bowlers at a number of positions, and the team dominated the AFC for nearly a decade. During the late 1980s and early 1990s, the Bills won seven division titles, made eight playoff appearances, and advanced to four straight Super Bowls, the first of which was that heartbreaking loss in Super Bowl XXV.

Kent played a tremendous role in all that success, appearing in 121 consecutive games—the equivalent of almost eight straight years. He was tough as hell and committed to a fault, helping Buffalo's potent offensive machine keep whirring. The only problem was that his body paid an incredible price, and he often needed painkillers, injections, and other interventions to get him out on the field every Sunday. I had no clue this was happening and as I understand it, not many others did either.

"I called him 'Tough,'" Bills linebacker Darryl Talley—the definition of toughness himself—said in an interview with Jerry Sullivan of the *Buffalo News*. "Because he was one of the toughest guys I ever saw. He dealt with pain on a consistent basis. But it didn't matter. He knew he had a job to do and he was going to do it. He'd get hurt and say, 'I can't come out of the damn game.' He instilled that mentality in the rest of the O-linemen. He held them to that standard."

He was always there. And once the games began, he somehow played better than a lot of guys who were fully healthy.

"I would talk noise on the field only because I knew that he'd be there every time to defend and protect me," Bills running back Thurman Thomas told the Associated Press. "I owe a lot of that stitching on my Hall of Fame jacket to Kent Hull."

Over the course of his career, Hull played in 170 games, was named an All-Pro twice, and earned three trips to the Pro Bowl. But with a man like Kent, statistics don't tell you nearly enough. The people who know him best do a much better job.

"His physical toughness, work ethic, intelligence, character and sense of humor made him an undisputed leader on a team filled with Hall of Famers and stars," Polian wrote in a statement describing Hull. "He was a fine man, a good friend and a true professional."

Hull and his good buddy Kelly both retired after the 1996 season. The contributions of Kelly and Hull were always obvious on the field. But inside the locker room, Hull's loss probably loomed even larger.

"I've decided I'm going to have to close this chapter in my life," Hull said at his retirement press conference. Head coach Marv Levy sat nearby, blinking back tears.

"This has been a great ride for me. I've had the opportunity to play with some Hall of Fame players, a Hall of Fame coach, and without a doubt the greatest fans in the world in western New York."

The entire city of Buffalo would miss him dearly. Hull retired to his home state and stayed active with his cattle farm and a variety of charitable causes, which included the Make-A-Wish Foundation and the United Negro College Fund. He often returned to Buffalo for team reunions and fund-raising events, keeping a firm hold on his connection to the city.

But we were all spoiled to have him as long as we did, and Kent was soon called up to a place much better suited for such an incredible man. He died in October 2011 at the age of 50 from intestinal bleeding caused by chronic liver disease. All the painkillers, injections, and constant abuse his body endured in sacrifice to his team might have played a role, but knowing the exact cause wouldn't heal all the hurt anyway.

His death tore holes in hearts from Buffalo to Mississippi and a whole bunch of places in between. Kent was the cornerstone on which so many things were built.

Love. Friendship. Football.

With the foundation gone, everyone was shaken.

How could a man who never missed a game be missing from their lives?

It didn't seem possible.

"I'm so deeply saddened," said Bills coach Marv Levy, a legendary man of intellect and decency himself. "I coached for 47 years, and he honestly was one of the very most memorable individuals who was my privilege to coach."

His old friends and teammates gathered in Greenwood, Mississippi, to say goodbye and the toughest among them were reduced to tears. Bruce Smith. Darryl Talley, Thurman Thomas . . . others. I passed through the receiving line seeing somber faces that had been filled with laughter in earlier times. His grown family and his good-looking son Drew were present. Many years earlier, we had thrown a birthday party for Drew in Hawaii when his father played in the Pro Bowl there.

Amid all the sadness, Bill Polian and I found each other at some point in the service. We were old adversaries who once battled over Kent's contracts, trading expletives and anger and maybe even an occasional threat. We hugged each other hard along with Coach Levy and cried in each other's arms, all of us weighed down by heavy hearts and moist eyes.

Even in death, Kent could bring people together. And his passing wouldn't undo all the connections he made or any of his contributions either.

The Bills were a special team, one with enough grit to survive four Super Bowl losses and a crucial kick that sailed wide right.

Hull always held them together.

And he still would even now. All the bonds, memories, and smiles that he made in his life can never be stripped away.

Whether in heaven or on earth, Kent Hull isn't just a Buffalo Bill.

He's the heartbeat.

Mark Stepnoski

The Linchpin

I WANTED TO KICK JIMMY JOHNSON'S ASS.

That probably surprises everyone who knows him. Or maybe it doesn't.

Our history went back about 20 years, to a feud that started during my playing days as a Pittsburgh Panther. In 1971, I had just finished an All-American season at linebacker and was picked for the North-South All-Star Game in December (to this date, it's the only Christmas I've ever been away from my family). Jimmy Johnson was one of the coaches and really pissed me off by playing some stiff from his own school ahead of me, even though I had been named captain by my teammates.

I've wanted to fight him ever since.

Twenty years later, it looked like I finally had a chance, but I didn't want any part of it. Kicking a coach's ass is not exactly an ideal entry on an agent's resume.

It was the early '90s and we were in Mobile, Alabama, for the Senior Bowl, a collegiate all-star game held for pro-bound players in advance of the NFL Draft. Jimmy was scouting the talent there as coach of the Dallas Cowboys and I was recruiting new players for Cindrich and Company, which was growing in both clients and contracts every year.

One of my existing players was Mark Stepnoski, a center for the Cowboys who played college football at my alma mater. Stepnoski had small hands and only weighed about 269 pounds coming out of Pittsburgh, but he was filled with all the intangibles that couldn't be found on a scale or a stopwatch.

Smarts. Savvy. Toughness. Technique.

"Step" got picked by the Cowboys in the third round of the 1989 NFL Draft, following quarterback Troy Aikman and fullback Daryl Johnston, who were picked in the first two rounds. Those three players—along with Tony Tolbert, who followed Stepnoski in the fourth round—helped transform a Cowboys franchise that had finished 3–13 in the previous season, the last one under legendary coach Tom Landry.

Despite playing exclusively at guard in college, Step became a Pro Bowl center and was a key cog in the Cowboys machine, serving as the signal caller for the offensive line and the closest protector of Aikman, the face of the franchise.

Dallas desperately needed to keep Step around, but his rookie contract expired after the 1991 season. Jimmy and I were both bracing for a holdout that might get Mark the money he deserved. And there was a little animosity between us already, with my all-star snub back in college and a previous holdout that we weathered when Mark was a rookie.

On this particular night, we were both inside the same bar and unfettered by any negotiations. Jimmy was sitting with Cowboys owner Jerry Jones, some of the team's staff, and some of my former coaches as well. They were all behind the velvet ropes of a VIP-type section, a place reserved more for NFL royalty than for hard-ass agents from Avella, Pennsylvania.

I caught eyes with some of my old coaches in Houston and they invited me over. Jimmy and the Cowboys staff were sitting across the table from them.

As a general rule, NFL head coaches aren't typically pleasant. Duh! They're salesmen, generals, and often stubborn SOBs who drag their teams through whatever they have to in search of success. Marv Levy was one of the exceptions.

Jimmy Johnson was not, but he was pretty damn good at his job and even I knew that.

Jimmy was born in Port Arthur, Texas, and played college football with Cowboys owner Jerry Jones at the University of Arkansas. Then, he started hitting home runs as a coach, recruiting Terry Bradshaw to Louisiana Tech, turning around the program at Oklahoma State, and winning a national title at the University of Miami. Jerry brought him to the NFL and Jimmy and Jerry transformed a downtrodden Cowboys franchise into a Super Bowl dynasty.

He and a lot of the other NFL people made a habit of drinking themselves through the Senior Bowl week. It wasn't unusual to see several of them closing down the bar one night and then sitting in the hotel lobby a few hours later trying to put the pieces back together, a black coffee in one hand and a lit cigarette in the other.

That was often the sad reality of the coaching profession, a job that wasn't nearly as cozy as you might expect. Coaches and everyone else in the NFL may have some fame and fortune, but they all work their asses off—way beyond normal hours. The job often has a way of overtaking your soul, swallowing up family, fatherhood, and all the other wholesome elements of outside life. Jimmy didn't seem to care about much of anything that night other than his next drink.

My old coaches, Larry Peccatiello, Richie Petitbon, and Joe Bugel, waved me over across from where Jimmy was sitting. And I take invitations seriously, a byproduct of A. J.'s advice that still echoes even today.

"Where you are wanted much, go little. Where you are wanted little, go not at all."

But this was a homecoming of sorts; those guys were my friends and clients, same with some of the scouts and personnel people who were also hanging out behind the rope. I had to go.

I went over. I'd have a drink with my old friends. I represented all of those guys, although with Bugel it was just advice that I provided when he took a coaching job with Al Davis and the Oakland Raiders.

I didn't make it a habit to represent coaches—it is a conflict of interest with your players—but some guys were special. My old coach at Pitt, Foge Fazio, was in that category and I was happy to represent him too. I consider it an honor to be asked by old coaches and sons of fathers I represented.

Plus, I was stone cold sober, fresh off a nice dinner with a recruit and his family. I wasn't one to mix alcohol and work when recruiting, but it wouldn't hurt to have one or two here with old friends. What could possibly go wrong?

Almost everything.

As I made my approach and sat down, it became obvious that Jimmy was trashed, knee-deep in drinks and seeming to drown in more of them every minute. Business as usual.

I tried not to engage him. I looked away. Where I'm from if you stare in a man's eyes you want to fight.

"You better not hold out Stepnoski," Jimmy said, unprovoked.

I ignored him. I didn't say a single thing and I don't think anyone else did either. You know how tough that was for me? Even though we were in a bar, this was still a place of business for the NFL. And it was a terrible place to throw down.

But Jimmy wouldn't let it go.

"You better not fucking hold out Stepnoski," he said again.

If there was one thing I remembered as an old Little League catcher, it was that you got three strikes before you were out. Or at least Jimmy did.

I was so pissed I wasn't seeing straight. My lip was quivering. My friends had invited me over. Who the fuck was he to talk to me that way?

"You say that one more time, asshole, and I'll kick your ass back to your college days and the Arkansas piggies."

If there was one advantage I held over all my adversaries—from Al Davis to Bob Irsay to Bill Parcells—it was the ability to get in their face without a single twinge of fear. In a world of testosterone-fueled, fully erect dicks, I always believed I could take just about anyone down in under five seconds, make him cry for his momma, and then send him off to sleep.

All you needed was a Chinese chokehold, a move we practiced back on the wrestling mats a million times.

Short arm drag to spin him around. Left arm locked across the throat. Right arm crossed under the chin.

The pass-out time is pretty damn quick—a worrisome fact we learned a few times in wrestling when someone went under.

"You fuckin' better not hold out Stepnoski!" Jimmy said even louder, swaying as he said it.

He started pointing his chubby little finger in my face. Now, my feelings were hurt. What had happened to my cordial invitation?

I was ready to fight a few seconds ago. All this other stuff was just adding gasoline.

"Let's go, asshole."

I wanted him now. Jimmy got up wobbly—a little too wobbly—perhaps acting overly intoxicated so someone would stop it.

I didn't want to fight in a place where everyone could see. I'd get banned from the Senior Bowl and do even more damage to my reputation, but Jimmy was asking for it.

I left the bar area and pointed to the bathroom. I was completely out of my mind. Maybe I'm a jagoff, and maybe I deserve to get my ass kicked, but it wasn't gonna happen here, now, or by him.

We cleared the corner of the wall leading into the door where the men's room was located. I felt a little bit of relief. No one else could see us now. Neither party would get sucker punched. That first strike puts you way ahead and I had been sucker punched once in college at the Greek Club.

The whole time I had trouble following him. I wanted to just forearm him in the back of the head but as soon as the corner came, I grabbed his ass and spun him around. And pulled back . . .

Bobby Ackles, Jimmy's personnel man, a great guy and an equally good friend who was about 5'6", intervened on Jimmy's behalf, grabbing my arm before I ever got a chance to use it.

Jerry Jones flew in next and stood between the two of us. Jimmy slithered away. It took Jerry a few moments to figure out who the hell I was. I moved back a couple of steps in case of a sucker punch—oh hell yes he would—but he immediately recognized me as the guy in the Herschel Walker trade, and decided to back the hell off.

Years later, after Jimmy and Jerry went their separate ways, Mary and I were celebrating a birthday and anniversary in Palm Beach, Florida, where the NFL held its annual owners' meeting. I saw Jerry in a ballroom where a band was playing and he was screaming something from across the floor. Moments later, the band suddenly stopped and the words became clear.

"And I should have let you kick his ass!"

Everyone heard it.

Later that same night, Jerry was reliving the story again to a healthy crowd gathered around, inviting Mary and me over to share in his Cristal champagne as he replayed the Cindrich vs. Johnson feud.

It was probably best for both of our careers that Bobby Ackles was around and I never got that Chinese chokehold on Jimmy.

"I told Ralph that if things had escalated and he would have dropped Jimmy, we would have erected a statue in his honor in the Cowboys players' lounge," Stepnoski joked.

Mark and I ended up holding out late into that summer, but it resulted more from the Cowboys' tight fists and roster composition than anything else on our end. In the previous season, the Cowboys had made the playoffs for the first time in several years and seven or eight players on the team—good ones too—had expiring contracts. Stepnoski remembers working out with the other holdouts throughout the summer. Each week it seemed that one of them would disappear, the absentee finally signing a contract and returning to the team.

Training camp came and went and Mark was the only holdout left. He headed back to his hometown, Erie, Pennsylvania, and laid low until everything got settled. Two days before the Cowboys first regular season game, we finally got him a fair contract. Mark missed that game and then another one in week two as well, thanks to a team maneuver that didn't give him any chance to play.

"They put me on that two-week roster exemption," Stepnoski remembers. "I was planning on playing in the Giants game in week two. That was purely vindictiveness. . . . That was one of the few starts that I missed and that's still a sticking point with me."

I was lucky to represent a guy who cared so much about each game. Once Step returned to action, he justified his new contract pretty quickly. He started every remaining game that season, earned a berth in the Pro Bowl, and helped propel the Cowboys to a playoff run that ended with Step and my good buddy Jimmy Johnson beating the Bills 52–17 in Super Bowl XXVII.

Step made it to another Pro Bowl a year later, but just barely. He blew out his ACL late in the season and was worried no one would vote in an injured player, so we all kept quiet, avoiding the media's requests for more information. Jimmy Johnson took care of him too, keeping him off injured reserve so the injury stayed a secret and he was still eligible for the Pro Bowl. In the end, the strategy paid off perfectly and

Step was a Pro Bowler again, even though he wouldn't be playing in the game.

The ACL injury cost him a lot of leverage in free agency, but he received a decent one-year contract from the Cowboys thanks to the improved conditions of the free market. He rewarded Dallas with another Pro Bowl season and then finally hit free agency in full health.

In 1995, he signed a four-year deal with the Houston Oilers that averaged about $2.3 million per season. He played out that contract and then re-signed another one with the Cowboys before retiring in 2001. In all, Stepnoski played for 13 years, made five Pro Bowls, and won two Super Bowls with those star-studded Cowboys teams. He also blocked for the league's all-time leading rusher (Emmitt Smith), snapped to a Hall of Fame quarterback (Aikman), and played next to two of football's greatest guards (Nate Newton and Larry Allen).

It was a hell of a run for a player who entered the league at 269 pounds and had never taken a single snap at center in college.

"I would have taken that in a heartbeat, that's what everybody hopes for," Stepnoski said. "Honestly, if I would have known that ahead of time, I would have been thrilled."

Step lives in Vancouver, Canada, now and is fairly healthy as well, his body not irreparably harmed after fighting for 13 years in pro football's trenches. He's the player you don't hear about nearly as much, the one who has been through all the battles and comes back from all of them okay, his body, mind, and spirit still relatively intact.

"I'm very grateful. Anybody who plays that long is gonna have issues and I have mine, but they're pretty manageable," Stepnoski said. "As time goes on, every year there are guys I played with or guys I played against—in some cases guys younger than me—who are dying or are in pretty bad shape, even handicapped. I have my things to contend with, but I'm not on any prescription medicines and I'm not getting surgeries every month."

I can't say that I'm surprised that Step has remained strong even in retirement. He was such a pleasure to represent that I can almost forgive him for making me deal with Jimmy Johnson.

I said almost.

Some things just aren't so easy.

Tim Ruddy

The Genius

THE PLANE WAS GOING DOWN.

All of us on board were convinced of it. It was January of 1994 and I was on a recruiting trip to see Tim Ruddy, an eastern Pennsylvania native who was a solid center prospect coming out of Notre Dame.

Somewhere high up in the clouds, it became clear that our plane had some serious problems. It was far colder than it should have been inside the cabin, a problem that had been persisting since before we took off on that early morning flight. There were obvious mechanical flaws, none of which seemed minor when you're flying about 30,000 feet above ground.

As we approached South Bend, they informed us that there was a problem with the wheels. At some point, we reviewed crash positions. And we all figured we were toast.

Take out all of your pens and other sharp objects. Bend over. Grab your ankles. And kiss your sweet ass goodbye!

They had already covered the runway with foam, something that was supposed to keep our plane from catching fire and save all our asses if we crashed.

Yeah, right.

They moved me to an emergency exit row. Since I was a former athlete and a pretty big guy, everyone figured I was the safest bet to open the door and get us out of there after impact. I took the responsibility seriously. I knew if I did somehow survive the crash, I wouldn't know straight from sideways or my butt cheeks from the plane pillows.

Football players need practice so when they get their head banged and brains scrambled, they can respond on instinct. I probably practiced my routine 50 times. Not a single person laughed.

Right hand to the seat belt to release it. Other hand over to the emergency exit door. Then, I'd mimic how to release the door and prepare myself to throw it open when the plane hit. I did all that over and over and over, searing the movements deep into my muscle memory.

Embarrassing? Well, I suppose, but only if we made it out alive.

Then, I took out a pen and wrote my last letter to Mary.

I told her how much I loved her. Told her to remarry when she was ready and move on with her life. Be happy. And make sure our children Michael and Christina know how much I love them too.

Goodbye.

I put the letter in my coat pocket. Then, we all figured it was over. After circling the airport for what seemed like hours, we started our descent. And we braced for impact.

There were probably prayers going up from every seat in the plane with a soul in it. Some people were crying. The ground grew closer. Our wheels hit it.

It was a hard landing, with a huge thud and a bounce or two, but we had survived the initial impact. The second bounce was a little softer and the brakes eventually screamed enough to slow us down.

We were alive. All of us.

There was a huge commotion in the cabin, hugs and high-fives and the kind of relief you can only feel by surviving what seems like certain death. A guy behind me came up to me and shook my hand and said he was scared but knew two things: One, if anyone was getting out of this alive, it was me. And two, he was blessed to be right behind me! Many of the passengers from Pittsburgh took a bus straight back.

The ground never felt so good. But even then there was no time to waste. I was late for my meeting with Ruddy and that's usually a deal breaker to begin with. Players move on to other agents who show up on time and don't care about excuses, even though I had a doozy with this damn-near crashed plane and everything that had happened inside it.

Luckily, I was still on schedule for a meeting in Madison, Wisconsin, with Joe Panos, a smart Greek kid who once worked at his family restaurant and now works as an agent. I made my connection to Madison.

And somewhere along the way, I got an urgent call from home. It was Mary.

"The dogs are barking down below [my champion beagle hunting dogs]. *It's pretty cold here. I know you put Pumpkin Patch and Bob in the pen together to keep them warm but I think something's wrong with Bob. He won't leave Pumpkin Patch alone."*

Who the hell knew a dog could be in heat in the middle of winter? Bob got lucky that night. Me, not so much. Pumpkin Patch was a loaned champion. Now, she was pregnant.

I suppose Bob did have a certain charm to him. And by that I mean he'd walk up to you any chance he got and piss all over your leg. He did it all the time. And I swear he always saved a little piss for his next target. I loved that about Bob.

I somehow helped Mary sort out how to handle it by saying something like, "Oh, you're upset, the dogs are barking? Bad day is it? I came within minutes of being Indiana bacon and I can't freaking do anything right now!"

I may have been a little annoyed. I hung up and went back to my agent work. She wouldn't find out just how dramatic my plane flight was until a week or two later, when the dry cleaners found the handwritten note tucked inside my suit coat and gave it to her. If there was any doubt how I felt about her after two kids and all the other challenges of raising a family and running a business, I think the letter probably made it clear. The Thunderbolt was alive and well.

Looking back on it, my near-death experience wasn't nearly as traumatic as you might expect. Since it was early in the morning, cold, and I was dead tired from all the recruiting, I wasn't as afraid as I should have been. If it had been a bright summer day and I was on a pleasure trip, well, I probably would have left a present on that seat.

Fortunately, Ruddy didn't give up on me either and I headed into the 1994 draft as his agent. The flight that almost ended with a fiery crash had been worth it after all.

Ruddy was an ideal client, a player who possessed two qualities that were imperative at the center position—brains and brawn. He had a perfect GPA coming out of Dunmore High School in Scranton, was an Academic All-American twice at Notre Dame, and started 23 games at center for the Irish's potent rushing attack. In the pre-draft process, I was told he aced the Wonderlic too, a brief intelligence test that's completed in about 12 minutes or less.

As the 1994 NFL Draft approached, Ruddy was viewed more as a mid-round prospect. He was a little undersized (6'3", 295) at a position where you often have to block behemoths weighing 350 pounds or more. But with his intangibles and a run on centers occurring earlier, he ended up getting picked in the second round, at No. 65 overall, by the Miami Dolphins. After serving as a backup during his rookie season, he was elevated to Miami's starting lineup and never left it, starting 140 games in his ensuing nine seasons with the team. He was selected to the Pro Bowl following the 2000 season and was a near-permanent fixture in front of superstar quarterback Dan Marino, missing only four starts in an entire decade with the Dolphins.

I negotiated extensions for Ruddy in 1997 and 2000, but neither approached the war we had with John Offerdahl, since Joe Robbie was gone and a more reasonable ownership group had taken over.

In fact, after the near plane crash I encountered when trying to recruit Ruddy, everything else in his career went rather swell. He helped me carve a deeper niche at the center position, among the players with gifted minds and enough guts to identify defensive formations and blitzing backers and block every last damn one of them.

Before Ruddy, I had Kent Hull and Mark Stepnoski. Later, I'd add Jeff Christy, Mike Flynn, and many more.

Centers with all their grit and grime were my kind of people. One of them even earned the nickname Dirt. And when his career was over, he'd have a yellow blazer and bronze bust.

But I had to get him a couple of contracts first.

Dermontti Dawson

The Mainstay

I'LL BE THE FIRST TO ADMIT THAT MY PROFESSION IS COVERED IN A shitload of slime and sleaze. Some agents recruit players with cash and cars and girls and anything else that might seduce a kid in his late teens or early 20s. Others siphon more money than they should, collecting unfair percentages or charging extra fees for a number of dubious services.

It made it hard as hell for someone like me who played it straight. And it also complicated things when someone got screwed over before I got them. Suddenly, I had to rebuild trust, restore faith, and prove to everyone that not every agent is crooked.

Dermontti "Dirt" Dawson was one of the wounded. Dermontti was brought up near the bluegrass pastures and white-fenced farms of Lexington, Kentucky. He's a devoted father and a devout Christian and speaks with the courtesy characteristic of a southern gentleman.

But beneath all the pleasantries is a big man (6'2", 288) who became a force on the football field. And his contract became an NFL landmark, an innovative deal that created echoes around the league like the ones signed by Bill Fralic and Will Wolford.

Dawson played college football at the University of Kentucky and was picked by the Pittsburgh Steelers in the second round of the 1988 draft. His first agent got him a decent deal, and he started five games at guard as a rookie. In his second season, he replaced Steelers legend Mike Webster at center, a position he would soon redefine. His career was pointed in the right direction.

But trouble began brewing off the field. Dawson and his agent had pooled their money for a horse farm in Florida. For Dermontti, it was a hobby and a piece of home all folded up inside an investment. But the agent he trusted had wrecked the relationship.

"He was a good agent [before that]," Dawson remembers. "I was with him for the first three or four years and then we got a horse farm down in Florida. We started doing stuff with money together and some of the money came up missing. We found out the guy was taking money out of the account."

Dermontti had to find a new agent. Someone he could trust.

That's where I came in. I had already negotiated some contracts for Will Wolford and some of his other friends and they ushered Dermontti in my direction. (Will was always great with referrals, and he brought me a lot of solid clients just like Dermontti.)

Dermontti probably went into our first meeting pretty apprehensive. I couldn't blame him if he was still afraid of agents, but I worked hard to gain his trust. I did honest work, gave honest advice, and fought like hell every time I had a chance to negotiate for him.

Over time, his previous wounds were healed and he joined the family I had formed with all of my other clients. We shared conversations and trust and everything else that matters between a player and agent.

Dermontti was an avid hunter and I'd invite him down to my parents' property in Avella, where you couldn't sit for too long without having an unsuspecting deer amble across your scope. The deer were so plentiful down in Avella that you saved your bullets for the big bucks long before there were minimums required by law.

Every once in a while, Dermontti would rush back from his Sunday games, grab a meal at Denny's or Eat-N-Park, and perhaps join a few other players in tree stands out near my parents' house, waiting amid the occasional snowstorm for a deer big enough to take down. He got a few nice bucks out there. And in the offices, I got some good contracts for him, as we eased into a solid relationship built on mutual appreciation.

Unfortunately, you can only hold hands and sing "Kumbaya" for so long in the NFL.

Soon, we had a big battle forming with the Steelers. Dermontti was in the last year of his contract. He was a standout player and wanted a

BIG deal in line with his performance, something that could secure his financial status far into the future. Who doesn't?

The Steelers have always been pretty tough in negotiations. A team with six Super Bowl trophies isn't run by a bunch of spineless bastards getting beat up by people like me. They're street fighters. Brawlers.

I often thought of their old negotiator, Buff Boston, who was both old-fashioned and frugal. He wouldn't move off a contract number if you lit a cherry bomb under his ass. And Buff's idea of getting creative was shifting cheeks when he farted.

Dermontti was the best center in the NFL, making the first of seven straight Pro Bowl appearances in 1992. He was a centerpiece of the Steelers' power running game and was quick enough to pull from his position, sprinting around the end of the offensive line to demolish a linebacker or defensive back who didn't have a chance. Pulling centers were almost unheard of in football. And no one did it better than a former guard like Dermontti.

Not surprisingly, the Steelers were desperate to keep him from hitting free agency after the 1997 season. But they were tight against the salary cap too. On our end, Dermontti recognized how well things were going in Pittsburgh and he didn't want to screw it all up by chasing a few more dollars and signing a contract somewhere else. The Steelers were going to give him a fair deal anyway.

Too many players—and agents too—get caught up in every last cent of their contracts and send their careers sideways by taking a little more money to put a square peg in a round hole. If a player is productive and happy with a team and its surrounding city, you don't want to mess with that too much. Dawson was on his way to Canton and I knew that. If a new team offered an astronomical contract, things might be different, but no one expected anything like that. I was fortunate to have a lot of smart, loyal guys like Dermontti who were able to see past all the extra dollars and extended their careers by taking long looks at the big picture.

Dermontti was in camp and the first game of the season was approaching when I began negotiating his new deal. As an agent, you can't let the player know everything that is going on in contract talks while he is playing in games. Players need a clear head to be successful and contract numbers have a way of clouding it. Your best bet is to have a firm idea of the contract parameters well beforehand and whatever you do, you have to make sure your player stays focused on his next snap.

In Dermontti's case, "Da Money," as he would eventually become known, stayed productive on the field and I kept working behind closed doors. To protect Dermontti for the rest of the season and beyond, I decided an option bonus would work, something that had never been done my way before and never been approved either. Why not give it a shot?

It worked like this: We'd sign a contract that had an option year like many other NFL contracts. Usually, option years are voluntary, but in reality they're often jammed down players' throats, allowing teams to keep a player for an extra year at 120 percent of the present salary, a modest raise that's often not in line with market value. And if a team wants to move on from a player, there's no penalty for pointing the guy to the door.

Our option was going to be different though. Instead of seeking a small increase over Dermontti's previous salary, our contract option was aimed at the Steelers. If they didn't exercise the option that included Dermontti's NEW contract numbers, they would pay him an even greater signing bonus and single-season salary—for nothing. And Dan Rooney didn't like nothing.

It protected us because if Dermontti got hurt during the remainder of the season and the Steelers decided they didn't want him, they had to pay him a higher signing bonus to walk away. It was a no-brainer for both parties, but only if I could get the landmark contract approved by the league. I did.

The Steelers were committing to a king's ransom, but now they had Dermontti's contract finished. The centerpiece of their offensive line was locked up. And they sure as hell didn't want to lose their All-Pro center.

I ran all the details by Steelers executive Dan Ferens, a tough negotiator who watched all of Dan Rooney's dollars. As I did with the maneuvers I mention in the Jeff Saturday chapter, I tried to sweeten the pot a little with everything else already in place. The deal was almost done, but I was hoping to put a few extra dollars in Dermontti's wallet. Even when a player had the right team for just about the right amount, it didn't hurt to push for a little bit more if you knew what you were doing.

I told Ferens that the deal was going to be a hard sell to Dermontti. He was a leader on the team and needed to be happy and a little more money might just do it. Ferens told me he'd check with the Rooneys and get back with me. Meanwhile, I called Dermontti for the first time since we started negotiating and he was ecstatic, ready to sign the contract yesterday. I told him to hold tight and wait until Ferens called me back, there were a few more things I was still fighting for.

Ferens called me back about ten minutes later and said the team was done moving. I told him I'd have to check in with Dermontti, perhaps that deal wouldn't be enough.

"That's fine," Ferens said. "But by the way, I just saw Dermontti in the hallway and he kissed me. And my back is still hurting from his bear hug."

"Oh. How soon can you have those contracts to me?"

When the fight was finally over, "Da Money" got a whole bunch of it, signing the contract between the first and second games of the season. Dermontti ended up with a landmark deal that made him the highest-paid center in the NFL. He got $7.405 million over three years, which worked out to a 425.7 percent increase between his 1993 and 1994 compensation and a 335.3 percent increase over his prior contract average. And the landmark bonus/option buyout clause sailed through just fine, a contract maneuver that would soon be copied, distributed, and popularized by agents all across the league who were looking to get their clients new contracts and also save teams some salary cap dollars in the process.

And most importantly, the deal gave Dermontti security and stability, in both a football and financial sense. Overall, Dermontti played 13 seasons for the Steelers, appearing in 170 consecutive games (which ranks second in team history), seven straight Pro Bowls, and earning a spot on the NFL's All-Decade Team of the 1990s.

"For me, I was proud I was able to be a one-team player and start and finish my career with the Steelers," Dermontti said. "I am proud of the career I had and that culminated when I was inducted into the Pro Football Hall of Fame. I'm proud of the way my career turned out. I never thought I would have had such a career."

I watched in 2012 when Dermontti got the ultimate recognition at the Pro Football Hall of Fame. My own playing career never took me anywhere near Canton, Ohio, but there's a huge sense of pride that hits when one of your clients is there. Up on stage in a yellow blazer, next to the bronze bust reserved for football's immortals, was a guy I helped. A guy I fought like hell for. I knew he appreciated my efforts. I knew he trusted me. And I knew I had done everything the way that you're supposed to.

There's a lot of satisfaction in that.

"Thank you to the fans because you guys are what this game is all about," Dermontti said in the final moments of his induction speech. "Thank you for your years of support and [the] dedication you have shown to the Pittsburgh Steelers and the NFL. Without you, there is no NFL. I want to thank you. God bless you and good night."

Sometimes, even an agent like me has nothing left to fight. All you can do is smile.

So I did.

Trev Alberts

The Re-Inventor

He was completely knocked out.

This was back before concussions and CTE (chronic traumatic encephalopathy) were buzzwords that grabbed newspaper headlines and airtime on television shows. Back before helmet-to-helmet hits were frowned upon, flagged for 15 yards, and heavily fined by the NFL commissioner.

It was a different game before all the lawsuits and litigation arrived, making everyone pay closer attention to the players who just got knocked silly.

Back then, you'd wait just long enough for the cobwebs to clear and your bearings to return before getting your ass right back on that field.

Maybe I'm crazy, but I always loved seeing the stars after a huge hit, laying a ball carrier's ass out and needing a few moments to get up myself.

"Yeah, I didn't know where the hell I was, but I was out there, buddy!"

It was 1995. My client, Trev Alberts, was playing linebacker for the Indianapolis Colts in a Thursday night game with the Philadelphia Eagles on ESPN.

The Colts were making a playoff push and Alberts was in the thick of it, a top-five pick playing linebacker in the middle of the defense.

But on this night, everything went black. Two Eagles players hit Trev almost simultaneously and his head slammed hard into the artificial turf. His brain had just been through the football equivalent of pinball bumpers.

Trev was out cold.

He eventually regained consciousness, but he didn't remember leaving the field. And he didn't remember much of anything a day later. There was a screaming headache. And he threw up every time he tried the slightest bit of exercise.

Nowadays, we all know better. Trev clearly had a major concussion, one that should have kept him out of action for an extended period of time, probably several games in today's more brain-conscious culture.

But back then things were different.

According to an interview Alberts did with Stefan Fatsis of the *Wall Street Journal*, this is what a team official told him then.

"Trev, a lot of guys have gotten their bell rung a little bit. You're going to be OK."

"The medical staff of the Colts was encouraging me to play [in the next game]," Alberts said in the same article. "They were not suggesting or forcing me to play, but they were encouraging me."

I had other ideas. I knew from all the symptoms and surrounding evidence that Trev had suffered at least a Grade 2 concussion. I had my own concussions as a player. *You think I got this way naturally?*

I also made sure I learned about the cumulative effects after my client, Al Toon, suffered several of them, so I was ahead of the curve—and ahead of the times—in regard to head injuries.

I didn't want Trev to play. I cared a lot more about his health than I did the Colts' postseason chances or the criticism that would arrive if he sat out.

The reason was simple, as it is supposed to be: I wouldn't have allowed my own son to play. I owed Trev the same protection.

Trev was a good-looking, clean-cut kid from a farm in Iowa, a lot like Robert Redford in the baseball movie *The Natural.* He had a great life ahead that didn't need to be ruined by a single, stupid-ass NFL game.

My mind was made up. I knew in advance that I'd get a lot of shit for holding him out of the next game and supposedly overplaying my role.

You're an agent. Who the hell are you to take a key player out of a critical game?

I didn't give a single shit about what anyone thought. I was a lot more concerned about the commitment I made to Trev's family and the promises I gave as I looked in his parents' eyes.

Don't worry, I promise you if I represent him I'll do my best at all times to take good care of him.

The Colts sure as hell didn't feel the same way. General manager Bill Tobin wanted Alberts on the field a week later to help the team solidify their playoff spot. I handled it professionally, telling the team to shove it but also setting up an end around with an outside medical exam. I got Trev a consultation with Dr. Joe Maroon and had him advise the Colts' medical staff that in his professional opinion, Trev shouldn't be allowed to play. I believe Trev himself served as additional evidence because he ended up flunking a physical too.

Tobin was pissed, which didn't help, because as an agent, you always like to stay on good terms with clubs and their employees for the next round of negotiations. But this guy was such a dick I didn't worry about that much. And your first duty is to protect your client anyway. If my own son wouldn't play, Trev wouldn't either. I was doing the right thing.

I decided to call Tobin directly. When he answered the phone, I told him to kindly go fuck himself.

That seemed to work. Score one for tact.

Trev didn't play in the next game.

"He wouldn't allow me to play," Alberts said. "Even when it wasn't en vogue for people to take care of the head, Ralph stepped in. I took a week off and never suffered another long-term effect."

I can't say back then that I understood everything about concussions or CTE, the degenerative brain disease caused by the repeated head trauma that football players often endure. But I knew what was best for my client—and that was staying off the field until things improved.

I suppose that commitment to my players helps explain why Trev picked me in the first place.

Trev was from Cedar Falls, Iowa, a town of about 40,000 people in the northeast corner of the state. He grew into a star at the University of Nebraska during the school's glory years, when head coach Tom Osborne had transformed the team into a college football giant, perhaps the best team of the 1990s. Trev started getting handwritten letters from agents late in his college career and put his older brother Troy in charge of finding a reputable one. Troy narrowed the list to about 20 agents. He figured anyone who really cared about representing his brother would be willing to endure the lengthy travel to small-town Cedar Falls for a meeting. He may have underestimated the determination and desire of agents, especially for a top 10 draft choice.

In the end, it came down to me, Tom Condon, and Joel Segal, two other agents who were big names in the business. You always have to decide when to meet the guy when there are other agents involved. I'm pretty sure I went last, even though it was a difficult time to be on the road.

"I don't have anything negative to say about the other gentlemen; I just kind of connected with Ralph," Alberts said. "My dad was a part-time farmer and the rural life was important to us. Ralph spent a lot of time out in the country too, and I just had a good intuitive feeling and connection. I was impressed that he had played, and the fact that he had gone to law school while he was still in the NFL as a player, that meant a lot to me. [With him being] a former player, I knew if I called and expressed frustrations about coaching philosophies or schemes, he would be able to speak my language. I liked the people he represented too. He was pretty clear about the selective nature of who he represented. His character and his personal integrity were important to him. He didn't want to align with people who would embarrass him."

Trev signed with me and we soon began preparing for the upcoming draft. His stock was already rising after an outstanding senior season. He was a first-team All-American and won the Dick Butkus Award given to the nation's top linebacker, after finishing the year with 15 sacks and 21 tackles for loss. Even more impressive perhaps, or maybe even more sick, was that he dislocated his elbow in the final regular season game and returned to play in the Orange Bowl, recording three sacks and being selected as the game's Defensive MVP.

Trev was going to be a first-round pick for sure, with enough skills and intangibles to build a bunch of tents in the trousers of NFL scouts. We scheduled a pre-draft, private workout at Nebraska. Those workouts take a lot of time and effort and some football smarts too. Trev had to be in peak physical condition when his pro day arrived. We also had to consider a multitude of factors like other big schools' workout dates, but with Nebraska, it didn't matter. Everyone was going to be there.

I let Trev know what to expect with the upcoming workout, but this was freakin' Nebraska! They had an entire staff of lifting coaches, trainers, and everything else to get him ready. He was plenty prepared.

His workout day finally arrived. There was a circuit of drills to go through, with the 40-yard dash always being the most important, and always the first one on the schedule.

Trev was a superb athlete, and could soar in the high jump, which was sure to impress some scouts. He knew his ability well and insisted on doing that first.

"If I hit it like I know I can, I'm blowing the workout away. . . ."

As an agent, you don't interfere with confidence or conviction like that. Trev was so good at the high jump that I went right along with his plans. He'd nail that drill, the scouts would start drooling, and the entire workout would be a slam dunk, pushing him up to the utmost levels of the draft board.

It all made sense to me, but I warned Trev that some jagoff scout would certainly try to hijack the workout, pushing his own agenda and ideas at the expense of everyone else.

Sure enough, the same Jets scout who pissed me off at Paul Gruber's workout by publicly requesting an additional 40-yard dash tried to take over Trev's workout too.

"I called this workout," I announced. "Thank you for coming. Trev is doing the high jump first. He'll eventually do everything for everyone."

I didn't say, "You don't like it, go flip yourself." But I was thinking it.

I organized the workout and invited everyone there. I was in charge.

Trev did his high jump first and hit it. He nailed the entire workout and ended up getting drafted much higher than he ever expected, going No. 5 overall to the Indianapolis Colts. I went to work negotiating his contract with my old buddy Bob Terpening, the former Patriots executive now working in the Colts front office, and my old drinking buddy Bob Irsay.

I always had a plan before negotiations regarding what I wanted for my client and how I was going to get it. Most of the NFL executives are pricks. They're not going to roll over. With Trev's negotiations, we hit our goals on all the parameters—got the basics hammered out—and hit the numbers we were aiming for and had a chance to get something even better. Big Bob Irsay and I were buds!

But as far as contracts in the NFL are concerned, there's almost always more money available if you're willing to go after it at any cost. I let Trev know what our options were.

"I learned a lot from him," Alberts said, noting that this particular story has stayed with him now that he's negotiating deals in his current job as athletic director at the University of Nebraska Omaha. "I'll never forget this—ever. Ralph told me in our negotiation with the Colts that he thought we were pretty much there. But he said, 'Trev I want you to know that there's another percentage still out there. It's blood money that we can still go after. You can do what you like and I'll do whatever you want. We can go after that blood money and we'll likely get it, but it's probably counterproductive. Right now, the Colts feel good about it and it's a fair deal.'"

"I've often thought of that and used it here," Alberts said, from his phone in Omaha. "He was right then and he continues to be right."

Make no mistake; I've grabbed a fair share of blood money on behalf of my players. That's business. But I'm also smart enough to know that every dollar comes at a cost. And in Trev's case, we didn't need the extra price.

Trev signed a six-year deal for $8.15 million in 1994. Then, his pro career ran into a whole bunch of bad luck. In addition to that Thursday night concussion, he suffered a dislocated right elbow, a partially dislocated left shoulder, and a lingering hamstring injury according to the Associated Press. He started in just seven games and played in 29 overall in his first three years. Then, he retired from football, failed by his body and the lingering effects of all the injuries.

"I thought I'd play in the NFL for 10 years, live in Indianapolis forever and get ingrained in the community," he told Eric Olson of the Associated Press. "The NFL stands for 'Not For Long' for a reason. It's a man's game. There are a lot of variables that go into success."

I often wondered how Trev's career might have turned out if he had been drafted by a team that knew how to use him. He was not well suited to be a sit-and-read inside backer, and I thought the Colts and their coaches ruined him. He would have been much better as an attacking, pass-rushing type of linebacker, and I always thought he could have thrived in the 3–4 defense in Pittsburgh. With a better scheme and big bodies in front of him, his entire career could have been different.

Instead, it lasted somewhere near the league's average, which is about three to six years, depending on the statistics used. But as a No. 5 pick, he was a victim of increased expectations, perhaps even unreasonable ones. I could relate to almost everything. My own career had been slowed by injuries too, and I only lasted four years myself. But my pedigree was nowhere near Trev's, and not many others are either.

Fortunately, I knew firsthand that there was life after football and in many ways, it could be a better one. But that can often be hard to see, especially when you're a player staring at an end you may not have seen coming.

"If you can imagine, if all you've ever done since fifth grade is play football, then you play in college (and professionally) and then it's gone," Alberts said. "Not only that, but I was the fifth pick of the draft. There are tremendous expectations and pressure to do well. When you fall short of those, it can be discouraging."

"Ralph was very encouraging, trying to help you understand that life will go on. The same values that allowed you to be successful in football, you just apply those in different areas. He talked about his own experience and he also went to work on the transition quickly. I immediately went to work in broadcasting and was able to do that for 11 years."

I helped get Trev a job as a college football analyst, first with CNN/SI, and then with ESPN. He was a "natural," just like the movie, an easy and articulate speaker who sounded something like your next-door neighbor, with good looks and lots of smarts that made him an instant success in television.

He realized just as I did—and everyone else who ultimately leaves the NFL—that life does indeed go on. Success and happiness will often continue too. Trev had a beautiful wife and children who could help him find both.

But the reality of life, whether you're a football player or an agent or anything else, is that the best things are often earned by the people who work the hardest. Trev clawed his way right back into a couple of rewarding careers.

And I was still continuing my own climb as well, building my agency by fighting for the best interests of all my clients.

My next battle would take me right back to Indianapolis, and inside the office of the team's infamous owner, a man who had an unquenchable thirst and a long history of stomping on hearts.

I, of course, was up for the challenge.

Game on.

Bob Irsay

The Villain

HIS OWN MOTHER CALLED HIM THE DEVIL.

Bob Irsay had no problem pissing people off. Irsay took the Baltimore Colts, a proud franchise filled with legendary players, and moved them out in Mayflower trucks in the middle of the night, leaving an entire town without a team.

Bert Jones, a former quarterback for the Colts, once gave a description of Irsay to the *Baltimore Sun*.

"He lied and he cheated and he was rude and he was crude and he was Bob Irsay."

"He's the devil on earth that one," his mother famously said in *Sports Illustrated*.

Irsay made his fortune in the blue-collar heating and cooling industry and had a persona to match it.

Rugged build. Glaring eyes. A notorious temper and a never-ending thirst for booze.

I would soon find all this out for myself. Bob and I were headed for a war.

Irsay wanted one of my clients, Craig Erickson, a gutsy quarterback who took the Miami Hurricanes to a national title in 1989. After college, Erickson was drafted by the Tampa Bay Buccaneers in the fourth round of the 1992 NFL Draft. Paul Gruber, another client of mine with the Buccaneers, always said he loved Craig—"because he had stones."

But Craig was stuck behind fellow quarterback Trent Dilfer, who was picked No. 6 overall in 1994. I wanted to usher Craig out of Tampa and get him a significant raise in the process. All I had to do was work out a trade with Irsay and the quarterback-starved Indianapolis Colts.

The Colts were interested, but their front office people wanted to see Craig go through a workout first, which wouldn't help my client in the slightest.

Craig wasn't a workout warrior. He didn't have tremendous arm strength or any of the other physical attributes that impressed people in one-person drills. He had a bunch of intangibles that couldn't be measured by a stopwatch or a scale, and won a lot of games with leadership and guts.

But if Irsay saw him practice live, it might kill the whole deal. So I stalled. And Irsay got pissed.

Turns out multimillionaires are used to getting what they want. *Who knew?*

Worse yet, Irsay had one of my old friends working for him. Bob Terpening, who drove me to the airport after I got cut with the New England Patriots, was on the Colts' staff.

Terp was an ever-present pain in my ass. If he drafted one of your clients, he'd be happy to sit on him until he signed. This time, Terp kept calling me, demanding a workout with Erickson. I told him to pound salt. Over and over and over again.

"What am I supposed to tell Bob?" Terp asked, like we were old pissing buddies.

"Tell him I said to go fuck himself. That's his problem."

Deep down, I kind of enjoyed throwing gasoline on Irsay's fire and jacking around tough guy Terp. I lived for these wars.

Before long, Irsay started calling me himself, his rage building with each ring. I let the calls go through to my answering machine. Then, I'd return them when I knew Irsay couldn't be reached. I could be a devil too.

It was cat and mouse with old Ralph in Pittsburgh and big, bad Bob in Indianapolis. Eventually, we'd have to meet. The shit couldn't avoid the fan forever.

To hell with it, Irsay finally said, he'd seen enough on film. We'd meet in Indy to settle the terms of Erickson's new deal.

Praise the Lord!

I can be a religious son of a bitch too. Part I of this terrible script was over.

But a second act was soon to follow. I called around and did some reconnaissance on Bob. Every person I talked to told me he was equal parts asshole and drunk. He started drinking at noon and his mood soured soon afterward. If I were smart—and decided to operate that way for once—I'd be out of his office before he ever finished his first glass.

I scheduled our meeting for early in the morning—7:30 a.m. Since Bob was a construction guy, he was fine with it. He was used to those blue-collar hours.

We met at his estate ranch and soon got down to business.

Hours passed. The 7:30 meeting turned into 8:30, then 9:30, 10:30, 11:30, and—damn it!—noon. We hadn't taken a single break. Both of us were frustrated, moving closer and closer to a fistfight. I wanted a BIG signing bonus—which is the only part of a contract that's completely guaranteed—with few qualifications and high base salaries and additional bonuses. Bob wanted lots of incentives, protecting his pocketbook if Erickson didn't produce. Well, I loved Craig but I didn't like Bob's plan one bit. That sure as hell wasn't going to work.

We were going nowhere—and it continued like that for a few more hours. Noon became one, then two or so. We were both pissed, nearing the point where violent ends seemed like a pretty good idea. I looked at my watch. Irsay was snorting—literally snorting with anger. He wanted blood. Outside of the swine world, snorting is probably not a good sign.

"I'm having a drink, do you want one?" Irsay demanded. The prick asks for nothing.

He didn't want me to have one.

Neither of us wanted to reach any common ground, let alone a mutual drink. But he jerked me around with my time and my money so . . .

"Sure, what the hell," I said.

At this point, I figured things were about to get ugly. But after a full day of utterly wasted time, ugly was a reasonable approach; maybe fucking ugly was the only approach this late in the afternoon to get the anger out of me.

I looked around and the only other person I saw was his driver outside the office. He was stocky, but not real big. If we threw down, I liked my chances. Maybe the driver knew kung fu or some other martial arts shit, but I was a champion wrestler and a linebacker tough enough to play in the NFL. If I got into his body first—and I would—I could twist and turn him to see parts of his body he had never seen before.

As for Irsay, he was an old man but still a mean, thick, son of a bitch who reminded me of A. J. I could get him in a Chinese chokehold or a headlock and make him call his momma a whore. But given what she said about him in *Sports Illustrated*, I'm guessing he might do it himself now that he was one drink deep.

Hell, at that point, I was angry and itching for a fight myself. King Kong or Bob Irsay, either one, I'd kick them in the nuts if I had half a chance. Everything I had heard about Irsay was coming true right before my eyes. He was mean, ugly, and angry and seemed certain to sucker punch me if the situation arose.

"What are we drinking?" I asked.

"Vodka, you want some?"

"Is it any good?" I jabbed him a bit more just to send his blood pressure higher.

He stopped, looked at me, sensed that I was being a smart ass, but also knew I was more than willing to fight too. Old Bob had no easy exit. I wasn't backing down.

I was waiting for his pour or his punch, whichever came first. And I figured with his private bar and big band music playing in the background, he'd pull out some Waterford crystal or a couple of nice glasses if we were going to be drinking.

I was wrong.

Irsay grabbed a sleeve of Coca-Cola stadium cups that were probably stolen from one of his concession stands. He put two of them on the table and filled one with vodka about a quarter of the way. He poured mine to the same level, but I upped the ante, pushing my cup up farther and asking for more. I was a lot like Dan Aykroyd calling for more champagne in the restaurant scene from *Blues Brothers*. Bob and I locked eyes, played chicken, and Irsay said nothing else. He poured mine up even higher—half full. But we hadn't agreed on anything yet, so there was certainly nothing to toast.

He took a sip and looked at me. I followed by chugging mine—all of it—and slammed my cup down so hard he must have jumped two feet.

I needed that first drink just to settle my nerves, but my actions had other consequences too. I had just thrown down the gauntlet in front of Irsay.

Bob's eyes were wide open and perhaps he was still snorting too. He chugged his own vodka and slammed the cup down in a thundering response.

Somewhere in the past few minutes, logic and reason had left the room. I was doing what everyone said not to, going against all the plans I had so meticulously made. I was drinking with the devil.

It went back and forth like a spirited game of Ping-Pong, each round ending with more vodka sliding into our stomachs. Before long, he was running up and down the bar like a jolly old elf, laughing along the way, grabbing whatever vodka bottle seemed to suit his fancy.

"Here, try this one from Poland. Here's another one made from. . . . Here's another . . . "

We were both hammered in an hour or so. I never expected this. I hadn't eaten anything all day except for a half-assed, hurried breakfast early that morning. You learn in my business to eat when you can. I didn't have any Pepto Bismol and wasn't sure what I might do to recover.

At one point, I went to the bathroom knowing I had to go, or should go, but if nothing else had to get away for at least a few seconds and maybe splash some water on my face. My whole body was pretty much numb when I approached the urinal. My apologies to the cleaning lady if I missed, and I probably did.

It reminds me of a well-known coach turned announcer who took a piss in the owner's closet mistaking it for a bathroom. Just a regular night for him.

In my case, I was drunk and vulnerable and in dire need of a hotel room. I had to get the hell out of there.

"Did you bring a coat?" Irsay asked me.

He was asking if I had a sport coat, some suitable attire for a social event. I did. A. J. always had me take a coat, and at a minimum, a roll-up tie just in case. I never went anywhere without it.

"Come on, you're going with me to a barn party."

Irsay took me to a barn party that was one of his charity events, a literary reading featuring notable authors and their published works. He led me around to each of the social circles, introducing me to everyone—and I mean everyone—as his own son.

"Hello, how are you?" he said. "This is my son . . . Ralph."

Har! Har! Har!

He laughed after each introduction, then moved onto the next group and did the same thing, again and again, laughing his ass off each and every time.

There was an auction as there always is at those types of events, and Irsay bid way too high on something in my name, laughing the whole time the price was flying up. I didn't know about it or see it, but I received bills from that night for three straight years.

Nowadays, I would have just paid for the damn thing to end it, but I never did back then. Terp likes to bust my balls and still asks me to this day if I ever settled my debt.

The hijinks continued for a few more minutes. Big, bad, Bob Irsay was having the time of his life. We left the party after one tour around, having made our social appearance.

Somewhere amid all that nonsense, the devil had lightened up. He told me to meet him early tomorrow morning for coffee and doughnuts.

I told him that I didn't like doughnuts, that I'd rather have bagels, just to let him know who was still boss.

Bob gave me the infamous glaring eyes, but they melted quickly into a much softer smile.

Bagels it is. I figured I was family now.

We met the next morning and finished the entire Erickson deal in an hour. I got everything I wanted—a big signing bonus and a great base salary with incentives to boot.

It was an outstanding contract. And I had beaten big, bad Bob Irsay but he didn't give a single shit. I don't know how many of those fun evenings he has shared with others.

To this day, when I pour some vodka I think of him.

Cheers to you, Bob. And your shitty stadium cups too.

But, I prefer to raise a nice Waterford glass and drink it all down with my toast:

"I don't know where you are, Bob, but wherever it is, I know this—if you were cremated, you're still burning."

Rodney Hampton

The Giant

THE CLOCK WAS TICKING.

Rodney Hampton knew the numbers. The average player only lasts three or four years in the NFL and for running backs it's probably less, having been worn down by a grueling position and tossed out by front office types looking for fresher legs. And Hampton, a bruising runner with a big laugh from the University of Georgia, had just finished his third season, a Pro Bowl one to be exact, after rushing for 1,141 yards and 14 touchdowns in 1993.

He deserved a raise. And he needed to get it now, before a knee blew out or the New York Giants decided to move on to someone new.

Hampton's first deal was negotiated with the help of his sister. George Young was one of the few folks you could do that with. Most other GMs would take advantage and have you walking around like you had a cornstalk stuck up your ass. Now, Rodney needed an agent to help secure a new contract, and his teammate Brian Williams recommended me.

Williams and I had a connection that served as a subplot to the whole thing. Brian's father was a former quarterback at Notre Dame who became a gynecologist after college in the Pittsburgh area. He was the doctor for many of the females in the Cindrich family, but because of his incredible ethics, I learned that from the ladies, not him.

Dr. Bob Williams was dying when his son Brian, a standout center from the University of Minnesota, was heading into the NFL and looking for an agent. Not long after I met Dr. Bob, he told me I had earned his trust and he was certain I wouldn't screw over his son. That was important to him because his days were numbered. And I never forgot that in all my interactions with Brian. So Brian and I had a special relationship and some of that probably got relayed to Rodney as a reference.

Now, came the hard part. I had to get Rodney a new, more lucrative contract with a year still remaining on his old one. And general managers are rarely in a hurry to renegotiate.

George Young surely wasn't. George was the Giants general manager at the time and he was also one of my favorite people to work with, a good, solid guy who served his employer's best interest and gave gold-plated quotes to members of the media. He never cheated a rookie if the kid didn't have an agent (Rodney was Exhibit A) and he built the Giants into a consistent winner as well, presiding over two Super Bowl teams during his two-decade tenure in New York. He's deceased now, but he deserves to be in the Hall of Fame, immortalized among all the legends with his face cast in bronze.

George was a pretty easy guy to negotiate with, though he never parted with dollars easily and he often relied on the slotting system to set the price. Most think this is fair. His draft picks usually got paid a little more money than the player picked behind them and a little less than the player picked in front. It was a common practice all across the league.

Unfortunately, I didn't operate with such easygoing ideals. I always wanted the best deal I could get for my client and didn't want to be tied to what had been worked out by the other teams and agents that bordered us. I wanted to overachieve and I usually did when the signatures hit the contract.

Within those constraints, I was pretty amicable though, and George and I often found a lot of common ground. With George, we never approached the nuclear wars that Bill Polian and I always launched. Quite frankly, my language was a lot better, but I can't say the same about George. He was educated at Bucknell and beyond, but he swore like he was in a street gang, sending F-bombs all over his office as his lovely secretary answered phones in the background.

George and I liked to negotiate on Saturday mornings. Tea and crumpets I would always say, bringing back warm memories from when I studied law with my wife during a summer abroad in Exeter, England.

George was reluctant to renegotiate Rodney's contract—it would set a bad precedent for all the other players on the team—but it became pretty obvious it was in the Giants' best interest. I was going to hold Rodney out of camp as long as I could otherwise. And he was a critical piece of the Giants' offense, having averaged four yards per carry in his first three years and appearing in two straight Pro Bowls.

Rodney was due to earn $425,000 in the last year of his rookie deal. We wanted something more in line with what the top running backs were paid, about $2–3 million annually.

Our initial tea and crumpets session did not go well. We were miles apart and stayed that way throughout the summer. Training camp began and I held Rodney out as he played the malcontent player role perfectly.

"I wouldn't say I'm irritated, but I am kind of bothered that it has taken this long," Hampton said to Mike Freeman (a good friend of mine on Twitter) of the *New York Times*. "I'm kind of surprised. I held up my end of the bargain, now it's time for the Giants to do their part. I want to get this done, over with. It wasn't supposed to take this long."

Rodney eventually reported to camp after holding out for two weeks, but it was only to make sure he'd satisfy all the rules that would make him a free agent at the end of the season. We still didn't have a new contract. And I had no problem floating the idea that he might eventually find one somewhere else, maybe even from a bitter rival within the same division.

"This is a guy you should take care of," I told the *New York Times*. "If you have a salary cap problem, do it now because next year when the cap is in place, it'll be too late. If he goes on the open market, there are teams like Philadelphia or other teams that don't have those cap problems and will pay him."

The threat of the Eagles swooping in to steal him away was my ace in the hole. George and I had a little more tea, a few more crumpets, and got the deal done. Rodney got the big raise he deserved, with a contract that averaged $2.3 million over three seasons and paid $3 million in the first year alone, a front-loaded deal that would help the Giants with the salary cap that was arriving a year later. For the time being, he was the second-highest-paid running back in the entire NFL.

He earned every dollar in that deal too, rushing for over 1,000 yards in each of those three seasons. Even more impressive was that he had sidestepped all the pitfalls of the running back position and was entering free agency as a healthy and productive rusher who would generate interest on the open market.

Some of it came from the San Francisco 49ers, a frequent postseason rival that was more than happy to enter into a public pissing contest with the Giants in pursuit of their star player.

George Young started it all by placing the transition tag on Rodney, a shrewd move since it let the Giants match any offer Hampton could get, and it would also scare some teams away from bidding in the first place. The Giants were already preparing for his departure anyway, having drafted Michigan running back Tyrone Wheatley in the first round. By using the tag, the Giants could keep Rodney around for at least one more year before handing off the position to his younger replacement. And after another year of wear and tear, Rodney's earning power would be greatly diminished anywhere else.

So I hated that plan and did my best to serve as a fluffer for San Francisco, driving the price up and making the offer more difficult to match. I went looking for a poison pill once again.

Carmen Policy was the 49ers president and general manager at the time, and I always enjoyed my interactions with him. Carmen was something of a salary-cap wizard, a creative guy who often seemed to find loopholes, shortcuts, and innovative solutions to better serve San Francisco's team. Perhaps he was a little sly, but that didn't make me like him any less. I had spent the better part of my early life in Avella searching for any mischief I could find. Who was I to throw stones?

Carmen always called me the Italian version of Ralph—Raphael— just as my Aunt Rosie did, and I enjoyed that too. I sometimes hated my regular name, so I was more than happy to envision myself as a Renaissance painter.

In the case of Rodney's contract, I had some creative ideas of my own that might torpedo the Giants. I had earned a doctorate degree in pissing off the NFL, and this situation was a perfect fit for my skills.

Carmen was willing to entertain whatever I came up with and that was half the fun. He knew as much about football talent as I did about gynecology, but one of his personnel people—a good guy, John McVay—made it clear that Rodney could really help a team that already had Steve Young and Jerry Rice.

So we started getting groovy, good-time vibes in the land of the hippies, and I began working on an offer sheet to send Rodney out west. I wasn't going to get another *Blind Side* contract where the 49ers would agree to keep him as the highest-paid player, not with Montana, Rice, et al. And the 49ers weren't willing to give the Giants a draft pick to get the deal done either, so we had to do something creative with the contract language that would squeeze the Giants and maybe even scare them off.

I put together an offer sheet with San Francisco that included a feature player clause that guaranteed Rodney would be the starting running back for the duration of the three-year deal.

What's the big deal? Well, try telling the momma of that draft pick and her superstar son Tyrone Wheatley that he ain't starting. For at least three years! The Giants wouldn't be happy with it either since someone from the outside was dictating something very personal to the team.

I sold it to the 49ers front office, reminding them about the creative language in Will Wolford's free agent contract that seemed like ancient history now. They finally saw things my way and were okay with including that clause.

The Giants were not. They didn't like the deal and Wheatley wasn't going to sit on their bench for the next three years. And on top of that, Hampton's contract offer was worth $16.45 million over six years, a hefty price tag that could put the cap-strained Giants in a tough spot with so much invested in a single position.

We had it all. I thought.

But George Young complained to Paul Tagliabue, the commissioner of the league. And Tagliabue went to law school with Carmen Policy at Georgetown, so the circle was a pretty tight one. Paul called Carmen and he decided to toss out the clause rather than tick off his college buddy and the rest of the NFL.

And that let the Giants back in, as they matched the six-year, $16.45 million contract with a signing bonus worth $3.7 million. Rodney returned to New York, which was fine with us in the end, because he was getting a big fat raise once again.

At the press conference to announce the deal, Giants co-owner Robert Tisch fired one final volley in the pissing match between the two teams.

"San Francisco was trying to figure out how to outsmart us. No way were we going to let that happen," Tisch said, according to Freeman's article in the *New York Times*. "They were holding press conferences every day. We didn't say anything. We did a good job of not blowing our own horn the way they did."

Hampton finished his career with the only team he ever played for, making it two more years before all those other factors he outran for so long finally caught up to him, and the team released him in 1998.

I could have gotten him another contract, maybe with Philadelphia or Kansas City, but Rodney was ready to retire. He had played well during his time in the league, with five straight 1,000-yard seasons. He had made enough money, surviving for eight years at one of the league's most destructive positions. And he had played his entire career as a New York Giant, something that didn't seem possible when the numbers were coming together out west.

"I played hard, left everything on the field and knew what it took my body to get through it," Hampton said. "I wanted to walk away on own terms."

Hampton returned to his hometown, Houston, and has spent his retirement running a family business involving exercise equipment, and conducting "Hamps Camp," a football camp that provides positive messages, support, and instruction for kids.

One of my next clients would take me on a path that would run almost parallel to Hampton's. James Farrior was drafted by the other team in New York, and their head coach was Bill Parcells, who won a Super Bowl in Hampton's first season with the Giants.

But Farrior's first negotiation wasn't going well.

I was brought in as something of a hired gun.

And I was ready to take aim.

James Farrior

The Steeler

THINGS WEREN'T GOING WELL.

James Farrior was a football player. He wanted nothing more than to get into training camp and get back on the field, put on his pads, and get right down to work. But football players can't be blind to the business. They're all running sole proprietorships, every single one of them serving as a CEO in the business of their body.

And Farrior was staring back at a bad business deal. Almost every rookie draft pick gets some guaranteed money up front—a signing bonus—and a contract that's typically three to five years in length. Farrior was expecting both after being selected No. 8 overall in the 1997 Draft. He was a standout linebacker at the University of Virginia and would be an immediate asset in a Jets defense that was being rebuilt by new head coach Bill Parcells. He deserved to get paid accordingly.

But the Jets were tight against the salary cap and were trying to squeeze him. New York offered him a bait-and-switch six-year contract that had no signing bonus, but unlike all other NFL contracts would be guaranteed up until the very end. It was a shell game by the Jets, who were presenting the offer as a better one because it was fully guaranteed, but in reality it would hurt Farrior twice.

There was no money up front. And he'd have to wait longer than others to hit free agency and reap the rewards of the open market.

Worse yet, Farrior's agent, according to James's mother, the representative responsible for knowing better and getting him a fair deal, was failing to deliver.

Was Farrior's agent being bullied by Bill Parcells, the biggest personality in the Jets' front office? Was he in over his head? I don't know all the answers, but Parcells has certainly been known to manipulate people and their circumstances too, if it might help his team in the end.

In this case, it was obvious things weren't working out as they should. So Farrior and his mother Becky stepped in. Becky had liked me when we first met, and she had good instincts about the business side of things. She also sensed that this deal was a terrible one. And her son James was plenty wise to know she was right on point.

"The deal I had at first wasn't the deal I wanted," Farrior said. "I knew with Ralph he would get me the deal I wanted and would get a good deal."

It wasn't easy switching agents, especially since the deal was nearly done and James was only a few days away from training camp, but players have to protect their business interests better than anyone else. Teams will often trample them all in their own selfish pursuits. And that's exactly what the Jets were doing.

But not anymore.

Here I am, boys! We don't like the contract at all. Let's start over. And everything else you were planning to do with the money you were saving on that shitty contract, say adios, my friends.

I spoke pretty good Spanish for an Italian Croat.

Anyway, Parcells was plenty pissed. He told the *New York Times* that the deal was 95 percent finished when Farrior brought me in. And Parcells, who was probably feeling some pressure in his first year with the Jets, just watched his first-round pick move a few steps farther away from the field.

But Bill and I had done this dance before and I was sure we'd do it again soon. Parcells always seemed to want a team-friendly deal that came at the expense of your client. He also wasn't above bullying agents or trying to work out some deals that might compromise one of your clients. But I was never afraid to call him out on it, and we could usually find some common ground when it came to contracts.

Alongside Parcells was Mike Tannenbaum, who started his career as the New York Jets director of player contract negotiations. Neither

Tannenbaum nor Parcells was interested in moving back to a more traditional contract, something that would give James a signing bonus. But I sure as hell was.

Parcells said I grew hoarse yelling at Mike. And I can confirm that I was M.F.-ing him every chance I got. But we eventually made progress and I got the Jets to move away from the hard-line stance they had previously taken.

Parcells should have been used to my operating procedure by now. One time, he asked me if everyone from Pittsburgh was crazy or if I was the only one. I thought that was funny, but it was also the reputation I wanted to have in negotiations. Truth be told, an agent who is always nice and agreeable probably isn't doing a very good job.

In the end, I usually tried to leave my negotiations on a positive note, saying nice things about the involved parties and sometimes even sending gifts. In Parcells's case, after a time I M.F.-ed him when he called the old agent of a new guy I was representing, I sent a couple of cases of Pittsburgh's Iron City beer once everything got worked out.

This time around, after a little more deliberation, we worked it out again, getting James into camp before the fourth day of practice. He signed a deal for five years and $8.8 million with a signing bonus of $4 million fully guaranteed. It was a quick turnaround considering how messy everything had been. I even left the Jets with $30 to spare under the salary cap.

"I tried to pick up the $30, but they drew the line there," I said, according to Gerald Eskenazi of the *New York Times*.

For James, it was a welcome end to all the stress and strain from the business side of things. He could finally return to simply playing football, something he had been doing since he was eight years old.

"That meant everything to me, to finally get everything over with," Farrior said. "The whole process is really a long, stressful process. . . . I was so happy to be back to playing football and feeling my way around being a rookie. It was unbelievable."

That first negotiation gave Farrior an early education into the business of pro football. Inside the locker room, he found a lot of other players who had been through something similar. This wasn't just a game that everyone watches on Sundays. Players had to be aware of the bottom line.

Farrior went into the league with his eyes wide open and kept them that way for the remainder of his career. But he also trusted me enough to have some autonomy as his agent. Over the years, we worked together to make the most of his playing days.

After five years with the Jets, where Farrior played mostly outside linebacker, he became a free agent in 2002. He was fresh off a season in which he started all 16 games and had 106 tackles, three forced fumbles, and two interceptions. But surprisingly, the market was milder than either of us expected. I blame almost all of that on the Jets. James was best suited as an inside backer and the Jets insisted on playing him outside. In free agency, I figured we'd find a place that would play him inside and maximize his talents.

Pittsburgh was one of the few teams that showed interest and I pushed him in that direction. I knew the Rooney family would pay him if he produced. I also knew that the team was well run from top to bottom, a model organization with a strong defense and more Super Bowl wins than any other team. "He kind of sold it to me," Farrior remembers, thankful for everything that happened next.

Farrior signed a three-year deal with Pittsburgh in 2002 and the team soon moved him to middle linebacker in their 3–4 defense. Both parties shared a significant amount of success in the years that followed.

The defense seemed to finish in the top five every year. With Farrior in the middle of their defense, the team made three Super Bowl appearances, winning two of them. Farrior flourished, finishing second in the NFL's Defensive Player of the Year vote for the 2004 season. It was an ideal fit on all fronts, with Farrior playing behind massive nose tackle Casey Hampton. He was also coached by one of football's legendary figures, Steelers defensive coordinator Dick LeBeau, who had returned to the Steelers in 2004.

"He's everything," Farrior said of LeBeau. "He should be doing the Dos Equis commercials. He's really the most interesting guy in the world. I think he played a musical instrument back in the day. And when he was in Detroit, he used to hang out with the Motown guys and a bunch of singers. He's just a Mac Daddy guy. When he walks in a room, it's like his show."

Amid the expertise of LeBeau, Farrior became an institution in the middle of the Steelers' defense. In his ten years as a middle linebacker, a position that endures the equivalent of a car crash on every play, he only missed six starts. He was a captain for eight years and led the team in tackles every year from 2003 to 2009.

And for a town built in part by the continued sacrifices of shift work, Farrior was a fan favorite. Someone nicknamed him the Ultimate Farrior, a playful reference to a superstar wrestler. And many of the black-and-gold fans twirling terrible towels in Heinz Field would spend their Sundays wearing No. 51.

It was a loving marriage for both parties that lasted a long time in NFL terms. Many people believe Farrior is the best free agent signing in Steelers history (he's also been ranked as one of the top 20 free agent signings in the history of the NFL). And before he retired, he became Pittsburgh's career leader in tackles (742), an impressive feat considering the legends who have lined up in black and gold.

Following the 2012 season, after 16 seasons in the league, a few contract extensions, and an entire decade with the Steelers, Pittsburgh had to move on from Farrior, Hines Ward, and a few other veterans to squeeze their roster under the salary cap.

Farrior could have played another season or maybe two—and part of me thought the Jets would have been an ideal fit with Rex Ryan's regime in place—but James wanted to retire as a Steeler and leave the game on his own terms. He didn't have a burning desire to play anywhere else. And I was okay with that too.

Business had been good for several years. It was time to close the doors and count his blessings.

I wanted to slow down in my own career too. My kids had moved out to California, with Michael working as an attorney and Christina getting gigs as an actress and television host. A granddaughter would be arriving soon.

And I wanted to take more time and trips to see them all, focusing on all the things that were more important than football. A long walk with my wife. A laugh with a little baby. A pasta dinner on Sunday and maybe a stiff drink too.

I'd let all those simple joys fill up more of my time in the years ahead. But my belief in the importance of family led me to another client too.

One of my first clients had a kid who was entering the NFL.

And there was no way I could let him be represented by anyone else.

Nick Toon

The Legacy

I was the guy from the Christmas cards.

Concussions forced Al Toon to retire before Nick Toon turned five. So Nick grew up away from the business of professional football, mostly unaware of all the contract negotiations his father went through and the agent who represented him.

His most frequent interactions with me arrived every December, when the Cindrich family Christmas cards showed up outside his door. Our office sent a large number of cards every year, to clients, executives, and employees all across the league. I could be a bulldog in negotiations—more than happy to mark my territory too—but I wasn't above sending a few warm wishes around the holidays. And I actually liked most everyone when I wasn't going one-on-one with them in a contract war. So that's how Nick first knew me. But the kid grew up quickly, taking an interest in football and following in the footsteps of his father.

The concussions that ended Al's career prematurely and left him with headaches, memory loss, and a sensitivity to light for years afterward weren't enough to scare Nick away from the game. But Nick has certainly seen the dangers of football closer than most, with evidence that goes all the way back to when he was four years old.

"I remember vividly right after he retired and he got his last concussion laying on the bed with him and hanging out, and we couldn't turn the lights on or anything," Nick said in an interview with Gary Myers of the *New York Daily News*. "It seemed like he was in there forever. Obviously, kids are impressionable at that age. I don't know that I was really aware of the severity of the situation. I think my mom and dad did a good job handling the situation because it didn't scar me."

Certainly Al Toon has felt some anxiety when his son is between the white lines of a football field. I sure have.

My own son Michael suffered a nasty concussion during a high school football game in 1996. He got smacked on a special teams play and had trouble getting up. His eyes rolled back a bit—an obvious concussion, Grade 2 to be exact. Even though I had a few of them myself, I was flooded with concern, enduring one of my scariest days as a dad. I lost sleep. And I wasn't sure when—if ever—I should let Mike return to the field.

Back then no one knew what they do now about head injuries, so I called around to gather what information I could, contacting a number of NFL doctors and trainers, and of course, Al, who had become an unfortunate expert on concussions.

That experience also led me to commission a survey in 1998 that covered concussions and a number of other pressing issues in football. I polled 100 draft-eligible players and found that 45 percent of them had suffered at least one head injury and 25 percent had endured multiple head traumas. But perhaps even more revealing was that 72 percent of the players said they believed playing in the NFL would be worth it, even if it would limit their physical activity in later years.

In the end, the implications were clear. Football is dangerous. But not nearly enough to scare a lot of people away.

"Everybody gets hit in the head playing the game of football. If you get dinged up or get your bell rung a little bit, every time that happens, you know, they call it a concussion. It's the risk you take playing the game," Nick once said on an episode of ESPN's *Outside the Lines*. "If you accept it, great, go out and play. If you don't, don't play. . . . I love the game of football and I'm gonna play it until I can't play anymore."

"I think about my career and the dangers of the game and that kind of thing," Al said on the same episode. "But I don't think about it a lot. Nick knows the dangers of the game."

Just like my son Michael, who eventually returned to his high school field, Nick Toon always believed the rewards outweighed the risks. In time, Nick became a football star much like his father. He was a tall, tough, fleet-footed wide receiver, an apple that didn't fall very far from a rather remarkable tree.

Nick was a high school All-American at Middleton and followed his father to the University of Wisconsin, near his home in Madison. After a redshirt year, he developed into a solid receiver for the Badgers, finishing third in school history in both receptions and receiving yards. Nick even eclipsed many of his father's totals, benefiting from a game that was much more fond of the forward pass.

After his senior season, Nick was invited to the Senior Bowl and the NFL's scouting combine, the subway stops just outside the professional game. Agents were already circling, selling their services and making all kinds of promises, some of which were certainly empty. Nick needed to pick someone from that pool and thankfully, his dad had done it all before. But Al refused to run the whole process. He offered his advice, but wanted his son to be in charge of all the important decisions, learning from everything along the way.

"I felt it was important for Nick and my daughters to experience and do research and interplay with the options that were presented and ask them [the agents] questions so they can think about their own perspective on things," Al said. "Ralph ended up being a good fit for Nick, I promoted Ralph as a great possibility, we did interviews with several others, and he did a few on his own that he eliminated. It was a great process, he learned a lot, and I wanted it to be his decision. I think it would have been a negative if you take that experience away from him. I think it would have stifled his maturation process."

Al's philosophy was about the same as mine, but I had other plans as well. I hoped Nick would select me so I could represent him as a partial payback to his father. Al did so much for me and my career that I could never repay it all, but I thought representing his son pro bono would be a nice way to say thanks.

So about 27 years after I made a pitch to the father, I did the same with his son. I wasn't actively pursuing new clients in 2012, but I didn't consider Nick a client either. He was family. And I didn't want to see him represented by anyone else.

My office put together a proposal that sold our strengths.

We had negotiated more than a billion dollars of contracts since 2000. We had eight top 10 draft picks over the years and our clients had played in more than 40 Pro Bowls and won a number of Super Bowl rings too. We had the NFL's highest-paid player twice and have represented the highest-paid player at every position except kicker. (No big deal. Kickers are usually nut jobs anyway.)

I also included one of my favorite quotes from the *Newark Star-Ledger*:

"If God had an agent like Ralph Cindrich, maybe we might have gotten a better deal down here. . . . The man is widely regarded as the No. 1 negotiator in Pro Football, which isn't easy to be when you're also known as one of the most ethical."

We finished our proposal with an itinerary that detailed plans for Nick from January all the way through his first NFL game, including key dates for a number of important milestones.

In the end, Nick followed the footsteps of his father once more. He chose me as his agent, making me one of the rare agents to represent both a father and son in the NFL.

"When it came time for the meeting with Ralph, we sat down and met," Nick said. "He had a no-BS approach, which he kind of has in his life too. That was what I wanted. Someone who was straightforward, honest, kept it real, was trustworthy, and had my best interests and my family's best interests at heart. Unfortunately, there's a lot of dishonesty and BS—if you will—in the industry. I knew I could trust Ralph and he would look out for me. . . . He's been a part of my family for many years. I was in a unique situation. The fact that he's still involved in the sector was a blessing for me. It's probably pretty rare and pretty unique to get the opportunity to represent two generations. It's kind of cool and I'm glad I made the decision I did. It was definitely the right way to go."

It was pretty cool to see my career come full circle too. Truth be told, it also made me feel pretty freaking old, but that happened with a lot of things.

Nick was drafted by the New Orleans Saints in the third round of the 2012 draft, and we signed his rookie contract at the end of July, without the prolonged holdout or war of words that preceded his father's deal 27 years earlier.

The times are simpler now, with all the salaries connected to draft positions and a percentage increase from previous years. There's little room for a negotiator like me to rattle a few cages and collect another extra dollar or two in negotiations. But I still helped Nick navigate the process and prepare for everything that would arrive in his rookie year.

And it gave his father some peace of mind. No matter what happened in the future, Al Toon knew Nick's agent was a friendly face, someone who could be trusted to take good care of his son and give honest advice whenever it was needed.

"They're not very many years—if you make a mistake at that stage with your first agent, it could really affect you," Al said. "It's one of the most important decisions you make as an athlete, signing appropriate representation."

Nick had a lingering injury and got off to a slow start in his first two years with the Saints, but had 17 receptions and an expanded role with the Saints in 2014. He also scored his first NFL touchdown in Pittsburgh as my family and I looked on from inside Heinz Field. It was a milestone moment that I won't forget anytime soon.

With a few more solid seasons and some good health to go along with them, Nick can build a solid foundation to secure his future in football.

And when his contract is up, I'll really be able to negotiate again, maximizing the market for Nick and driving up the demand. I'll argue and scream, maybe swear a few times if I force it, and enjoy the process as best I can. Now that I've slowed down some there aren't nearly as many negotiations as there used to be.

I soak them all up.

And in the end, I'll make sure Nick gets a good deal, just as his dad always did.

Like father. Like son.

I've been blessed to know both of them.

Jeff Saturday

The Center

Thirty-two teams passed over him in the NFL Draft.

He finally signed as an undrafted free agent with the Baltimore Ravens, but they soon released him, cutting him loose less than two months later, before he ever played a single snap in a game.

The dream was dying. Hope was slipping away.

A lesser man might have given up. But Jeff Saturday had a bunch of faith, both in his football abilities and a power much higher than that, believing God would work it all out in the end.

Jeff went to work as a manager at an electric supply store in Raleigh, not far from where he made All-Conference at the University of North Carolina in Chapel Hill—a beautiful campus I visited as a recruit out of Avella.

Saturday worked as a manager for months, learning the business and occasionally wondering if he'd be inside that store forever. He thought about playing in the arena league or maybe Canada, but he never gave up. Never quit. And when he wasn't surrounded by all those conduits, connectors, and crimps, Jeff stayed in shape and stayed ready for the opportunity he hoped would come.

He always seemed to have an uphill climb anyway, an undersized lineman (6'2") with what scouts called alligator arms (they were supposedly too short), a player who seemed to start each game with two strikes already against him. But he made up for the supposed shortcomings with smarts and technique and toughness and all the other things that weren't so easily measured.

According to Tim Layden of *Sports Illustrated*, Saturday was a star player in high school and yet struggled to find scholarship offers. His coach phoned in a favor to get one from North Carolina and head coach Mack Brown. And then Saturday became a starter as a freshman, carrying the Tar Heels to a winning record they weren't accustomed to and Brown to a better job at tradition-rich Texas.

"We were lucky to get him," Brown told Layden. "He was so tough. And so smart. And he loved to play football."

And yet, the NFL seemed to ignore all that as the scouts locked in on the size of his body and the length of his arms.

After Saturday's pro day in Chapel Hill, a number of NFL scouts talked to him about his future in the NFL. And it seemed to be a bleak one.

"The day the pro scouts were in town, Jeff comes walking into the store," James Spurling, an owner of a gas station where Saturday worked in college, recalled to Layden. "I say, 'How'd it go?' Well, Jeff starts getting choked up and says, 'I guess I'll be pumping frickin' gas and fixing tires for the rest of my life.' He was really upset. The scouts told him he was too short and his arms were too short to block those big pass rushers."

"He told me, 'Man if it ain't football you're gonna be successful in something,'" Saturday said. "'You work hard. Don't give up on your dream.'"

A few weeks later, Saturday fell through the bottom of the draft. And then he fell out of favor with the Ravens.

But NFL fortunes are often made or lost on the smallest of margins.

A single yard on fourth down. A few inches of goalpost. A heel that hits out of bounds. "*The inches* we need are everywhere around us. They're in *every break of the game*, every minute, every second . . ." Al Pacino said in the football movie *Any Given Sunday*.

Saturday gained the inches he needed and got the big break he deserved with the help of a former teammate, an Indianapolis Colt named Nate Hobgood-Chittick who had enough backbone to walk into the office of Bill Polian, a Hall of Fame general manager who had built several Super Bowl teams, and provide a reference for a friend.

"I had no footing at all with that franchise," Hobgood-Chittick, a former Tar Heel, told *Sports Illustrated*'s Layden. "So I stood outside Polian's door in my dirty sweats, saying a prayer. I walked in and said, 'There's a guy selling electrical supplies in Raleigh right now who whipped all those first-round draft choices at North Carolina every day.'"

"Polian looked at me and said, 'I love it, let's get him in here for a workout.'"

This was vintage Bill Polian, a prime example of what made him such a skilled executive. His open-minded pursuit of players had origins in the lesser leagues he worked in, where you had to kiss a lot of toads, but only needed a single prince to change your fortunes.

Jeff was just that. He had fared well in college practices against three Tar Heel defenders who were taken in the first round of the 1998 draft. And that, along with Polian's instincts, was enough to bring him in. Saturday signed as a free agent with the Colts in January of 1999 and began his first season as a backup guard. Injuries gave him two starts later that season, and he played surprisingly well, impressing me in a game against Denver. A year later, he started all 16 games at center for the Indianapolis Colts, the first line of defense for future Hall of Famer Peyton Manning.

Over the years, Jeff and Manning would become cornerstones of the Colts franchise and leaders of a no-huddle offense that was notoriously complex, with Jeff often pointing out defenders and Manning constantly flailing his arms and pumping his leg to communicate calls. The two were something of a synchronized swimming routine, with the audible reaching the other players just as it was supposed to, and the snap always seeming to arrive on time.

The guy who wasn't good enough to be drafted started 85 consecutive games for the Colts from 2000 to 2004. And Manning, the quarterback taken No. 1 overall in 1998, was there for every last one of them. I imagine Manning had his hands on Jeff's butt more than his wife's. "They kind of think the same at times," backup quarterback Curtis Painter once told Joe Capozzi of the *Palm Beach Post*.

Jeff signed with me just as his first contract was about to expire. He was looking for an agent to help him as he approached free agency and a number of friends recommended me. We hit it off the first time we met. And I knew Jeff was a valuable commodity to the Colts, someone who deserved to be one of the highest-paid players on the team.

The Colts started off with a reasonable offer as was Polian's style. And Jeff, who had played all his previous years with a meager salary not far from the NFL minimum, was ready to jump at it. Saturday was much more grateful than greedy, and we both wanted him to stay in Indianapolis anyway. Jeff also remembered his time in that electric supply store so well that he couldn't possibly take a contract offer like this for granted.

He was ready to make a deal.

"I remember Ralph saying, 'We're not taking it, this is step one,'" Saturday recalled. "I remember other players saying it was a great deal. Karen [Jeff's wife] and I were praying at night. We wanted to stay in Indy, we loved the area, it was a good team and we were considering all that. I was coming from the place where I was on the street working a regular job."

"But Ralph was like, 'We're absolutely not going to take this.'"

So my old friend Bill Polian and I got to battle again. Polian called Jeff and said he couldn't get anywhere with me, he needed to speak to him alone. Bill never did this in Buffalo, but for God's sake this was his free agent, not mine. I told Jeff not to do it, that Polian was trying to drive a wedge between us and perhaps deliver a less lucrative deal in the process. But Jeff wasn't going to leave the city he loved without at least talking it out with Polian.

In that meeting, Bill arrived at a better number. I wanted Jeff to be the highest-paid center in the game, but the Colts were somewhat strained by the cap, with Manning and some other high-profile players already earning big contracts.

Jeff likes a buck but he loved his team. Polian promised to guarantee a large part of the contract, ensuring that Jeff could at least be confident in the dollars that were actually included.

Jeff agreed. I did too, earning a sizable share of my client's trust in the process.

"He [Ralph] will drive it until the end but he'll never let his pride overtake it," Saturday said. "He knew what my wife and I wanted and he'll never let his pride get in the way. He didn't care that he wasn't the last guy on the phone call. He was happy for us. He said, 'I think it's a fair deal, if Bill is giving you his word, it's good, he has never gone back on a deal.'"

And I meant that, one of the highest compliments that I can ever pay Polian. He always kept his word. Always.

Jeff signed a six-year deal that kept him in place as Manning's center, and the Colts won a Super Bowl in 2006. Manning and Saturday eventually set an NFL record with 172 games together as quarterback and center, breaking a streak that was previously held by one of my other clients, Kent Hull, and his quarterback Jim Kelly in Buffalo.

"He certainly has made my job easier over the years. . . . Just the great consistency we've had there," Manning said to Mike Chappell of the *Indianapolis Star*. "A lot of communication, a lot of conversations."

The beauty of the NFL is that once you're on the field, your status gets stripped away. Everyone who plays the game will experience that. A future Hall of Famer might sack a rookie. A seventh-round pick might block a sixth. And a center who went undrafted might snap the ball to a quarterback taken No. 1 overall, one of the best players ever at his position.

Saturday and Manning shared rows on a bus and aisles on a plane and opinions about what plays to run on the field. Manning was easily the more noticeable one, but Jeff was a key component to the Colts success, an unsung hero of a team that won eight AFC South Championships in addition to that Super Bowl in 2006.

"Jeff had equal say with number 18 [Peyton Manning]," former Colts guard Ryan Lilja, who played with both Manning and Saturday, told Tim Layden. "And Jeff won his share of those battles."

Jeff's performance set me up for another war with Bill Polian in 2009. Free agency approached again and even though Jeff already had a decade of wear and tear in the NFL, plenty of teams were interested, including the Pittsburgh Steelers. Once again, he hoped to stay in Indianapolis.

The Colts got a break with the league's salary cap being higher than what was expected, and the contract offer for Saturday was pretty solid from the start. Bill didn't want me to go fishing in the free market. We had the deal in place—all the important stuff was set—and I wanted to push for a little bit more. This is when I had the most fun as an agent. Good football people NEVER lose a deal at this stage anyway.

"Ralph calls me and says I'm gonna get your wife some new jewelry, a new bracelet—it's going to be gorgeous."

Jeff's wife Karen has never been one of those jewelry-obsessed plus ones and I certainly knew that. But she always made my job easier (the wives are important in contract negotiations too) and I wanted her to know I appreciated her support. Plus, she was always fun to be around when we hung out together at the Pro Bowls.

So she deserved some new jewelry in my mind. Even if she never asked for it.

I called the Colts' offices, but Bill Polian was out of town and I got his son Chris instead, who was working as vice president and general manager at the time (Bill was the president). I liked Chris too.

"Ralph calls back and says, 'Tell that beautiful bride of yours we just got another 50 grand for a splash,'" Saturday remembers with a laugh.

At the time I thought Jeff would probably donate it. He's a quiet man with a big heart.

I was rolling now so I decided to try my luck again a little bit later. I needed another 25 grand to complete the deal. I called the Colts again and Chris answered. But Bill was back from his trip too and overheard what was going on. So did Colts punter, Hunter Smith, who had recently played his last game with the team and was making the rounds to say goodbye, at what turned out to be an inopportune time.

I pushed once again for just a little bit more money. And the elder Polian lost it. His F-bombs and mofos started flying in my direction and a few other profanities followed them.

I never spoke that way around Jeff. He never cared for or paid attention to bad language, but he was strong in his faith. And he didn't chastise you if you sometimes spoke like a sailor.

"You tell him if he can go out on the open market and get 10 million, do it," Polian said to me, as Saturday recalls. "I'm bending over backward, there are other centers out there I can get. . . . I'm gonna pull the deal off the table."

The story eventually got relayed to Saturday by Smith.

"I don't know what was going on, but somebody's agent was catching hell."

That was me. I had pushed it as far as I could and Saturday signed with the Colts for three years and $13.3 million, with an extra $50,000 or so designated for his wife.

"That's the part that [Ralph] loves," Saturday said. "He loves the negotiations, the battles, cussing at each other, telling each other to die, and an hour later they're back on the phone [as friends]. You know he loves to fight as much as anyone."

Saturday finished that deal, and then became a free agent again in 2013, when Peyton Manning left Indianapolis to become the new quarterback of the Broncos. For the first time in his career, Jeff considered a team outside Indianapolis, and eventually decided to leave, signing a two-year deal with Green Bay to become the center for Aaron Rodgers.

"I wanted him to work for [the] team full time but he wanted to go at it one more year," Colts owner Jim Irsay—Bob's son—wrote on his Twitter account. "He's as good of a man as it gets."

Jeff spent his last season in Green Bay, snapping to Rodgers, another expected Hall of Famer. It was far from his best season, but he was voted to the Pro Bowl anyway, an honor awarded to him for an outstanding career as a NFL center.

In the Pro Bowl in Hawaii, across an ocean and far away from Denver, Green Bay, and Indianapolis too, Saturday and Manning crossed conference lines and shared one last snap, one undrafted legend snapping to another one drafted No. 1 overall.

"That's something special, I'll always remember it," Saturday said.

And so, a career that started out on life support, down in an electric supply store in North Carolina, ended at the NFL's all-star game on Hawaii's biggest island. Saturday finished his career with six Pro Bowls, 211 games, and the longest starting streak for a quarterback-center combo.

The scouts and their stopwatches were off base. His intangibles couldn't be measured. His determination couldn't be quantified.

Jeff Saturday proved them all wrong.

Zach Strief

The Saint

In theory, I was slowing down.

I sold my agency, Cindrich and Company, to DeBartolo Sports in 2005 and stepped back a little bit, specializing more as a consultant, expert witness, overseas professor, and negotiator, shedding some of the responsibility required of full-blown representation. I quit actively recruiting clients soon afterward. The laws scared me to death and I always operated clean, but I didn't take shit from college coaches, and I was afraid one of them might set me up.

Slowing down was not one of my strong suits. I kept working for my clients who were already in the league, taking care of the people who had earned my loyalty long ago. I also kept busy by teaching a sports law program in Florence, Italy, sending my expertise overseas to the country of my ancestors. And I picked up a couple of other clients too, players brought to me by friends whom I was happy to represent.

One of them was Zach Strief.

Zach is a big (6'7", 320), smart guy who is very low-maintenance as far as clients go. Sometimes as an agent you have to wear a whole bunch of hats—friend, therapist, motivator, even parent—but that's never been the case with Zach.

"Some guys use agents for a lot more," Strief said. "Some turn them into travel agents, some guys need emotional support, some guys need to be told every day that they're good enough, and some guys need someone to complain to."

That wasn't Zach's style. In fact, he even told his first agent that he'd only call him about once a year, and when—or if—he did, things had to get done. Early in his career, he called once and his agent failed to deliver, forcing Zach to remind him over and over.

After a while, Zach had enough. He told his financial planner, David Szafranski, who is a good guy who has become a good friend, that he wanted to switch agents and a little bit later he ended up on my doorstep.

Zach and I were a perfect fit. I always sought bright, high-character clients instead of goons. I never wanted any players who would bring a whole bunch of drama into my work.

So Zach, with his easygoing nature and Northwestern education, was a great guy to have, especially in the closing stages of my career.

I flew down to see him and talked about what I might offer as an agent. He listened. And he couldn't help but wonder if I would ever slow the hell down.

"Ralph is a unique and interesting personality. You're immediately comfortable with him; he's a very inviting guy. He's very personable and animated," Strief said when asked about his first impressions. "The one thing I remember was that Ralph's mind kind of runs 150 miles per hour. I felt like half the time I was playing catch up. I remember walking out of the meeting and knowing that I liked him, but not knowing exactly what he said."

Zach signed with me and went to work building his NFL career. After starting 40 straight games at right tackle for Northwestern University, he was drafted in the seventh round by the New Orleans Saints in the 2006 NFL Draft, not exactly a lock to make the team. Players drafted that late usually don't survive the club for a single season, and they face an uphill climb to make an NFL roster, never mind a starting lineup.

But whatever Zach seemed to lack, it was not enough to keep him off the roster. He had all the qualities to make it happen. He was hungry and smart and determined to do everything possible to improve his position. He was a modern day Ralph Cindrich, someone willing to play multiple positions and on any special team that needed an extra body. Not surprisingly, he made the team as a backup offensive lineman and a situational player and eventually became such a valuable commodity that the Saints couldn't afford to lose him.

New Orleans kept him around by giving him a restricted tender twice. NFLPA rules provide that agents will not charge a fee on tenders.

On the field, Zach was moving closer and closer to a starting role and finally earned it in 2011, turning all those paid dues into healthy dividends. The Saints' offense exploded that same year, setting an NFL single-season record with 7,474 yards, while Strief and his teammates earned the Madden Protectors Award given annually to the league's best offensive line. He finished two other seasons in similar fashion, starting 15 games in 2013 (he missed just one because of injury) and playing extremely well on the edges of the Saints' high-powered, pass-happy offense.

According to *Pro Football Focus*, a website that monitors player performance, Strief and Drew Brees were the Saints two best players in 2013. And Zach was rated as the seventh-best tackle in the entire league.

During the season, we approached the Saints front office about an extension. Zach had been in New Orleans for his entire career. He had been an offensive captain for the past two seasons and active in the community as well, a frequent visitor to the needy in New Orleans' hospitals and the students in the city's schools. He didn't want to play anywhere else. But sometimes, those things aren't so easy to control.

Zach gave me his targets for the total dollars and the years of his next contract, and it was my job to get them both, preferably in New Orleans, but if needed, he was willing to go somewhere else.

He liked the deal that had been recently signed by New England Patriots right tackle Sebastian Vollmer. Vollmer was an unrestricted free agent in 2013 and ended up signing a four-year deal with the Patriots for a little over $20 million, $7 million of it guaranteed via a signing bonus. The Saints were pretty tight against the salary cap, and we couldn't work out an extension with the team during the season.

"We want him but I can't promise you," general manager Mickey Loomis often said. I hated that.

So when the Saints' season ended, after a 23–15 playoff loss in Seattle, Zach couldn't help but wonder where he'd play next.

"I was telling guys, I don't think I've ever actually cleaned my locker out empty. I've cleaned it up, but never emptied it. You know? It's not the fun part," Strief said soon after the season ended, to a pair of reporters gathered at his locker. "You know what I mean? It's the part you feel like you don't have any control over really. It's kind of like my work is done and now it's up to other people that are not me to make those decisions. Obviously this organization has been a big part of my life and I feel like I've been a part of the success here and you don't wanna leave that. And yet, it's probably my last opportunity to sign a contract in this league. They understand that and I understand that. You hope that everybody at some point comes to an agreement to where you can stay. That's how I feel. I think that's how they feel upstairs too. And yet, sometimes that doesn't work out."

So for the first time in seven years, Zach was heading into an off-season with a great deal of uncertainty. New Orleans was home. He was happy. But most everyone understands that the NFL is a business above all else, and emotions must be moved to the side.

Beginning in March of 2014, Zach would be an unrestricted free agent free to sign with any team in the NFL. I went to work selling all the other NFL teams on why they should sign him.

We put together a briefing book on Zach that we sent out to all the teams. It compared Zach to other tackles, including the unrestricted free agent tackles at that time—Michael Oher of the Ravens, Austin Howard of the Jets, and Breno Giacomini of the Seahawks. Overall, Zach had better stats when it came to pass blocking efficiency, rushing yards over the right tackle, and other important measurables. We also pointed out that the Saints ran more of their running plays over the right side of the line, Zach's side, than the NFL average. The Saints also did better than the NFL average when it came to short-yardage on a third or fourth down running play.

We also compared Zach to tackles who had received contracts in 2013: Gosder Cherilus from Detroit; Anthony Davis from San Francisco; and Phil Loadholt from Minnesota. Zach was as good or better than those players in sacks allowed, pressures allowed, power run success, and percentage of rushes over right tackle. Of course we also highlighted the fact that Zach was a team captain, played left tackle when needed, and rarely missed playing time because of injury.

We made sure to consult the National Football League Players Association as well. The NFLPA represents the interests of all players.

We were able to get contract numbers for offensive tackles and also an overview of each team's salary cap situation to help us formulate what we believed would be a good deal for Zach. We also contacted Mark Levin at the NFLPA to go over the Saints cap situation specifically and discuss the general structure of a deal that would work for both Zach and the team.

Heading into free agency there were a handful of teams that had starting right tackles who were unrestricted free agents, including the Panthers, Dolphins, Raiders, Jets, and Seahawks. The Saints were also in that group, since Zach was no longer contractually bound to them. When free agency opened, we sent all of those teams our briefing book, and expected that any interest in Zach would most likely arise from one of those teams. We also checked in with head coaches, GMs, offensive line coaches, offensive coordinators, personnel directors, and even owners if we knew the owner played a hands-on role in determining who to sign.

These days, a lot of an agent's interaction with teams when negotiating a contract is via e-mail and telephone. You can schedule a face-to-face meeting if need be, but if both sides are comfortable negotiating over e-mail, then you might as well save the time and money and skip it. As free agency rolled along, both the Jets and Dolphins showed interest in Zach and I kept the lines of communication open with the Saints.

We talked numbers with the Dolphins and they wanted to bring Zach in for a visit. The problem was Zach had a prior commitment with his high school in Ohio, so the visit in Miami never came to fruition.

While all this was taking place, I kept working to get Zach a fair deal from the Saints. He was thriving in New Orleans, and there was no point in sending him somewhere else if the numbers were close. I know the NFL. You don't meddle with success, especially if you've been a late-round draft choice and found a system that suits you well.

Zach had a pretty good grip on the process. He figures free agency is only easy for maybe 15 guys, the high-profile players who have coaches chasing them with fistfuls of cash as soon as the transaction window opens, or in some illegal cases, even before that. Everyone else has to sweat it out as he did.

Uneasy. Uncertain. Unsettled.

I kept an open dialogue with the Saints and did my best to keep Zach calm, which was pretty darn easy. I was confident that we could all eventually find common ground, especially since I had done a lot of work up front and Zach's contract targets were realistic. (My initial reaction was his targets might have even undervalued what he was really worth to the team, but I always feel that way about my clients. So I had to be careful.)

We went back and forth with the Saints over a number of days. Initially we submitted an offer with total money similar to the Vollmer deal that Zach liked, but with a higher guaranteed amount. In the NFL, guaranteed money is just as important, if not more important than the overall dollar amount of the contract. For marketing purposes and headlines, many agents and the press like to emphasize the total, big dollar amounts, but the fact is, most of the time that figure is unrealistic and the player will never actually see all of that cash. Contracts in the NFL are not guaranteed. Players can get released. Deals can get restructured. The guaranteed dollars are the most important ones.

The Saints responded to our initial offer with similar total dollars, but there was a large gap in the amount of guaranteed dollars.

We submitted our second offer, lowering our demand on the total dollars, but in return asking for even more guaranteed money. The Saints sat on our second offer and in fact even pulled back from the negotiations.

Throughout the process, I was in contact with Zach and providing updates. He was pessimistic at that point, thinking it was possible he wouldn't be returning to the Saints. I didn't sugarcoat it, just told him to sit tight and see what happens.

I checked in with the Saints GM Mickey Loomis and stayed in contact with Khai Harley, the Saints director of football administration, whose duties include negotiating player contracts and salary cap management. I also made sure to keep head coach Sean Payton in the loop since he and Zach had a good relationship.

The Saints finally came around and responded to our second offer. They moved to a guaranteed number that I thought Zach would like since it was higher than Vollmer's deal. I called Zach again.

I suppose I got excited a few times, accelerating my speech. As I said, slowing down isn't exactly my strong suit. I love the hunt and the chase, but when you're closing in on the kill, you don't delay a single second. Things happen fast in this business. So I've always had to operate that way too.

"He's got so much energy and he wants to get so much out, I can't tell you how many times we have a conversation and I end up little confused," Strief said with a laugh. "I think that energy helps him as an agent though. And he gets charged up when he's negotiating. You can tell he enjoys it. That's good to have."

Zach was happy with the offer, but I got the green light to squeeze for a little bit more, which ended up being a half million more in incentives, tied to things such as being named to the Pro Bowl.

In the end, all my energy worked out in our favor and the Saints offer was good enough to keep Zach around. He wouldn't have to empty out his locker and move on.

He was staying home.

"We are excited to announce that Zach will stay with us into the future," Mickey Loomis said after Strief was re-signed. "Not only has he done an excellent job at the right tackle position, but he has served us well as an offensive team captain for the past two seasons and has always been a great asset in the community since he first came here in 2006."

Zach's deal was worth an estimated $20.5 million over five years, and while you never know, it will likely keep him in New Orleans for the rest of his career. We also made the contract friendly in regard to the salary cap, helping the Saints re-sign other key players and continue their success. In return, they gave us more guaranteed dollars, $8.4 million to be exact, which hit Zach's comfort level as it would for most his age. The majority of that money arrived in a signing bonus, combined with guaranteed salaries in 2014 and 2015. There are also yearly roster bonuses and a per game roster bonus starting in the third year of his contract. With the annual roster bonus, the Saints agreed it would be paid the fifth day of the league year in the 2016–2018 seasons. From an agent and player's perspective, it forces the team to make the payment or cut the player loose at the beginning of free agency. If your client is left without a job, you'd rather know at the beginning of free agency when you have the best chance to secure a contract with another team.

In the end, things worked out as we hoped they would, one of those fairy tales where everything aligns perfectly for both the player and team. I was happy to facilitate it and enjoyed working alongside the Saints.

The whole thing was so downright amicable that I didn't even have to swear that much. But I probably dropped a few expletives anyway just to let the moldy bastards know I meant business.

Zach's contract or perhaps Nick Toon's next one will likely be my last. I only have a couple of remaining NFL clients and there's no chance of me pursuing or accepting any more. I like what I have. I'll settle those contracts when they expire, perhaps write a textbook, take on the NCAA if I get the chance (but I hope by then there is change), teach and lecture to share some of my expertise, and then turn west toward the sunset.

When I finally walk away, there's only one question that will matter. And it's the same one that Arthur J. Rooney asked.

"Did you do the best that you could do?"

Even now, I know the answer.

And it's one that I will be happy with.

Life Now

The Grandfather

THERE AREN'T AS MANY FIGHTS AS THERE USED TO BE.

There are times when I miss them dearly, times when I wish I was back in the arena more often, collecting more dust and sweat and blood and battling the NFL owners more frequently on behalf of my players.

But I've cut back on clients and contracts, and mostly represent a few players I've had previous relationships with. I kill some other hours by teaching, leading law students and college kids in classes or workshops on ethics, methods, and other matters that might arise in the legal system.

The NFL has changed too. Rookie deals are tied to a more formalized system, with contract amounts dictated by draft positions and percentile increases over previous years, so there isn't as much wiggle room for a negotiator like me.

"I always thought that when we were in the 1970s, '80s, '90s, and 2000s, up until the most recent CBA, everything was a knock-down, drag-out fight. Once the new CBA came into effect it was mostly etched in stone," said my buddy Bob Terpening, a former general manager for the Indianapolis Colts. "You're not gonna have the same knock-down drag-outs that you used to. In the old days, it was a knock-down, drag-out fight every time."

Terp often turned those negotiations into full-blown wars. And I love him for that.

But deep down, there are a lot of moments in those wars that I won't miss. At all.

The media is monitoring your every move. People are saying bad things about you. You learn to sleep every night with cold sweaty hands and feet.

There was a lot to worry about then. But when things went right, it was magical. Something special happened when all of those dollars and cents were in flux, when all that money, testosterone, and argument mixed together. The adrenaline pumped. The mind raced. Not a single second was dull. And in the end, there was always a story.

Times have changed though. My life has too. These days, my biggest adversary might be my own body, which has been a little beat up by all the athletic battles I've been through. In recent months, I've had surgeries to replace a bum knee, a torn rotator cuff and bicep tendon, and a case of two drooping eyelids from scar tissue. A lot of other football players have it ten times worse, and I consider myself lucky to have the health that I do.

All in all, my life is better than good. You might say I've mellowed a bit and you'd be absolutely right. But it's tough to be a hard-ass when there is sun in the air, sand between your toes, and your granddaughter grabs you by the hand and walks you down to the water.

That stuff is special.

My kids, Michael and Christina, are still in California, so I fly out there as often as I can. Michael has a booming legal practice and a beautiful wife Courtney and my granddaughter Mackayla.

Christina is making her name in television. I was in the audience when she won a regional Emmy for her television show *Private Islands*. And I couldn't help but get a few goosebumps during her acceptance speech.

"My parents, you guys are my everything, my rock," Christina said. "And your love and support is what gets me through every day of this journey."

I hear those words, see everything I have and everywhere I've been, and can't help but wonder what I did to deserve such an abundance of blessings.

And nowadays, I'm taking more time to celebrate them all.

A long walk with the wife. A giggle with my granddaughter. A pasta dinner on Sunday and a few glasses of really good wine.

As my brother Ron says, we're getting too old to drink bad wine.

Life is good. I'm reminded of that almost everywhere I go. Last spring, I was inducted into the Western Pennsylvania Interscholastic Athletic League Hall of Fame, an honor that recognized my athletic accomplishments all the way back to my days at Avella High School. I got to share it with my family, friends, and a collection of old coaches, the guys who elevated me to that night's stage. Just before that I won a Legal Intelligencer Award for my law career and was recognized by the Pennsylvania Hall of Fame for my athletic endeavors. I've had so many great people help me along the way, that it's impossible to thank them all (I'll try like hell in the acknowledgments though).

When I was inducted into the WPIAL Hall of Fame, people from my little town took out more ads than anyone else in the program, outnumbering the well-wishers from much bigger places. There were old pictures of me in wrestling singlets and football pads, hair parted to the side with a whole lot of life waiting up ahead. The other ads were bought by my brothers and sisters, Avella's football and wrestling boosters, an old coach, and some businesses too—all of the ads filled with sincere congratulations.

Lots of things may have left Avella over the years, but pride was never one of them. I still drive down there every so often, eyes open to the wildlife and wide-open spaces I so thoroughly enjoyed as a kid. I'll scout the hillsides, see a bunch of hawks circling overhead, and sometimes drift back several decades in the memories filling my mind.

I talked to all the boys at Avella High School recently, hoping to breathe life into a football program with barely enough bodies for a team. They made it to the playoffs last year with fewer than 30 players on the varsity roster. Around town, they're still fighting uphill battles. It looks like there's a bit of blight scattered about, an abandoned house here and some boarded-up windows there.

But if I stop for some broasted wings at the Breezy Heights Tavern, slide into a booth, and stare out the window, I can see the future.

There's a gas well. And another. And another.

The town that was built upon a spirit of resistance might have one more opportunity, one more fight left in it. And the next hope is arriving underground, the same place that the coal did.

Shale wells are popping up everywhere around Avella. Trucks and workers are pouring in, and a good bit of money is too. Maybe there will be enough of it to spark a revival—and some people are trying like hell to make it happen. A local historian acquired a train car and restored the train station in town, transforming it into a historical society that tells the story of Avella. Before my mother died, she gave some money to support the cause. And there are rumors that Lincoln National Bank, which crashed when the stock market did 20 years before I was born, is targeted for restoration too, bringing a second local institution back to life.

No one can foresee everything in Avella's future, but I do know this— I wouldn't bet against any of the people there.

As for the future of football, I'm not one to predict doom and gloom or lay a bunch of blame all around the game I love. Football helped form my life. And it gave me pretty much everything I have.

Sure, it has some problems. College football is completely corrupt and the NFL is what it has always wanted to be, a big-time business worth billions of dollars. But I'll love the game and the guys who play it until the day I die. And I think there are enough people like me to sustain the sport far into the future.

Maybe it sounds like I've grown soft in my old age, but there's still some brimstone in my belly waiting for a chance to come out.

Sometimes public figures and policies piss me off and I'll take to Twitter and wage a few wars, skewering people—and maybe satisfying some too—every time I type. And I'm still a bulldog in the NFL's board-rooms, willing to fight anyone, anywhere, if it benefits my clients.

But my biggest fight—and perhaps my final one—is protecting the contents of everything that was once covered by a helmet. I read the headlines and hear the stories about friends and former teammates who are losing the games going on in their minds. I'm haunted by the calls from former teammates who have lost it.

The brain becomes inept, unable to execute as it always had before. Memories are fumbled away. The mind is lost.

It's the greatest tragedy in our sport and I ache for all those affected.

But I've already made my own plans to battle back. There are too many laughs, too many stories, too many warm memories being stored in my mind to ever let them go without a fight.

Inside my head, the Thunderbolt from when I first met Mary still surges. The fish blood on Bill Fralic's contract is still fresh. And all the other stories you read about in this book are still alive and well.

So I'm training my brain as I did my body during all those athletic years, hoping a strong mind will prove more powerful than any opponent that it might encounter.

I read a lot. I trade thoughts, memories, and opinions all across Twitter, getting a good bit of mental exercise inside each of those 140 characters. And I've memorized quotes, speeches, and poems for years, often unpacking them to test the mind, or match the occasion.

As the last breath hung on my mother's lips, I held her hand and recited poetry to send her softly on. Even then, my mind held firm.

I don't expect to lose a single memory, but if I live long enough it's possible that I could suffer some of the same CTE symptoms that have befallen so many others.

No matter what happens inside my mind, I know there are certain things I'll never forget. The fence I fell off in Avella. The West Coast beach I walk with my granddaughter. Those memories have made my life. And I do all I can to protect them.

In the years ahead, there will be more play and less work and lots of time with a family that might grow even bigger. Maybe I'll write another book too.

But someday, I'll retire for good as an attorney, an agent, and a teacher. I'll walk out of the arena Teddy Roosevelt talked about and wipe away all the dust and sweat and blood.

I'll move forward. And when I do look back, I'll smile.

Because with a little bit of effort, I can still see Mario in the middle of the rain, teaching us all how to take life's punch. I can find Mary across the room in that winning white dress, with a Thunderbolt waiting for me up above. And the Chief is sitting amid the shadows of his office, sharing the wisdom that a young man won't soon forget,

Did you do the right thing?
Was it the best you could do?
I can answer yes to both.
That's all that really matters, isn't it?

Barstool Stories

I met a bunch of big-time athletes thanks to Al Abrams, the *Pittsburgh Post-Gazette* editor, who established a Dapper Dan Banquet that was one of the best in the country. As a high school senior, I sat on a leather couch next to Al while he discussed race relations with baseball legend Roberto Clemente, who was extremely animated in this particular conversation. This was the late '60s and racial issues were a hot-button topic. Al was saying he understood—he experienced discrimination as a Jew—you just have to give it time. I really don't think anyone other than Al could talk to Clemente that way back then. Al was given tremendous respect by all the professional athletes, writers, and guests. Al eventually introduced me to Clemente and Roberto acknowledged me at the introduction with a head shake.

When you're honored in high school by the Dapper Dan Club they put you up on the dais with all the greats and I mean all the greats: Joe Frazier, Muhammad Ali, Stan Musial. I was just a good athlete from Avella and I sure as hell didn't belong, but I was happy to have that spot. I sat next to Fritzie Zivic one year—a well-known Hall of Fame boxer and a fellow prick Croatian. He was one of the dirtiest fighters during his time and never ashamed of it. Anyway, Fritzie's right next to me and former Steelers running back Frenchy Fuqua goes up to the podium dressed in one of his wild costumes: glass shoes with goldfish, a plume hat, and a satin, gold overcoat or cape. Fritzie gives me a shot in the ribs and leans over.

"That guy know how to fight?" he asks pointedly.

"Well . . . I don't . . . I don't know, Fritzie, you know, he's a football player. Why do you ask?"

"He dresses that way he better know how to fight!"

—◆—

My youth football coach Ab Rush was a big part of my athletic success and my life in general. His wife, Jane, was too. One night, many years after I moved on from the Pee Wee league, I was all dressed up for a formal party in a black suit and pink tie.

"Ralph, Abby would look good in that tie, why don't you give it to him?" Jane said.

"Wait a minute, Jane," my brother Ron said. "What if Ralph asked you for your panties?"

Without missing a beat, Jane responded, "If I was wearing any, I'd give 'em to him."

—◆—

I carved my biggest niche in the NFL with offensive linemen, but I had a handful of quarterbacks too. One of them was among the biggest Cinderella stories pro football had ever seen. Jeff Blake went "from the waiver wire to Waikiki" (for the Pro Bowl), as Cincinnati writer Geoff Hobson put it.

Blake led East Carolina to an 11–1 record and a No. 9 ranking as a senior, but wasn't drafted until the sixth round by the New York Jets in 1992. The Jets cut Blake after two seasons and he signed with Cincinnati as a third-string quarterback. But Bengals quarterbacks David Klingler and Don Hollis both got injured in the same game, and Blake got a golden opportunity. He made the most of it, taking the starting job and holding onto it for six years. He earned the nickname "Shake-N-Blake," became famous for throwing deep balls that seemed to drop from the moon, and made the Pro Bowl in 1995, throwing a record 92-yard touchdown in that game. As his agent, it was fun to watch everything come together. And according to Blake, it all happened so fast, he never got to savor it as much as he would have liked.

"It all happened so fast it seemed like, it was kind of unreal," Blake said. "I never got a chance to indulge in it. The one thing I wish I could do is go back and have the opportunity to reflect. Sometimes things happen and you never get a chance to indulge in your victory or your success."

Blake played in 120 games over the course of his career, following his stint in Cincinnati with stops in New Orleans, Baltimore, Philadelphia, and Chicago. He currently works as a coach and trainer preparing the next wave of elite quarterbacks.

＊ ＊

One year with the Cardinals, a few of us agents—Frank Bauer, Frank Murtha, and myself—banded together and refused to deal with the lead contract guy of the Cardinals, Bob Wallace, a good guy working for a tough, old-time owner who at the time was, well, cheap. Bob was not easy to deal with and he used all of the abundant leverage available to him. We used what we had. Every time he would call, we would all hold tight and refuse to negotiate. Then, we'd call the other agents of the draft choices of the Cardinals and pretty much leave a message—"Rabbit on the Run!"—knowing the other side was holding tight.

"Rabbit on the Run" was a bonding, stonewalling, and teamwork tactic to let each other know an NFL call was coming. Bauer says I folded on our little game before the rest of them, but that's a bunch of BS. You can only hold tight when it's football smart to do so. If you have a punter who's a fifth-round draft choice and you're holding him out, you better know what the hell you were doing. Yeah, Bauer's guy held tight. He was a freakin' top choice.

And he's still busting my balls about it. I had John Bruno, a sweet kid and punter from Penn State who later developed skin cancer and died.

I eventually quit that holdout, bonding, "Rabbit on the Run" chit pretty quick when I got served with one of the two lawsuits the NFL laid on me in my career.

You see, things changed when Gene Upshaw, president of the NFLPA, the NCAA, and the NFL, all agreed to their own rules. You are not permitted on either side—player or agent—to collude in labor law (agree with another party to not deal with someone on the other side). It used to happen all the time. But once the new CBA came into play, you could find yourself in deep trouble if you carried on that way.

One of those lawsuits was for $500,000. And I don't even count the subpoena I and the whole Houston Oilers team received at a training camp in Huntsville, Texas, which was a gift from God. That one required us all, *Praise the Lawd!* in Texas talk, to leave that hot, humid hellhole of Huntsville, Texas, one summer. It was divine intervention. If the United States is a body, Huntsville, Texas, in the summer is by far the butthole. Though it had, I'm told, some of the most fair and beautiful ladies of Texas.

———◆———

During the draft, I used to give legendary Steelers announcer Myron Cope a bunch of inside information. I loved him just as everybody else in Pittsburgh did. But he knew next to nothing about the draft prospects and he loved to call me right before the draft began, even when I had multiple picks in the top 10 and a phone that was ringing off the hook. But because it was Myron, I always told him everything I knew. I got a lot of information from reporters who were calling teams across the league, and I also learned a few things from the pro people I was talking to about my clients. With all that info, I usually helped Myron predict the draft pretty closely, even though he knew nothing about it. Our record was 13. It's hard to believe, but we nailed the first 13 picks one year, correctly predicting two trades as well. Pretty impressive. Yoi and double yoi!

———◆———

I had a run-in with Bob Griese long before I represented his son Brian.

I was playing for New England and Bob was the opposing quarterback for Miami. The Dolphins had the ball near the goal line and legendary fullback Larry Csonka was in the backfield. Griese was the quarterback.

As a linebacker, I was thinking that if I didn't drill Csonka before he built his momentum, I was gonna end up underneath his cleats. So what if I had the tight end in man-to-man coverage defense?

I had seen the play Griese was about to run a hundred times and I still fell for it. The tight end, Jim Mandich, blocked down and fell down into the traffic jam. I filled the hole and smacked Csonka before he got his feet underneath him. Unfortunately, Griese pulled the ball back for a perfect fake. And that tight end I had in man coverage just got back to his feet, perfectly completing the tight-end fall-down play.

Griese was smiling so big he could have broken his helmet. Instead, he tossed a soft pass to the tight end for a touchdown.

Maybe he remembered that play when he was looking for an agent for his son. Bob's college roommate at Purdue, John Luckhardt, was the coach at Washington and Jefferson, not too far from Avella. Luckhardt gave me a sterling review and I ended up representing Brian, who ended up starting 83 games as an NFL quarterback.

⚊ ⚊

Big Daddy Lipscomb was my favorite football player. Big Daddy was flashy and colorful. He once said about one of his ex-wives, "I don't miss her but I sure do miss that car!" Big Daddy played for the Steelers from 1959 to 1961 and worked as a professional wrestler in the offseason.

He died young though. He allegedly took an overdose of heroin and was found dead in a Baltimore apartment. Some of the facts didn't add up. I studied it. The needle he allegedly used was injected into his dominant hand

If you're a righty, you're going to use your right hand. It didn't make any sense that Big Daddy would use his left. Roger McGill said they had to find players to hold him down to give him a shot. He was deathly afraid of needles and would never take them voluntarily. Roger was close to all of this, and he left with me with no doubt he thought there was foul play. Theories abounded from a mob hit to making some enemies by fooling around with too many strange women.

⚊ ⚊

People in Pittsburgh can recognize the voice of local radio announcer Bill Hillgrove a mile away. Bill was lucky enough to see my ass during a training camp in Meadville, Pennsylvania. He also saw me getting a painkiller injected into it from a team doctor. Bill said I didn't flinch. I told him my son was going to play golf, not football. But that plan didn't work out either. My son Michael is a lot like his dad. He always seemed to enjoy strapping on the pads and knocking people around.

Bears general manager Jerry Angelo played college football at Youngstown State, which is just 45 minutes from Pittsburgh, so we always shared a little bit of a Rust Belt connection. There was mutual respect between us and our interactions were always friendly and productive. One year, during the second day of the draft, I was sending out notices to teams about my clients who had yet to be picked. Jerry contacted me and said he was interested in one of my clients if he didn't get drafted. I told Jerry that unfortunately we had a better opportunity already, so it wasn't going to work out.

I hoped I hadn't hurt our relationship, and as it turned out, everything was fine.

Angelo and his Bears drafted my client in the very next round.

My Life and Wisdom as a Negotiator

I think you either like to negotiate or you don't. I was never smart enough to do it the way I would have liked—smooth and clean like a kid going to church. I used the only tools and training I had available, all of which came from contact sports.

When I was first married and my wife worked for the airlines, we went to Israel and the sites of the Holy Land. I negotiated there with every street vendor who would say things like: "Sir, this is a beautiful bible covered with wood from this sacred place? How could you negotiate on a bible?"

"Look bub, there are about 50 others just like it from vendors at the stalls over there. My final offer!" That worked all through Europe and especially in Italy.

There was nothing nice about me during negotiation times. My personality changed. There were constant fights, wars, and moves designed to break the Man.

Now, let's be real though, tell me what options a kid has—and I like using kid here for my purposes—when the player is taken by a team who has exclusive rights to him for one year no matter what?

You don't get anything in negotiations for being a nice guy. Things have changed now. The amount a player receives coming out of college really is set in stone depending on their draft position. It hurts the players and the agents, but it's set in stone.

Times have changed.

SEVEN LESSONS IN NEGOTIATIONS

Follow these seven guidelines and you'll become a better negotiator right now.

1. The general rule is that the place and setting of bargaining may influence outcome. The common belief is that power is in your own place. My position is that that just isn't always practical or true. Take the Bill Fralic negotiations as an example. Fralic's contract was negotiated at a fishing hole. And I may have secured Craig Erickson's contract at a barn party with Bob Irsay.

2. The second general rule or common theory is to always negotiate in person. This, likewise, is not always practical, depending upon the industry. Al Toon's second contract was negotiated on a San Diego beach. Furthermore, outrageous demands can sometimes be made over the phone much easier than in person.

3. Preparation is of paramount importance. This is the most important part of negotiations: obtaining facts. Know the secretaries. And the negotiators too, through research or experience. For example, with people like George Young it was fairly easy coming close to what you wanted, whereas with Bill Polian you were always trading or splitting.

4. Many people have questions about whether you should ever have your clients involved in the negotiations. I had a few extreme examples where my clients were completely unavailable. Paul Gruber was so secluded in the woods of Wisconsin that there were rumors the Tampa Bay Buccaneers had hired former FBI people to find him. Mark May had to walk into town in Franklin, Pennsylvania, to find a phone. And Al Toon spent a good bit of his holdout with the Jets on a boat in the waters of Wisconsin. All their contracts worked out well. As a general rule, don't have clients involved. That's why you're hired—to go through all the aggravation. And people usually don't represent themselves well in their own negotiations.

5. An expert in the field once remarked that adjudications equalize power and juries penalize the powerful. It is extremely important to

not misrepresent facts, but also not to disclose the position of your client. Your duty is to your client. The Herschel Walker dealings were a great example of keeping quiet until the contract is done and never disclosing your position in advance.

6. Confirm favorable agreements. Never be embarrassed to require that it be put in writing. It will always save you in the end. Do not trust oral agreements or memories. Tape them if possible with notice and consent of the other party. The Miami Dolphins went back on their word with John Offerdahl and his first agent. Offerdahl had to hold out to get the renegotiated contract he was once promised.

7. There are times when you do not go for the jugular vein. You beat up champions, not the weak or poor. Trev Alberts still revisits the advice I gave him on blood money. You can go after it, but it comes at a price, and often it's one that may not be worth it.

For more anecdotes, tips, and tactics concerning law, client representation, negotiations, and more, check out Ralph Cindrich's upcoming textbook.

Afterword

The Blessings

My whole life has been football, most of it in the NFL. In the past, I've wondered whether a life in football was a wasted one. Critics of the business want you to believe it is. They're wrong. Football has given me everything I have in life—all of it. It was a privilege to play.

I owe football big time. It kept me out of trouble, provided an education, paid for my first new car and house at a young age, and put me through most of law school. I met my bride because of football. I live a charmed life because of it.

I know now why I blew out my knee. I would have played longer—and better too—but I almost certainly would have suffered even more damage to my brain.

I believe I was able to write about my experiences and share them here because I didn't have a long career on the field. I learned in college from this sawed-off runt of an English professor, Abe Laufe, that for a work to be considered literature, there had to be a moral. I hope you found one.

My heart is in here on every page. Did I mess up somewhere, maybe get something incorrect? My nightmares involve reading something that I misrepresented in this book. I have extensive, rather excellent notes, but there have to be a few screw-ups. I did my best—just as Mario and the Chief always wanted. But I've been hit in the head too. Repeatedly. Don't you get that?

I've been blessed beyond belief from the day I was born, starting with a brilliant mother who helped me overcome a serious speech defect. I think about where I came from and my experiences throughout the years, and I often remember the *Pittsburgh Post-Gazette* Dapper Dan awards dinner in 1967. It was my first honors banquet and I was named the MVP of WPIAL Class B. My youth football coach Abby Rush escorted me. Big-time Westinghouse high school star Lloyd Weston looked like he fell out of the pages of *GQ*. I looked like a dirt-poor farmer. I wanted to leave. Coach Rush put me at ease. "Ain't nobody care what you look like, Ralph, or where you've been—only where you're going."

Abby, along with Mario Gabrielli, in absentia of course but with me like old times, introduced me at the Pennsylvania Sports Hall of Fame induction ceremony in 2014.

I've been blessed all along the way. I've been in the business so long that I'm now representing the sons of clients. I'm at a point where I don't have to charge if I don't want to and can help out a client's charity too. I'm thankful that I was able to make it to this point.

My family, my hometown, my coaches, teammates, and clients are the reason why.

I've been blessed.

INDEX

ABOUT THE AUTHOR

A star linebacker at the University of Pittsburgh, **Ralph Cindrich** played for the NFL's New England Patriots, Houston Oilers, and Denver Broncos. In the 1980s he became one of the pro game's most prominent player agents. Soon he was ranked among the most powerful people in sports. *USA Today* called Cindrich "the undisputed free-agent champ." His pioneering work for left tackle Will Wolford was featured in Michael Lewis's *The Blind Side.* Today he represents several second-generation clients, teaches sports-law classes, and serves as an expert witness in multimillion-dollar labor cases. He lives in Pittsburgh with his wife, Mary. Visit him at cindrich.com.